*You're holding an anthology of 110 stories submitted by women
who made the first move and found the loves of their lives.
They displayed courage, pluck and a firm belief in their convictions.
Result? Every single one is single no more.*

Here are summaries of some of the stories you'll read:

Katy drove two-hundred-fifty miles to confess her love to Ryan, only to find out that he had met someone else and wanted her blessings. Losing him to another woman was not an option.

They met at a resort and spent an amazing weekend together. He promised he'd contact her when he got home, but he never did. She even e-mailed him. Still, nothing. With no other way to reach him, but truly believing they had hit it off, she got in her car…

Anna did everything but stand on her head to get his attention. When he *still* didn't notice her, a bold-faced lie did the trick.

This Pennsylvania woman awoke one morning to discover she had fallen in love with her best friend. Telling him might ruin their friendship; what if he didn't feel the same way?

Jamie was so subtle, that the man of her dreams ended up marrying another woman. When she heard of his divorce years later, she was determined that this time things would be different. It started with a stakeout…

*N*o more relationships! He had just ended a miserable one, and was not looking for another. But she had other plans...

*M*eagan did something thoughtful for a co-worker she had a mad crush on. When he asked how he could thank her for her kindness, she surprised him with four simple words.

*D*onna lived in Southern California and was having recurring dreams about living in Florida that she just couldn't ignore. So she packed up everything, moved to The Sunshine State and ran into the mysterious stranger she'd been dreaming about every night, right down to his white pickup truck.

*A*t forty-two and widowed, she summoned the nerve to go on her first blind date. Unfortunately, her date never showed up. Rather than go home disillusioned, she stayed, and made a move that would change the rest of her life.

GRAB YOUR TIGER

How 110 Women Made the First Move
to Capture the Men of their Dreams

An anthology of true stories,
compiled and edited by Kathy Schwadel

Published by
Keen Publications, Inc.
New York, New York
212 570-2009

www.GrabYourTiger.com

Published by:
Keen Publications, Inc.
254 East 68th Street, 6th floor
New York, New York 10021
(212) 570-2009
E-mail: keenpublications@aol.com

Website: www.GrabYourTiger.com

Printed in the U.S.A.
Cover Design: Howard Goldstein

To order this title, please call (212) 570-2009 or visit our website at www. GrabYourTiger.com

Publishers Cataloging in Publication Data

Schwadel, Kathy, 1954-
Grab Your Tiger: How 110 Women Made the First Move to Capture the Men of their Dreams, 1st Edition
Includes index.
1. Man-Woman Relationships. 2. Mate Selection. 3. Single Women

ISBN 13 # 978-0-9630801-2-7

To my husband, Peter

You are my love.
You are my inspiration.

You are my sweet tiger, forever.

Grab Your Tiger

TABLE OF CONTENTS

Grab Your Tiger

To single women everywhere:

*H*ow is it that seven and a half years into a new millennium, we pursue the lifestyles, careers and vacations we covet, but when it comes to meeting a man for a serious relationship, we'd just as soon let coy smiles, innuendo and gratuitous laughter do our talking? How ironic that so many of us still opt to place our romantic fates squarely in the hands of the same sex we're quick to pronounce clueless, once we're with them!

No matter where you fall on the subject of women making the first move, know that subtlety rarely works when it comes to men. Studies show that men miss our flirting signals with great regularity, an astonishing *three out of four times*. Make eyes at him until your lashes fall off—it's no guarantee he'll walk over, no matter how polished your seduction skills.

Ladies, isn't it time we assumed the same parity with men when it comes to relationships, as we do in other areas of our lives? When we allow ourselves to fall victim to the anachronistic, societal whisper that labels us 'desperate' if we approach a man first, we diminish ourselves and run the risk of *never* meeting the very men who appeal to us. Worse, simply standing there makes us fodder for the annoying, gregarious fools who prey on females for sport. And, most important, we may miss out on a real sweetheart, especially if his fear of rejection exceeds ours. If women don't pick up the ball at least some of the time, both parties remain at a stalemate. Nobody wins and everybody loses.

Grab Your Tiger celebrates 110 women who empowered themselves and followed their hearts. They found ways to approach the men they found compelling, to recast their platonic relationships and to forge the marriages and long-term commitments they longed for. They employed everything from directness and candor, to clever ruses and bold faced lies, to initiate that first meeting. And they were right on target: Both scientific and anecdotal evidence reveals that men are thrilled by women who make the first move. In fact,

in a recent online poll of nearly 10,000 men,
93% say they would love to be approached by a female! [1]

Wisely, the 110 women in this anthology recognized that some men are shy, others fear encroaching on your space and, still others, have concluded you're out of their league, so they held their collective breaths, *and they took responsibility for their own happiness*. I think you'll find their tales delightful reading—and if you're single and still looking—a source of inspiration.

Kathy Schwadel

[1] Jeff Cohen, " About.com Guide to Dating and Relationships" 2006.

And now for a little Theory Debunking

I was forty-nine when I married for the first time. Despite the daunting Newsweek cover story stating that as a female over forty, I was more likely to be killed by terrorists than tie the knot, I managed to create my own 'happily ever after.' While it was not by design that I stayed single for so long, it was by design that I came to meet and marry my soul mate.

My dating agenda was simple enough. I sought men who shared my irreverent point of view, and because I'd wait before letting things get physical, I felt secure that my relationships were well-grounded. Mental energy, laced with a bit of cheek, was my aphrodisiac, but it never seemed to lead me to the long-term committed relationship I desired.

The big turning point occurred in my mid-forties—hopeful relatives had stopped toasting my impending nuptials and I discovered that tossing my hair seductively, tickled a man's funny bone more than his libido. More important, it hit me that for three decades, my arsenal of dating moves was limited to passive flirting. As a result, I was only dating men who approached me first —more often than not, glib, glad-handers who lacked the depth and character I sought in a life partner. What if there were a galaxy of wonderful men, who never did walk that gangplank out of fear? What if I were missing out on the cream of the crop?

So I debunked a theory. No, I obliterated this one—that tired female mantra, handed down by generations of women, that men love the chase and that it's the male's biological imperative to pursue the female. The unspoken corollary? Only sad, pathetic women approach a man first.

I began talking to men I found appealing and found that the more progressive ones are jazzed by females with the pluck to approach them, perhaps because it betokens the sort of partner they want to share their lives with. And so, at forty-six, I flipped the script, gave some serious thought to the kind of partner I wanted and where I might find him, and happened upon my best friend and husband, Peter. The change I made came down to this simple principle: I began taking an active role in matters of the heart. It involved three steps.

Step One: I lost the 'Man as Hunter' theory. Historically, both sexes have enjoyed the chase and both have the inborn capacity to do the hunting: Did you know that females invented weapons—presumably to keep up with male hunters who could rely on their brawn?[2] Diana, the Huntress, descended Mount Olympus to hunt evil and defend the weak, Queen Elizabeth I killed deer and stag with her crossbow and in some Phillipine cultures, women still hunt pig and deer with bows and arrows.[3]

Whether we chase deer, deerskin boots or the dear heart in the next cubicle—we all have the innate skills to grab ourselves a tiger. Isn't it time we got out there?

Step Two: I stopped reading relationship books that insist I take my cues from men. These books only served to limit and confuse me. 'Never call a man first.' 'Always keep him guessing.' 'Smile and look approachable.' This last one was lethal; instead of appearing inviting to men who appealed to me, I effectively became an idiot magnet. And more recently, the message in today's best-sellers is: 'Wait with bated breath for him to give you the nod.'

Just how is it that we ever let a gratuitous phrase like *He's Just Not That Into You* become the unchallenged mantra of smart, capable women everywhere?

Apparently, having a horrible day, fighting with his boss or nursing a boil on his rear must not count for much. More important: The authors of these books imply that if he doesn't call for a second date, or even propose a first one, that we come to the esteem-shattering conclusion that it's all about us; we're a little too chunky, boring or platinum-streak-challenged to suit him, thus, his inertia—not that he may be shy, intimidated or clueless that we're interested. Why not suggest *we* make a call to see what's up? As we reclaim our power, we may, perhaps, discover he's thrilled we did!

With one bold stroke of the pen, these books serve to diminish women and dehumanize the entire courtship process.

According to these so-called relationship bibles, if men aren't burning up your phone lines, it's because of *you! you! you! You* just don't tick all their boxes! And let's not minimize their sexist premise: The male is a paragon of perfection; when he likes us, will always call in the requisite number of days, or make that first move, hands down, no question. Reality check:

He's the same guy you'd be more than willing to recognize as splendidly *imperfect* if he were your boyfriend. You'd see all his flaws—twenty-twenty. So why on earth would you count on him to behave seamlessly in a first meeting—or any time after that?

If six days pass, and he hasn't picked up the phone, yet you felt sparks between you, *does it really matter who makes that call?* Before the momentum is gone, why not take a shot that can change your life? Even if you don't end up with the guy, the lift to your self esteem, when you cease viewing yourself as a pawn, is priceless.

I hear some grumblings from the bleachers. "Sure men want hot women to come up to them, or call them, but what if an average-looking female like me makes that move?" Worse case scenario? They'll talk to you for a few seconds— or not—and walk off. Since when does dismissed by a total stranger qualify as rejection? Take a deep breath and try again. Just keep your eye on the goal:

Increase the number of men you speak to, so you can decrease the time to find a wonderful man you can truly connect with.

Chances are you've already met your share of smooth-tongued lotharios. Assume that men with something more to offer are lurking in the shadows. It's up to you to find them.

Step Three: I became proactive. I came across an article that codified my nearly three decades of frustration; it stated that flirting, the way it is typically done, will rarely get a man to approach you. Digging deeper into the social science literature, I learned that men need dozens of signals to 'get' that you're smiling because you *like* them, and not because they have bits of lime in their beards. More about exactly what you can do to get his attention in *Chapter 1: If Flirting Were a Language, Men Would be Illiterate.*

The few men who do pick up on your tweaks, twitches, smiles and purrs, and find them irresistible, may still be too nervous to come up to you. Don't declare them off limits because they don't approach you first; you may miss out on some real gems. Check out *Chapter II: In Defense Of The Shy Guy.*

When you're convinced you should get out there and grab your tiger, you can improve your odds of a successful hookup by reading *Chapter III: Up Your Odds—Look Before You Leap!* Turns out, men subconsciously send out signals that they are interested in you, even if their feet stay planted in one spot all night. While their brains are reciting all the reasons you'll reject them if they approach you, their bodies can't lie. Spot these signs and traveling to his corner of the room will be a cakewalk.

If you're still not convinced that you're tiger-grabbing material, read *Chapter IV: Ten Great Reasons For Approaching The Next Interesting Man You See.* Then, move on to 110 wonderful and true stories, and prepare to be inspired.

My first and only experience taking the reins of my love life led me to the clever, accomplished, handsome man I married. At the age of fifty-two, I'm happier than I have ever been. A smart businessman of stellar character and a deep commitment to family and friends, my husband, Peter, is a self-proclaimed introvert. But for the fact that I approached him during his workout, we may never have met.

To celebrate this joyous period in my life, I began seeking stories from other women who'd also found the nerve to grab their tigers. What follows are their real-life adventures, as they they battled their anxieties and seized the moment—and, ultimately, the guy. Oops! That's not exactly true: A number of these accounts are written by males who had a first move made on them by females, and to whom they are forever grateful. I gathered these true stories by placing ads on fifty or so websites online; I received 626 stories in all and have included 110 of them here.

I think you'll enjoy the ones I've selected for you—they profile women of all ages, who, despite their fears, and despite stale, societal dicta, took proactive steps that would change their lives forever. *Enjoy!*

[2] Jill Pruetz "Savanna Chimpanzees, Pan troglodytes verus, Hunt with Tools" *Current Biology*, Vol 17, 06 March 2007, 412-417

[3] Headland, Thomas N. and Janet D. Headland. 2000. "Four decades among the Agta: trials and advantages of long-term fieldwork with Philippine hunter-gatherers." Notes on Anthropology 4: 79-88.

CHAPTER I:
If Flirting Were A Language, Men Would Be Illiterate

So you figure you can bat your eyes, lick your lips and smile sweetly, and by the end of the night he's yours? It's not a bad start and, at times, it might work. But if you rely on a handful of gestures, alone, to meet a man, *you'll miss out on a lot of wonderful men.*

Richard Bandler, a psychologist and the developer of Neuro-Linguistic Programming, found that his greatest challenge was getting his male participants to pick up signals the opposite sex was sending them. He put a group of men and women together in a room, having first instructed each of the women to pick a man and flirt with him. Result?

**Over seventy-five percent of the men
failed to notice that the women were flirting!**

Simply put: Offer him a smile and don't be surprised if starts checking his fly or feeling his chest hair for bread crumbs. A few provocative gestures *are not enough* to propel an interested gent to your side of the room. To increase your chances of flirting successfully, you must learn to *use numerous and varied signals,* according to Dr. Monica Moore, a psychologist at Webster University in St. Louis.[4]

Clearly, the more flirting techniques you employ, the better. Dr. Moore found that there are approximately fifty-two different "nonverbal solicitation behaviors" at a female's disposal, *and the more of these she sends, the more likely she is to be approached by her intended target.* After 2,000 hours of research in bars, malls, parties, etc., and she found that

**women who performed more than thirty-five flirting displays
per hour elicited greater than four approaches per hour.**

Translation: You need to send at least eight gestures in his direction to have a shot at getting his attention. Variety also factors into your success rate. When men are awash in signals from a woman, they start to feel liked; either they'll muster the nerve to approach or they'll welcome her approach. Dr. Moore also found that

**men are more receptive to high-flirtation women who are
average or even less than average-looking, than they are to
women who are more attractive, but who emit fewer signals**.

It's not who's most appealing, but who's most inviting, belying the view long-held by evolutionary psychologists, that women with the most symmetrical features or the best waist to hip ratios (think hourglass body) will attract the most men. You'd do well to keep Dr. Moore's findings in mind if a few extra pounds have you second-guessing yourself.

> **Get that flirtation ball rolling full throttle, and the curvaceous ice maiden standing a few feet away is toast.**

However, you need to put some words to the dance, lest you come off looking like a traffic cop. If you are clever, irreverent, outspoken, funny, outrageous, sardonic—lead with it. Rustle up some moxie, and insinuate yourself into his space, and into his life, with your unique brand of you. At the end of the day—whether it's a networking meeting or a singles party—it's the spirited, self-possessed woman who has the best chance of getting the guy. Remember, you're not trying to attract just somebody to date. You want somebody who adores you for who you are.

Statistics also show that you'll increase your chances of a successful hook-up if you flirt with men who are on the same attractiveness level as you.

> **Studies of couples conducted by the Social Issues Research Center (SIRC) indicate that most successful marriages and long-term relationships are between partners of equally good looks[5].**

Additionally, the SIRC confirms that "over eighty percent of women have a poor body-image, and underestimate their attractiveness," so they advise that

> **if you are female, chances are that you are more attractive than you think you are, so try flirting with some better-looking men.**

Here's a partial list of the attention-getting signals Dr. Moore and her associates observed. Incorporate them into your flirting repertoire and be sure to repeat them to get your interest across:

- a room encompassing glance when you first enter, ending your gaze with him
- short darting glances at the guy, fixing your eyes on him, looking away and then doing it again
- tossing your hair
- playing with strands of hair
- primping—smoothing out your skirt or other article of clothing
- running finger along the rim of a glass

- a coy smile
- caressing a part of your own body
- tilting the head to expose your neck
- aligning your body towards his
- solitary dancing
- licking your lips
- exposing your palms
- mirroring his moves

But know that even if you were to direct every one of these gestures towards your target, it's no guarantee he'll dash over, or ask you out; he's human and prone to self-doubt.

The men I interviewed for this book provided some interesting reasons for not jumping for the bait, no matter how enticing. Some had been burned before, by misread signals, others have sketchy social skills and still others think you're just being friendly and don't 'get that you're interested:

Joe S., 29, Bank Manager: "I can't figure women out. There are times when I know she's giving me the eye. She's practically hailing me down. Then when I walk over to her, she acts like I'm completely contagious!"

Lou, 31, Cook: "I guess I'm the shy type. At parties and weddings, unless a woman has a sign on her forehead that says 'Ask me out' I'll usually talk to her for a while, thank her for her company and say good night"

Robert, 54, Engineer: "I need a couple of drinks, before I can even think of approaching a female I'm attracted to. By then, either someone else has scooped her up, or I'm so tanked I'm afraid I'll sound like a jerk, so I let it pass."

Dennis, 49, Marketing V.P.: "I'd be afraid to go up to a woman at work and say something nice. My job has policies about this stuff. She could finger me for harassment!"

All the males I spoke with agreed they would love women to take them off the hook, at least some of the time, by taking the initiative. In the words of one fellow: "We're not mind-readers. Sometimes we need you to come right out and let us know how you feel!"

Still need convincing that men don't readily pick up on flirting? Have you ever been to a party where another woman makes a point of touching your boyfriend's arm and laughing just a bit too much at his jokes? When you mention it later, in the car, he says he never even noticed she was coming on to him: "She was just being friendly!" he protests, and he probably means it. He was completely oblivious, while you and every other female in the room knew exactly what was happening.

Bottom line: Feel free to flirt, just don't count on it. In the words of a popular lifestyle columnist for the Manilla Times—

"If flirting were a language, men would be illiterate."

[4] Moore, Monica, Ph.D., "Nonverbal Courtship Patterns In Women: Context And Consequences." *Ethology and Sociobiology* 6(4), 1985 237-247.

[5] Social Issues Research Center, *SIRC Guide to Flirting*, Oxford, UK, 1997

CHAPTER II:
In Defense Of The Shy Man

But I don't want somebody
Who's loving everybody
I need a shy guy
He's the kinda guy who'll only be mine
from the song "Shy Guy" by Diana King

*W*onderful men surround us each day and a large percentage of them are mind-blowingly shy around women. While an introvert may lack the social-assuredness to approach you first, once he gets to know you, he's more than capable of taking the lead. It never ceases to amaze me how chatty and communicative my normally quiet husband can be when we're together. I love it. The extroverted men I gravitated to in the past, may have been more practiced at smooth rejoinders and bombastic bon-mots, but I discovered that shy men are more than capable of offering the wit *and* substance so many of us crave. And contrary to another of my long-held prejudices, where I equated aggressive with manly, and shy with weak, shy men can be tremendous pillars of strength.

When I encourage my single girlfriends to approach quieter, less extroverted types, I get one of two responses. "If a man really likes me he knows how to put one foot in front of the other. If he can't do that, he's not worth knowing!" To this I offer several dozen stories, in addition to my own, in this very book, where men did not make a move for any number of good reasons. If he's not at the top of his game, what's stopping you from being on top of yours?

Then I get: "How do I know if the guy I go up to is the right guy? The short answer is you don't. But if you focus on quiet men, chances are pretty good you're not dealing with a player. Plus, a shy guy isn't grading you on what you say when you approach—he's just thrilled you're saying it to him. Best of all, you get a listener. Nice.

Chat him up and check out his body language (more about that on our website www.grabyourtiger.com). You can pretty much tell by his words, attitude and movements how he feels towards you. If the vibe is mutual, great. If not, move on.

The very fact that he kept pretty much to himself, and stayed so focused on his workouts, was one of the first things that attracted me to my husband. Unlike many of the men in our gym, he was not focused on every woman who wiggled by. I had no idea if he had any interest in me when I bounded up to him first at our new gym and introduced myself. Sure, I was anxious, but I just did it. The Sports Club L.A. in Manhattan had just opened and I was looking to make new friends and maybe even meet someone to date. Remember, I'd spent decades waiting in vain for the *right* man to walk over to me.

During my early evening workouts, I'd spot glorious sunsets through the huge windows rimming the ceiling, and without giving it two thoughts, I'd find my new buddy and drag him over to watch them with me. He was immersed in his weights. I was too excited to care. Early on he told me he was living with someone, so while he was he was off limits for a romance, he was great to chat with between sets.

I continued to practice approaching men who appealed to me, and in short order, found a nice guy to date. Verbally playful by nature, I'd often inject word play and double entendres into my conversations; it served to hide my nervousness and weed out the dullards. It encouraged the men to volley lighthearted rejoinders back at me, which reduced the tension and made us both feel comfortable.

Months later, when Peter was out of his relationship, he admitted to me he found my occasional repartee and spirited interruptions fun. I stood apart from the scores of women surrounding him, many of who had much better faces and figures than I, just by being me. After many months of small talk, we were able to accumulate information on each other's likes and dislikes, so that when he was ultimately free to date, we'd already cultivated a wonderful friendship.

Peter and I married three years after the day we met. Although he says he *had* noticed me early on and found me very cute, chances are his shyness and his circumstances would have kept him from making a move.

Peter is my best friend and the best thing that's ever happened to me.

He gives me license to be me—safe in the knowledge that if I fall, I'll always have a soft place to land. And I'll never stop being that soft place for him, either.

The first move. The best move I ever made in my life.

CHAPTER III: *Up Your Odds: Look Before You Leap*

Men send out signals they like you, without even knowing it. His brain may be holding him back because of nerves or a recent bad breakup, but he can't stop his body from talking.

If he displays six of these signals—in your direction, of course, you may assume he's eager to meet you.

Next move: *Yours!*

a) He'll look at you more than once.

b) Each time, he will gaze directly at you for at least 2-3 seconds.

c) His eyebrows will flash—they'll rise for an instant when he first spots you.

d) He'll make sure you see him checking out your body.

e) His lips will part automatically for a second when you make eye contact.

f) His nostrils will flare; combined with the parted lips and eyebrow flash, he is literally opening his face to you.

g) He'll step apart from the group he's in, or the rubber plant he's behind, so you can get a better look at him.

h) He'll exaggerate his movements, like putting his glass back on the bar with his whole arm extended so you don't miss it. He'll also stand tall, displaying his prowess.

i) He'll start preening, smoothing his tie, his hair, pulling up his socks.

j) You'll find his thumbs hooked over his belt pointing to his groin. If he's sitting, his legs will be wide apart.

k) While he's looking at you, he'll touch his face a lot. This is a combination of nervousness and a phenomenon known as auto-erotic touching set off by his attraction to you.

l) He'll start squeezing or rolling his bottle, glass or can from side to side

m) He'll pull out his palm pilot or some other nifty gadget to try to impress you.

n) He'll mirror your moves, subconsciously aligning himself with you.

Grab Your Tiger

CHAPTER IV:
Ten Great Reasons For Approaching The Next Interesting Man You See.

1) You get to be the chooser not the chosen. Remember, not every man you have your eye on is going to walk over to you. Don't ever leave again having never made contact, because you were both afraid to make the first move.

2) Men are obtuse when it comes to flirting signals—they need you to spell out that you are interested in them as a possible date; they're relieved if you go up to them first and break the ice. As long as you're reasonably well put together and have a genuine smile, there isn't a man I spoke to who would purposely make you feel uncomfortable.

3) You will never regret the times you make a fool out of yourself, but, rather, the times you *don't* try something, out of fear. In the words of one very smart man, who happens to be my Dad, *"If you don't reach, you don't grab!"*

4) You're making one of the biggest mistakes of your life if you're still thinking: "If he's interested, he'll come over!" For every guy who goes up to a woman, there are dozens who don't. Here's another direct window on why. I asked a group of men at my gym what stops them from approaching someone they'd really like to meet. These are their reasons for holding back:

    a) "If I just got blown off by a female five minutes earlier, I'd be done for a while!"

    b) "Some women are just out of my league; they'd never go for a blue collar guy like me so I figure, why bother?"

    c) "There are plenty of guys around her—she doesn't need another one."

    d) "I've got mustard on my tie and my eyes are bloodshot from a late night at the office. She's going to think I'm some drunken slob."

    e) "She's wearing a ring." (No matter that's it's not even on her left hand. Many a man has been put off because he erroneously assumes a ring on either hand means you're engaged or married. Best to keep your finger jewelry to a minimum.)

    f) "She's too pretty. She'd never go for me."

    g) "She'll look at me, but then when I go to look back, she looks away. It's cat and mouse and I'm not sure what to make of it."

5) Men love it when you approach them. Surveys show that more than nine out of ten men state that they would be excited and flattered to have a female initiate a date, or even a conversation.

6) Only a neanderthal would have a problem with a woman making the

first move.

7) If you walk up to that cute guy in the corner, you'll spend less time being the target of aggressive jerks who stick like glue to women who stand alone.

8) Chances are you'll want a true partnership if you end up with this man. So why not start things out as the strong, spunky, assertive woman that you are, instead of acting like a fawning, fragile gladiola?

9) Just because you got the ball rolling, doesn't mean that he's going to expect you to always take charge of things. Most men won't even remember who started the conversation. They'll just be pleased someone did.

10) Taking responsibility for your happiness is a great way to boost your self esteem. *When you go out and grab your tiger you are giving voice to your inner tiger and that's the greatest achievement of all.*

*My sincere thanks to everyone who
submitted a love story for this anthology.*

You give testimony to the joys that can
result from female self-empowerment.

May you always find the courage
to go out and grab your dreams!

Grab Your Tiger

110 ways to Grab Your Tiger...

Grab Your Tiger

First Base

After a six-year romantic relationship ended bitterly, I threw up my hands and vowed to spend the next four years focused on my education. I'd just aced the LSAT and had been accepted, with scholarship, to law school. I had no time for a relationship with anything but a book, which worked out well for my shattered and weary heart.

I spent the summer before my first year of law school hanging out with my best friend from high school. One weekend she announced she'd invited a male coworker to hang out with us: "I've always thought you'd hit it off with Randy," she said, refusing to catch my eye. "No way," I answered. "I'm done with relationships." "Still," she replied, "are you wearing *that*?"

I was relieved there were no sparks between Randy and me. He was funny and decent looking, but I'd always been attracted to rebellious, unattainable types, which was probably my problem. Randy was soft spoken and conventional—the kind of guy who coached little league. He didn't seem overly impressed with me, either. With that out of the way, we were able to be great friends with no complications. He hung around with us all summer and became the brother I never had. It was an effortless relationship. He'd seen me in nothing but a tee shirt with no make up and ratty hair and it neither repelled him nor peaked his interest. He often confided that he simply wanted a committed relationship with a sweet girl—the last thing I needed.

That's why I was happy for him when an old girlfriend suggested getting together to see if they could salvage their relationship. I found his nervousness at planning their reunion cute and endearing. I brushed off the unexpected jealousy I felt as stress from starting school. He would be starting a new life and so would I—just as I wanted. When the day came, though, I was

by
Shannon M. Dean

Odessa, Florida

I was crazed and pacing and fighting a weird, undeniable urge to call him and tell him I didn't want her there.

crazed and pacing and fighting a weird, undeniable urge to call him and tell him I didn't want her there. I am not an impulsive person, but it was without any thought, whatsoever, that I rushed over to his place to stop whatever was going on.

When he opened the door, looking completely confused and adorable, I grabbed him and kissed him—long and hard.

After he could speak, he asked "What's going on?"

"I just want to be with you," I answered, now embarrassed and wondering what in the world I was thinking. "I missed you. We've been together all summer. I can't help it."

To my complete amazement, Randy laughed, kissed me back and asked why I thought he'd been hanging around all summer?

The first impulsive moment I ever had in my life led to my almost ten-year marriage to Randy, my husband, the father of my two boys and the best little league coach our city has ever seen.

2

by
Janice Louise Anderson

Amsterdam, Netherlands

I met my tiger when I was well into middle age—something of a miracle according to my family, who, by this point, probably viewed me as an unmarriageable pariah. Throughout my dating years, I'd clung desperately to men who offered me very little, but seemed an easy antidote to being alone. One gem in particular was in my life for nine years, until I finally realized, with some therapy, that I deserved better. Only where were the decent men, now that I was ready?

One Spring evening in 1995, I was on my way to rent a movie when the magnet on my refrigerator caught my eye: *Insanity: Doing the same thing over and over and expecting a different result.* It's as if I had never really read it before. In fact, I didn't even remember seeing it before. Maybe the universe was trying to get my attention? Or maybe it was my mother, who'd come to stay the previous week.

So I chucked the movie idea and asked my friend, Beth, who, at 32, was fifteen years younger than I, to join me for a bite to eat; I was now actively bucking insanity by changing my routine and planning to share a mushroom pizza and some good gossip with a friend. When we got to the restaurant, I was seated directly facing the saxophonist of the local band that was playing; I squelched my urge to ask to be moved to a quieter spot and decided to enjoy the music.

Once I allowed myself to relax, the sweet notes from the sax felt like caresses. The guy playing it was no slouch, either; blue eyes, tousled silver hair and ten fingers that knew where to press and where to linger…I smiled reflexively at him and when he was done with his set, he looked straight at me, pulled the instrument from his lips and smiled back. Periodically, I'd glance over at the band, as Beth and I chatted, waiting for our order to come. She shot out with "You like him, don't you?" I ignored her for the moment; I was too busy hoping he was sneaking

> **"Go to the bathroom. I'll see if his eyes follow you."**
> **Here we were, two women in our forties, acting like teenagers.**

3

glances back at me, because then, maybe, I could screw up the courage to go up during his break and tell him how much I was enjoying his music. Taking his lack of eye contact with me as a sign that he wasn't interested, I shared my new and unrequited crush with my friend. "Don't jump to conclusions!" she offered. "After all, he *is* performing." Then she shared her plan: "Go to the bathroom. I'll see if his eyes follow you." Here we were, two women in our forties acting like teenagers. Naturally, I agreed to do it.

As I waited outside for the bathroom to be free, I recalled the quote about insanity and, against my normal instincts (which were to avoid talking to men first), I started chatting with the bartender: "Great jazz; love the sax—do they play here a lot?" Turns out the saxophone player was his best friend's dad; his wife had died suddenly three years earlier, so he left Atlanta and the corporate world to focus on his music. As the bartender explained, this man had learned the hard way that life held no promises and the time to 'go for it' was now. Was this the universe, giving me another subtle whack?

Heading back to my table, I noticed the music had stopped and the band was taking a break. Before I could lose my nerve, I strode outside where sax man was lighting a cigarette. I approached with a smile, he smiled back and I just stood there, letting the moment wash over me, praying that he would say something first. He didn't. So, out it came:

"You have such a gift; I love hearing you play."

Now he was beaming. From there, the conversation flowed like honey, and in the corner of my eye I could see my friend giving me a thumbs up.

When I returned to the table, I shared everything with her, including the business card he handed me.

"Did he ask you out???" she pushed, excitedly.

"No, I invited him to lunch tomorrow so we could continue our conversation. He gave me his card and made me swear I would call."

"I don't believe it! Girl, you rock!" were her exact words.

And so we began dating. I fell in love with this kind, handsome man who has taught me by example to see every moment as precious. During one private performance seven years ago, my sax guy asked me to marry him. We had a small affair with family and friends and then packed everything and moved to Amsterdam, to the town where he was born. I never thought I could be this happy.

Several times I've thought back to the night we met, and I realize it wasn't just showing up—it was pushing myself beyond my comfort zone—that has made all the difference.

On July 3, 1983, I awoke with the premonition I would find Mr. Right that day. Since I had rarely experienced psychic powers, but I *had* experienced unsuccessful relationships, I disregarded that intuition.

It was Sunday of a holiday weekend, and everyone had plans. I had that nagging feeling I should get out there, but I wasn't comfortable with the idea of going to a bar, solo. Finally, my instincts won. I would go alone, but act as if a pal had temporarily deserted me, for safety reasons, as much as a sense of bravado.

I also decided to choose, instead of waiting to be chosen. But in addition to physical appeal, how else would I choose? As I walked into the area where the DJ was playing to a packed dance floor, it came to me: I would look for someone my mother would like! How quaint!

I'm not sure why that made sense to me; I'd spent so much time defending my choice of men to my parents, perhaps I was just tired of fighting, only to find they were right all along. Maybe years of having their values instilled had finally worked and I was ready to see men with different eyes.

Within minutes, a man walked by who appeared to radiate kindness and gentleness—in addition to being tall, dark and handsome. Without hesitation, I walked over and asked him to dance, something I had never done before to a stranger. He seemed surprised, but danced with me. When the music changed to a slow number, we thanked each other, and went our separate ways. So much for my premonition and planning!

The rest of the evening was predictably non-eventful. My self-assuredness melted away, and I felt silly just standing there. What had I been thinking? It was like all of the other nights, and I didn't even have a pal to commiserate with! Just when I thought I would leave, the man I had approached appeared in front of me. This time he asked *me* to dance. Afterwards we talked and

by
Karen Amato Schwartz

Pittsburgh, Pennsylvania

> **So much for my premonition and planning!
> I felt silly just standing there.
> What had I been thinking?**

exchanged phone numbers. We were married the following summer.

It's been over twenty years, and the shirt he was wearing that night still hangs in the closet, for sentimental reasons. It's still remarkable that I felt an absolute need to go out that night, especially alone. I discovered that he never went out on Sundays either, and only rarely, to that particular club. We lived on opposite ends of the city and had no common ground where we would have ever met otherwise.

Serendipity is amazing, but it appears that one also has to trust their instincts when it comes to romantic premonitions. One more thing—my mother did like him!

4

by
Felice Shekar Harksel

Davie, Florida

We were standing close to each other. I could feel the electricity. I knew if I didn't act, he never would.

Dating was not the first thing on my agenda after getting divorced. I had two small children to raise, a business to run and my sanity to think about.

My days were full, which was a blessing. I had no time to think about being single with two children. I spent my free time working, which helped me to not think about my life situation. A friend of mine came to see me on a beautiful, sunny Saturday afternoon, only to find me working at my desk, dealing with the endless mountain of paper work that comes with being self-employed. He gently explained to me that I had better figure out what I "liked to do" and start doing it. I let him know that I was doing exactly what I wanted to be doing, which was paperwork, while the kids were spending the weekend visiting with their father. He didn't buy it, but let me off the hook, anyway.

He was right, of course. And it got me thinking. I had no idea what I liked to do. I had spent many years considering what my husband liked to do and adapting to that, all in the hope that it would make our marriage better, which of course it didn't. I then had to consider what my children liked to do and facilitate that. But me? I had no idea what I liked to do. I had to go all the way back to my childhood to find the answer, as it had been that long since I had the deciding vote on my own likes and dislikes.

Riding a bicycle. I had always liked to ride a bike. No, I loved riding a bike. In fact, I'd had a crush on the older boy who had taught me to ride a two-wheeler. Although I hadn't ridden since getting my driver's license at sixteen, I figured it was worth a shot.

I borrowed a bicycle from the teenager next door; if I was able to ride successfully, on three separate occasions, I would buy a bike of my own. A short time later, I became the proud owner of a brand new red Schwinn and began to

7

enjoy the same freedoms I had felt as a child.

On the alternate weekends when the kids would visit their father, I dressed in my riding clothes, matching sneakers and bandana, dusted off my headphones and headed down to the local beach boardwalk.

I'm sure you think that's where I met the man of my dreams. No so. What I did do was start to feel young, attractive, active, free and pretty again. While I did meet men on my bike, which did wonders for my ego, that is not where I grabbed my tiger. It was my first step into the jungle. And how can you bag a tiger if you don't venture into the jungle?

There was a regular customer who came into my shop a couple of times a week. He was pleasant and nice looking. One day in conversation he mentioned a steak restaurant he liked. I dropped what I thought was an obvious hint and asked him when he was going to take me there. He didn't respond and I felt he was just not interested, so I wasn't going to push the issue.

On another occasion we were standing close to each other without another soul in the shop. I could feel the electricity. I knew if I didn't act, he never would. So I leaned in and kissed him. Gently, sensually and for a long time. He then asked me out. When he asked what I wanted to do, I suggested bike riding, and we made plans to meet at the beach for our date. Little did I know that he hadn't been on a bicycle since he was about ten years old, and had to borrow one and practice. But he was a real trooper and kept up with me every inch of the way. It was only later that I found out that he hadn't been able to walk for a week after our first date! And the rest, as they say, is history.

My husband and I still ride bikes and have even taken a week-long bike trip to Vermont. He can now walk afterwards. That is how I grabbed that Tiger—by just living my life and venturing into the jungle, which is where the tigers live.

Trapping the Tiger

5

**by
J. Taylor**

Utah

I often joke with my husband that we need to come up with a better story of how we met. It's not really pathetic or boring. It's mundane. You see, we worked in the same building. Now, I know many people meet their significant others at work, which is why I joke about coming up with an exotic story to tell people. The truth is that we were just real people, meeting in a real way.

Timing was everything. He had worked there for six years, and I had worked there for three. It's funny how we had never seen each other until I was going through a long antici-pated divorce. I spotted him standing in line to buy lunch one day. He had prematurely gray hair and his light blue eyes were striking. I could tell he was young, but he looked so sophisticated. I formed a crush right then and there. I didn't say anything to him. I was still technically married, and someone that looked as good as he did must be married, or at least involved.

I continued to bump into him around the building. My crush grew, and I even told my Mom that I had it for this guy with gray hair, although I never really thought anything would come of it. Besides, even though the divorce had been years in the making, and I was not emotion-ally invested in the process anymore, I told my-self it would be a long time before I met some-one I could really be in a relationship with, so why should I pursue this?

I ate my words very soon thereafter. I was sitting at the lunch table at work with a new em-ployee on my team. He was sitting at the next ta-ble by himself. I figured since I didn't have much to say to this new coworker, I might as well use it as an excuse to invite him to sit with us. He happily accepted my invitation, and as he spoke I found myself falling for him. He was amazing.

> **In spite of the interest he was giving me, he didn't ask me out. I was confused...**

9

In the coming weeks we continued to bump into each other. He would compliment me, I would blush, and I wouldn't know what to say, so I wouldn't say anything. The possibility was quickly slipping away from me. I needed to do something about it.

One day, as I passed his desk, I noticed he had clothes hanging all over the place. How strange, I thought; I decided I would e-mail him about it, and make some funny remark. This would break the ice, once again. He was involved in a big system upgrade/conversion at work, and I was working a lot of overtime because of it, as well. I knew we were both burned out, and so I offered to accompany him on a walk any time he needed to get away. He took me up on that offer, and we started having daily walks. Our conversation flowed unlike anything I'd experienced before, and I was happy to learn that he had never been married.

In spite of this, and in spite of the attention I felt he was giving me, he didn't ask me out. I was confused and decided I needed to know his feelings before I made a complete fool of myself. However awkward it was, and however exposed I felt, I asked him how he felt about me. He explained that he didn't know if he should take the first step, since I had just been divorced. He was afraid of putting too much pressure on me and scaring me away. The very next day he asked me out on an official date. After a seven-month engagement, we were married.

Some people ask how I could marry the next person I dated after my divorce. My answer? Timing is everything. All I have to do is look in his eyes, or feel his hand on my back, to know that I made the right decision. We have a strong, happy marriage. I am so grateful that I took the steps necessary, despite my hesitations, to get to know him and find out how he felt about me. If I hadn't, I have a feeling I would be in a completely different place than I am now, and there is nowhere else I would rather be.

The Night That Never Happened

Ryan was a guy that I met after a serious breakup. He was my "guy's view."

He was living in Orlando and I was at school in Tallahassee. I couldn't see us "dating" since we had the long distance between us. We continued to talk, and I had a feeling that he wanted more from our relationship, but I still was wary of the distance.

Then one day, a package arrived from Ryan. It was a ring he saw that "reminded him of me." I turned to my best friend Jessica and said, "I think I like Ryan. No... I know I do." We decided to make a "road trip" to Orlando for the weekend and I would open my heart to Ryan and tell him how I felt.

When Jessica and I arrived in Orlando, we met Ryan at his apartment with another friend of ours, Amanda. He and Amanda were going to a wedding that evening, and then we would meet them downtown. I had "the perfect outfit;" the one that would make Ryan fall head over heels for me. When we got ready, I took my time, making sure my hair was perfect and my make-up, flawless. It was going to be a night we would never forget.

Needless to say, it was.

When Jessica and I arrived downtown, we met Ryan and Amanda at the bar. As we walked in, Ryan grabbed my hand. I turned to Jessica with a huge grin on my face. It was happening! We found some seats and ordered drinks. Ryan and I began talking; Jessica and Amanda started their own conversation.

Ryan turned to me and said, "There's something that I need to talk to you about...."

Oh! My! Goodness!

He is going to tell me what I drove down to tell him! My face beamed!

"...when I was in Chicago, I met someone..."

by
Katy Leach

Winter Park, Florida

**I didn't know
what to do or say.
But I knew
how I needed
to feel,
and I wanted
to feel numb.**

My face dropped. "What?" He told me her name and some other things, but I didn't hear a word. My bottom lip began to quiver. I saw Jessica looking at me and her face was the same; Amanda had just told her what I knew.

She mouthed, "I'm so sorry." Ryan got up.

I didn't know what to do or say. But I knew how I needed to feel, and I wanted to feel numb. We ordered shots. Several shots. I pretended like it didn't bother me. I was fine! We made our way to another bar and some guy started to talk to me. I couldn't tell you what he looked like or what he said to me. All I know is that Ryan was watching me from across the room. I turned to my mystery man, said "You'll do" and kissed him. I knew Ryan saw, and I knew it hurt him. He left the bar and headed home.

We hailed a cab and made our way back to Ryan's apartment. When the taxi arrived, we didn't have enough money so I walked up to Ryan's front door, rang the doorbell, and when he answered, I announced "There's a cab outside that needs to be paid" and walked in. He went out and paid the driver. When he returned, he said that Jessica and I could have his bed, and he would sleep on the couch. Fine with me.

But, as I lay in his bed, it wasn't fine. This was *not* how it was supposed to happen. This was *not* why I drove 250 miles down here. It was *not* going to end like this.

I walked into the living room and said "We need to talk."

And we did...for hours and hours. I cried and told him how I felt. He cried and told me how he felt. He said that he always liked me, but never thought that he'd have me. He figured that it was going to be that way.

I told him that it didn't have to be—that we could pretend that the night never happened.

I fell asleep in his arms that night, and when we awoke, I looked up at him and asked, "Well?" He kissed me, and that was the answer I needed.

Ryan and I were engaged a year later and married a year after that.

We are about to celebrate our two year wedding anniversary.

We still talk about "the night that never happened."

7

by
Keith Jones

Queen Creek, Arizona

We'd just finished a long day painting a church building in the crowded and impoverished 'suburbs' around Tijuana. I was one of the chaperones on a teen mission trip to assist some of the poorer churches in the area. A first year college student, I was pretty mature for my age, so I wasn't surprised when I was asked to help supervise.

Tired and hungry, we went to downtown Tijuana to grab a bite to eat at the Hard Rock Cafe. We were eager for something a little more American that we had been eating for the last few days at the work site. I took a seat with three girls I was friends with. Being one of the chaperones on the trip, I tried hard not to just be 'one of the guys'.

Once dinner was over, we sat around yapping about school and the like, when two of the girls got up and excused themselves to go the rest room. Brandi, a very good friend, decided to stay behind. We started talking, and in no time, things got awkward. We both stumbled for a while, and she finally blurted out, "Well if you haven't figured it out by now… I like you!"

I was totally blown away. While I had kind of suspected it, we'd never been more than good friends. In fact, two years earlier, she had been the off-and-on-girlfriend of one of my best friends. Evidently, I'd completely missed her subtle hints—like asking me to teach her to throw a football, or calling me while she was baby-sitting, just to talk. We'd spent quite a bit of time together during the day painting, but I hadn't chalked that up to anything more than just coincidence.

Like an idiot, I blurted out "Well, maybe we can go out sometime when we get back." She cocked her head to the side and gave me the weirdest look. The other girls came back from the rest room and the intensity of the awkwardness had now reached unprecedented levels.

> **When she took a chance, and made that bold statement, she did it knowing that I had been dating a girl back home.**

13

We all headed back to the church building for a pep talk from the youth minister before heading to bed. Having realized how badly I'd handled Brandi's revelation, I grabbed the seat next to her and sat down. Half-way through the talk, I reached my hand over and took hers. Ever since that night I have done my best to take a little better notice of her hints.

So far I must be doing a pretty good job. This August will mark eleven years since that fateful night. We've been married for the last eight and have three beautiful children. When she took a chance and made that bold statement, she did it knowing that I had been dating a girl back home. She had also noticed that another chaperone and on the trip had been spending long periods of time with me. What she couldn't have known, however, was how much that first move would totally affect the outcome of both of our lives.

Kind of funny how that works.

Three Little Words

The man of my dreams became mine forever with three little words. And no, it wasn't "I love you." Perhaps it wasn't as daring or creative as writing his name in the sky or threatening to jump from a tall building if he wouldn't be mine. Let's just say that I'm usually ultra-conservative, so bold is not exactly my forte.

I was twenty-one when I met him, an undergraduate about to enter my final year and living away from my parents for the first summer of my life. We knew each other in passing, but weren't exactly friends. Truthfully, I had always admired him from afar, although I thought I wasn't his type of woman. Then, one magical night, under the influence of alcohol, we got together. No sex, but lots of hungry kisses.

We played it cool for a while, 'hooking up' at parties where we both happened to be, him stopping by to see my roommate when he knew he was working, casually asking me if I would like to go to the park.

After a few months, we were inseparable. I'd wait in my dorm room for his calls, pretending to do homework. We spent every night together, slept in on Sundays, went out for lunch, and had some pretty mind-blowing sex. The months crept on, and graduation day crept closer. I had decided to attend another university to get my teaching degree; the problem was that it was two hours away.

In March, only one short month before I would finish my time in this lovely place, I began to worry.

"What are we going to do?" I asked him one night while we were lying in bed.

"I'll come see you on weekends, baby. We'll be fine," he whispered while softly stroking my cheek.

That didn't really suit me. Having tried

by
Krista O'Connell

Truro, Nova Scotia, Canada

> **So I summoned my courage, forgetting everything my parents had ever taught me about how a decent woman does things.**

long-distance relationships in the past, I knew that they almost never worked out. First he'd be busy on a certain weekend, then I'd have too much homework. Before Christmas, we'd probably be exhausted and reluctantly call it quits.

I realized, then, that I loved him, and that my life was simply better when he was there. So I summoned up my courage, forgetting everything my parents had ever taught me about how a decent woman does things.

"Come with me," I said, not having any idea what his answer would be. He had a steady job, friends, family, a life here.

I prepared to hear all of these answers and justifications of why it just couldn't happen—not right now. I would accept them grudgingly, knowing he was right, even though I would cry myself to sleep in secret. Instead, after only a moment's hesitation, he said that magic word.

"Okay."

That was almost three years ago. We've had our hard times, and living together hasn't always been easy. In fact, recently, we moved back to the place where we met, only a few blocks from where our first summer together happened. We've had fights, acquired a dog, gotten through the deaths of family members, laughed and cried.

But I'll never regret taking a deep breath, summoning all my courage, laying my heart on the line, and uttering those three little words.

How Guacamole Gave Me A Wife

**by
Ralph Nieves-Bryant**

New York, New York

The first time I saw the woman that would become my wife, she was presenting at a youth conference, screeching like her head was on fire. She barked about youth rights, fighting the power and other communist manifestos. My initial reaction was "Who the hell is this blabbermouth?" Who could know that five years later I would be trapped in her Master Plan by three slick moves and the world's best guacamole.

One year later, Anna and I met when we were mutually stiffed by a friend who made separate plans with us on a rainy Friday night. Abandoned on a corner, we decided to make the most of it by playing pool all night. We quickly became friends. Until…

"Interested in dinner?" she asked.

"Nah, not hungry yet," I replied.

"No, silly. I mean, let's go out on a date."

"Okay, I guess," convinced that this was not her desired reaction.

But she had knocked me for a loop. Girls usually needed a gigantic neon sign with the words "I like you!" flashing like a Times Square billboard before I made a move. By asking me out, she cut me out of the equation. This was *Slick Move #1*.

Raised by a Southern Grandmother who spent approximately 600 hours a week in church, I heard lots about being a man—ask the girl out, pay for the meal, open the door, pull out the chair…blah, blah, blah. And throughout my dating life, I played Mr. Gentleman and every woman I dated obliged. Except for Anna. Instead, she suggested her favorite Mexican restaurant. However, this did not make me do a Mexican Hat Dance.

"Mexican ranks just below Puppy Chow on my favorite foods list," I said.

"Do you trust me?"

> **If Anna could change my mind on guacamole, what other mysteries could she help me uncover?**

"Sure, but in 1982, I trusted God to give me a pony, and I'm still waiting."

"Don't worry. I'll take care of everything."

Montezuma's was darkly lit like Dracula's lair and made for romance, with mariachis singing songs of love and table candles flickering like lightning bugs. If not for the fluorescent light of the strangely placed aquarium in the middle of the restaurant, I would not have seen my food, let alone my date.

Once at the table, Anna took over by ordering for both of us, starting with the guacamole. Every guacamole I'd ever tried was more reminiscent of a green goop-like spackle substance, than edible food. But this was prepared table side and was so miraculously fresh I thought I had picked the avocado myself. If Anna could change my mind on guacamole, what other mysteries could she help me uncover? I thought. *Slick Move #2.*

It became clear we were destined to be together. Unfortunately, until then, no one told us. We already knew we both worked for nonprofit organizations. But we also learned that as teenagers we were both rabid fans of the Rocky Horror Picture Show, doing the Time Warp dressed like freaks from a bad Vincent Price movie. And we both grew up in the Bronx, where the only thing hotter than the New York summers were the burning buildings.

Four hours into dinner, our waiter circled us like a shark, hoping that we would leave before dinosaurs returned to earth.

"This is one of the best dates I've ever had," I said, reclining in the faux wood chair.

"I'm glad you enjoyed yourself," Anna replied, flashing her best smile that distracted me from noticing the check on the table. She quickly grabbed it. *Slick Move #3.*

"What are you doing?"

"I asked you to dinner so I'm paying," she said, with a stern look that I would come to know as her 'you're not going to win this one' face.

Into what sinister womens' lib plot had I just walked? "Give me the check," I demanded.

"No. Just drop it," she barked.

Feeling overwhelmed, I thanked her profusely and offered to take her home. While I did not pay, I could still try to be a gentleman.

When I got home, I called my best friend Greg and said, "I just went out on a date and a girl paid the check. I think I am going to marry her."

Guess what, I did. In retrospect, I know I was merely a pawn in her plan for world domination. After ten years together, I'm just thankful she chose to take me along for the ride.

A Song Of The River

by
A. Howard

Sydney, Australia

"You must meet Ann," they smiled. I was visiting some friends one weekend and they took me around to her house. My eyes widened as I went in through her open door. The house was full of light—sunlight glancing off the river and touching glass and silver throughout the rooms. There was a fragrant scent—lavender I think. Paintings and books adorned the walls. The house was an assault on the senses.

I was used to elaborate sets, being an opera singer, but this house had the feeling of a winning stage set. Ann walked towards me, her green eyes full of the same magical light. She smiled and my day smiled.

"I like your house," I stammered.

She just smiled, queen of her domain.

My friends took us both back to their home for cocktails. I watched Ann's slim fingers curled around her glass stem, her long lightly tanned legs stretched comfortably before her. She had such poise. I am well over six feet tall and she was up to my shoulder. I am used to women being attracted to me, but Ann seemed intriguingly polite, but distant.

She left after about an hour, and my friends and I sat in the garden, looking at the river, talking about my last performance. After dark, Ann returned. Her composure gone, she blurted out that there was a strike and she couldn't get to her publisher's by train, as she had planned.

"I'm frantic," she said, "the deadline is in two days."

"I'd be happy to drive you," I murmured.

Her green eyes settled on me. "You would?" "That would be wonderful!"

I felt that I was drowning in her green eyes. We left next morning early; the river mist hung about the road and I drove carefully while we chatted.

> **I showed her to the spare room. "If you need anything, just call me." Ann smiled and closed the door.**

"What do you do?" I asked.

Ann told me she was a painter and writer and had come to the river three years earlier. She had bought her house for a song—it was so dilapidated that plants had grown through it and birds were nesting in the rooms. She said her house was like a work of art for her. She asked me what I did. "Opera singer—London, Milan, Bordeaux, New York."

"Do you have a significant other?"

I told Ann that I had been married briefly, but that it had not lasted—the travelling and pressures in my career. I said I'd love to find someone special, but women wanted you to be there all the time.

"Look! Can you stop a moment?" Ann cried. We pulled over and watched as the sun climbed through the river mist, first silver, then rippling gold. Two birds took flight from the water and the ripples widened. Ann pointed out the birds and I felt the softness of her breast against me.

When I stopped outside her publisher's, I asked if she would be able to return home easily. She told me she hoped either her car would be fixed by the end of the day, or the strike would be over. I gave her my phone number and offered to drive her home.

I left with that special fragrance hanging in the air, hoping more and more that I would hear from her. Towards the end of the afternoon, Ann phoned. She said she would love to take me up on my offer, but she couldn't leave the publisher's until late evening and she thought it might be an imposition. Also, she had to be there early the next morning.

"I have a spare room," I said gallantly.

"Oh, wonderful," Ann breathed, "I'd be so grateful."

Mine was a bachelor pad, so I raced around and threw stuff in cupboards and washed up. I raced out and bought a dozen red roses and vacuumed, then sat with a scotch, thinking of Ann's green eyes. When I met her that evening, she was wearing a different dress, light yellow, with emerald earrings that flashed when she laughed. I vaguely wondered how she was dressed so well when she had been at work all day. She looked fresh and lovely, her hair, silvery blonde, like the sunlit river. We had dinner. I couldn't stop looking at her slim fingers and wanting them on my skin.

I showed her to the spare room. "If you need anything, just call me."
Ann smiled and closed the door. I had left one of the red roses on her pillow.

Of course, she did call me. We have been married now for twenty years and each day is better than the last. I found out in due course that there was no strike, she didn't even have a car, and that she had been following my singing career for years! Our mutual friends were part of her scheme. The minx!!

11

by
Dana Borden Wilkes

Billings, Montana

Before I could talk myself out of it, I pulled an old receipt out of my bag and scribbled a note on the back. Within seconds, I was mortified. What had I just done?

I was hardly an ingénue when it came to the world of dating. At thirty-eight, I'd clung desperately to more than my share of unsatisfying relationships for two decades, including one short-lived marriage. At the urging of my married sister, I took some time to evaluate how I was picking the men in my life. I stopped dating, period, so that I could, as her favorite book advised, 'date myself'.

Initially the concept totally irritated me, but then I started to flow with it. I spent my weekends engaged in activities I forgot I liked back when I was in my twenties and single, and forced myself to try new ones. In a year that included skydiving lessons (something I actually enjoyed in my twenties but which terrified me now), painting and writing a journal, I found that I got juiced by adventure, was totally in touch with my funky, creative muse and had a gift for expressing my thoughts on paper.

I also decided to work out more regularly, dropped eight pounds with early morning jogs, and joined the local Chamber of Commerce, expressly for the purpose of making new friends and maybe even meeting a man. This last activity was my least favorite, since I would have to network with total strangers. Still and all, I felt a sense of confidence—I guess my year of solitude had taught me that if I ended up alone, I wasn't such bad company after all. For the record, this would be the first time my sister has ever been right about anything.

The first Chamber meeting was a breakfast seminar on Internet Marketing. New to this as I was, I forgot my business cards. The speaker was a marketing executive named Robert Wilkes; he had plenty of good ideas to share and a warm, easy way about him. Being in the same field, myself, I nodded my head in agreement as he spoke; I had inadvertently (or was it?) drawn his attention to me, so when he looked over, I flashed him a smile. Safely ensconced in the audience, I figured I had nothing to lose.

Each time I flashed him a smile, he made it a point to smile back. Feeling emboldened by his response, I decided to up the ante and I raised my hand when he asked for questions. Coming up with a decent question was easy; it was keeping my legs from buckling as I stood up, that was hard.

I got his answer, long before he spoke a word. The electricity was powerful. I could sense by his eyes, as I opened my mouth, that he felt it, too. As our exchange continued, I felt spirited, even buoyed by his apparent interest, and found myself playfully challenging his willingness to take business risks. This pretty much forced him to make the point that he absolutely did take calculated chances when the circumstances and timing were right. I'd gotten a rise out of him, in a light-hearted way, and he had managed to volley a teasing comment or two right back in my direction. Wow…witty too. This one was a keeper. I decided I'd ride my bold streak and go up and thank him for a great presentation when the seminar ended. But it wasn't to be, as he was instantly surrounded by colleagues when he stepped away from the lectern.

During the continental breakfast that followed, I noticed he was seated at a large, round table, close to the stage. Before I could talk myself out of it, I pulled an old receipt out of my bag and scribbled a note on the back. I handed it to the nearest waiter and pointed out the gentleman who was to receive it. He obliged. A second later, I was mortified. What had I just done?

'How's this for good timing when it comes to taking risks? Eight AM, Saturday, at the Airsports Skydiving Center over on Lavender St. The instructors are certified and the class is on me. Are you game?' I signed it 'Dana'.

"I say you've got a date!" boomed the voice behind me.

I turned to find Robert, holding the receipt in his hand. I think he was even blushing.

"You know, I'm pretty flattered. A woman has never invited me to do anything— except, maybe, to take a flying leap. Wait, you're asking me to do the same thing, aren't you?" he laughed. Funny, too.

That Saturday was the first of many skydive outings together over the next two years. Turns out Robert was divorced and the custodial father of two. On the second anniversary of our meeting, he proposed to me on a cliff over the Pacific, just before our sunrise jump. I know it sounds corny, but my feet still haven't hit the ground!

12

I cannot forget the day of my friend's marriage to her Prince Charming. The glow on her face said it all. Her grinning and naughty smile appeared to be saying "Look I got what I wanted. I told you I will not be a loser." The memory of Natasha's wedding day is clearly etched in my mind and will always remain fresh in my memory, simply because she proved that if you want something in life passionately, and have the burning desire to get it, you will find a way to get what you crave.

Natasha was always a go-getter and someone who had a never-die spirit. I have never seen such a headstrong and optimistic girl in my whole life. She knew very well that the guy of her dreams, the man she loved madly, couldn't be hers, because some astrologer had predicted that if he married her, there would be a lot of complications after marriage.

Excuse me if you don't believe in what I am saying, but the people in my country (India) still show a lot of respect and faith in astrology, stars and match making by pundits (priests). I told her many times that she was fighting a lost battle, but she would always snub me and say, "Well, if it is a lost battle, let it be. I know how to turn it into a victory."

It all started when Kabir came to see her with his parents in response to the newspaper advertisement given by Natasha's parents for a suitable match for their daughter (something that happens even today in India). Natasha took an instant liking to Kabir after talking to him, and knew that all this time she had been looking for someone like him, only.

Kabir's parents liked Natasha, but were firm believers in astrology, and match making of kundalis (birth charts). Kabir, too, liked Natasha but was a shy guy. He felt some sense of responsibility towards his parents and couldn't go against their wishes.

by
Neerja Sharma

Chandigarh, India

She knew she was taking a risk. Her plan could backfire, too.

So when Natasha was told by her parents of the astrologer's prediction, she was heartbroken. She tried her best to forget Kabir, not think about him, but it was all in vain. What people call "pangs of love," she seemed to be feeling now. She tried to contact Kabir, to know his feelings, and realized he was helpless due to family pressures, and to his own fears, too.

Natasha couldn't take her state of misery any longer. She decided to do something fast as Kabir's parents were looking at, and meeting with, other short-listed girls' parents. She called and asked me to accompany her to Delhi, where Kabir's family astrologer lived. Being a loyal friend, I agreed, as I didn't want to leave her alone in that state of affairs. I asked her what she was going to do.

She replied, "Wait and Watch." That was the reply of my friend Natasha, the old, naughty, confident and always a winner, Natasha.

We reached our destination and Natasha went to meet the astrologer. She knew she was taking a risk. Her plan could backfire, too. What if the astrologer told Kabir's parents everything? What if he refused her proposal and request? But, being the fighter that she is, she counted to ten, took a deep breath and went inside the astrologer's den. When she came out, she was smiling and crying at the same time. When I asked her what had happened, she just smiled and made a thumbs up sign.

On the way back home, she told me how she bribed the astrologer and asked him to change his previous prediction about their marriage. Initially, the astrologer refused strongly, but when he saw green notes coming out of Natasha's purse, he agreed, and told Kabir's parents how his prediction was wrong; he had read the birth chart of someone else, not Natasha. He convinced Kabir's parents how good a match both Kabir and Natasha would make, and that by not agreeing to marry them off, they would be losing a very good proposition.

A week passed after this meeting between Natasha and the astrologer. Natasha waited with bated breath for the phone to ring. She didn't go anywhere, worried the phone might ring in her absence.

And at last the phone did ring. And the voice on the other side said, "We would like Natasha to be our daughter-in-law. What do you think, Mrs. Singh?"

13

by
Heather LaRee Carter

Paso Robles, California

**I'd had my
heart broken...
Now I ached for
someone who
believed in fidelity,
who was willing
to work on
building a
solid relationship**

The technique worked when I was a teenager, wanting to be homecoming queen, making the cheerleading squad and scoring several chosen boyfriends, so I thought, "what the heck, I'll try this." 'Programming the mind' was a tool of the guru-days of the 1960's. Envision the end result—the scene you desire—lock into it, feel the emotional quality of living it and then rerun the vision over and over, day after day. Act as if you have it: Be the person you see in that picture, and you'll attract what you want.

My vision included the ranch-style house, picket fence, cute kids laughing, as they chased each other in the front yard, along with my faceless hubby and me standing by—full of love for our life and each other. My vision held potent emotional quality and I zeroed in on "the feeling." I didn't know what he looked like or how much money he made. I'd already experienced the charming, gorgeous, unfaithful and unreliable husband who'd spun a web around me. I'd had my heart broken by the powerful, successful businessman who aggressively courted me and then couldn't commit. Now I ached for someone who believed in fidelity, who was willing to "work" on building a solid relationship—in addition to being healthy (good genetics for the offspring), not addicted to any substance and who loved me.

I wrote about it, tore magazine pictures and tacked them up. I ran "the tape" daily, adding "for my highest good" to keep my desire honorable. I stepped into my picture and immediately felt more joy, light, power and confidence.

Within weeks, a recruiting call came from an old girlfriend organizing our first high-school reunion. One of the calls I would make was to my old sweetheart from ten years before. I wasn't waxing or fluttering—just innocently calling to say "Hi" and encouraging him to come. The greater powers were at work and I didn't have a clue.

25

Something gravitational yanked me towards him during the reunion night. I moved in on him, like a dog in heat. He was surprised—but willing. We interlocked for the next two weeks, swept in nostalgia, deep stirring, lust and what I thought then, must be destiny.

We leapt into the current and took one of the most emotionally rapid-like rides of our lives. Apparently, before I could begin really living my vision, major "house-keeping" was required. We were thrown, tested, tossed, yanked and raked to the point I backed off. But he didn't. I thought the spirits had played a cruel joke on me. Or that I had monumentally duped myself. I no longer knew what I wanted, didn't trust myself—but he still wanted me.

He said, "Take your time. Do what you need to do. I'll keep working my life and I'm here for you if and when you need me to be."

Months of swinging on my own indecisive pendulum and perplexed by his steadiness and loyalty, I opened up the tiniest bit to reconsider. I sat down and made the pro-and-con list about him. I took a seriously logical business perspective. Invest-ment-worthy? I ran my vision, with him at my side. He had all the attributes from my former "must have" list. I did love him, but lots of "things" about him really bugged me. He could be critical, insensitive, self-absorbed and curmudgeonly. I whined for ease—for a sure sign. A sure thing.

I heard an inner voice, laughing at me: "Get over yourself and get to work. You're no perfect prize either."

I was not mooning in love, but a steady undercurrent of deep love resonated and I sensed wisdom deeper than me. I made myself the deal to commit to the path of growth through this relationship with him. Accepting that good growth requires work, exploration and trust to reap the true and lasting benefits, I asked to move in with him.

A short time later, during one of my meditations, I called in all the higher forces and my highest good. I asked for guidance and suddenly the vision of our wedding played across my mind's eye—a wedding that would be held at an event a month from that day.

Twenty-five years ago, Valentine's Day 1981, we were wed. Countless times throughout our growth-filled years together with our two precious sons, I've felt the overwhelming blessing of having my original vision played before me, affirming the power within.

Soul Mate

by
Robert Rohloff

Winnepeg, Manitoba, Canada

I met my soul mate at a Karaoke bar, twenty-one years ago to this day. I was there, drinking with friends, when out of nowhere this stunning dark-haired female came up to me and asked if I would like to sing "I Got You Babe" by Sonny and Cher. I said "sure," looking into her large, dark eyes. Once up on stage, she took my hand and held it while we sang. Every time we sang, "I Got You Babe," she would squeeze my hand tighter in hers. After the song was over, she gave me a kiss on the cheek, whispered her name, Diane, in my ear and then disappeared.

About two weeks later, while sitting with a friend having a beer after work in the same bar, I felt a tap on my shoulder. I turned; it was Diane. She looked more beautiful than I remembered. She said she was singing "I Got You Babe," and wanted to know if I would join her. I said I would. We sang the song, but this time she did not disappear. She stayed with some friends she was with, and asked me a couple times to dance.

The last dance of the evening, she pulled me out on to the floor. She draped her arms around my neck, and held me as tight as she could. I remember that it felt so natural holding her, as if she were made to be in my arms. After the song was over, we stood in the middle of the floor holding each other and dancing. One of her friends had to come tell us the place was closing. She kissed me, this time on the lips, and left.

I went back to the same bar every night for three weeks to look for her, but no luck. Then, one night, out of the blue, I received a phone call. It was Diane. She said she had gotten my number from one of my friends and we talked for over two hours. She revealed her husband had died two years earlier from a heart attack. I told her, I'd lost my wife to cancer. At the end of our conversation, she asked if I'd like to go to a movie

At fifty-two, I felt like a teenager going out on his first date.

with her. I said "Yes." She added that there was a midnight show and that she would pick me up in fifteen minutes.

And exactly fifteen minutes later, I saw a car pull up in front of my place. At fifty-two, I felt like a teenager going out on his first date. I ran from the house to the car, opened the door, and slid into the front seat. She said "Hi," and gave me a big kiss on the lips.

After the movie we went out for something to eat, and then took a ride out to her cabin by the lake. Leading me by the hand, she peeled off her clothes and dove into the water. I slipped off my clothes, and followed. Then we hurried back to the cabin ,where we made love for hours.

That was twenty-one years ago, and we are still in love with each other, as much now, as we were then. The only difference now, is that the physical lovemaking is gone. Now, we sit in our rocking chairs, holding hands.

Nobody Wants Me

Mom! Nobody wants me. I'm never going to get married. Nobody wants me!

That's what I cried for years.

I never dated much as a kid. In fact, I never dated much as an adult. This embarrassed my father. I'd overheard his phone conversations when I was a teenager. "No. She doesn't. Well, you know, all the men are in the Army and Navy."

"Dad, the war was over eight years ago. You can stop apologizing for me now."

When I was in my twenties, I met a nice young man in church. Quiet. Soft-spoken. He was shorter than I. But, hey, I couldn't be particular. He drove me home from church one Sunday night. I invited him in. My father started the conversation. "What's your name again?"

"Joe."

"What do you do, Joe?"

"I work for the government."

"How much money do you make?"

"Uhh."

"What are your plans for the future?"

"I've got to leave. I'm having a very busy day tomorrow."

Joe left. He never came back.

Mom! Nobody wants me. I'm never going to get married. Nobody wants me!

Oh, Virginia, don't say that. God has a husband for you. God will bring you a husband.

My father died when I was thirty. My mother was up in years. I was an only child. I thought, "If I don't get married soon, I'm going to end up an old maid orphan."

I read an article in the newspaper: "Ten percent of all single men and women who join singles groups get married." Wow! Based on this, if I join ten groups, that will give me one-hundred-percent chance of getting married!

I joined a ski club where I met Jimmy. He was a sweet guy and a great skier. He was from the South and had a charming Southern accent. We had a good time together. Almost every

by
Ginnie Mesibov

**Philadelphia,
Pennsylvania**

**"Ginnie, would you like to go steady?"
I said, "Steady? People our age don't go steady!**

---

weekend, we went skiing. When the weather warmed up, we went sailing.

Jimmy and I dated for six months. But nothing happened. When I say "nothing," I mean "nothing." So, I thought, maybe I should take the lead. I said, "We've been dating for six months now, and we haven't been the least bit affectionate."

"Ah know, Ginnie, ah know."

I gave him a little peck on the cheek. Well, Jimmy ran as fast as his long legs would carry him, and he never came back!

Mom! Nobody wants me. I'm never going to get married. Nobody wants me!

Well, Virginia, marriage isn't everything you know. Getting married isn't the only thing in life.

Oh-oh! My mother was giving up on me! Maybe God was, too! I quickly joined more groups—sports, political, social. You name it, I joined it!

My seventh group was a seashore group in the charming New Jersey beach resort, Surf City. Every weekend, ten to fifteen of us gathered for boating, tennis, and great meals.

I became friendly with Fred. He owned a sailboat. Fred was a big lug. He wasn't too cultured, but he had a sailboat. Every weekend, we'd sail the tranquil waters of Barnegat Bay. In the evening, we'd watch the sun set as it painted the sky with brilliant reds and golds.

One weekend, down the shore, my car broke down. I told Fred, "I have to leave my car down here to get fixed. You'll have to take me home."

"Gee, Ginnie, I can't do that. It's out of my way."

I was shocked! He couldn't take me home because it was a little out of his way? A couple girls gave me a lift. One of them said, "Ginnie, Harold is interested in you."

"Harold? Really? He's interested in me?"

I liked Harold. He was very sophisticated and had a great sense of humor. That week I called Harold on the phone.

"Would you be able to give me a lift down to the shore? My car's still there getting repaired, and I have no way to get there."

"Sure."

Harold picked me up. On the way down, he took me out to dinner. I was wined and dined. We started dating. He was an artist, so we went to art shows and the theater. We had dated for just six weeks, when Harold popped the question. The question was: "Ginnie, would you like to go steady?"

I said, "Steady? People our age don't go steady! We can date. But I'll date other men." I thought, 'I can't waste any time. I've got to play the field. But I've really fallen for this guy. Maybe my ploy will work.'

Harold thought, 'I can't let her get away. She's just what I always wanted. And I've waited so long.'

So, he said, "Well, then, will you marry me?"

"Yes, I'll marry you! Yes, I'll marry you!"

I went home.

Mom! Somebody wants me! I'm getting married! Somebody wants me!

Around The Coffee Pot

He was tall, dark, and handsome. He was interested and interesting, smart and funny. He was Jewish (well, half, anyway). In other words, he was absolutely perfect.

I leaned over the table, hanging on his every word. He was talking with his friends about that day's osteology class. I knew little more than "the head bone's connected to the neck bone," but if things worked out between me and Fascinating Stranger, I could take that class next semester, and catch up. I nodded, knitted my brows and did whatever else I could to look intelligent and competent, not like the college freshman I was.

I ate grapes from his plate, one at a time. He couldn't leave, if I was still eating his food, right? I snaked my hand past his roommate's dinner, ignored a lifetime of my mother's instruction and sent the attraction rays: I...Live...Near...You... And...I...Think...Your...Jokes...Are...Funny...

He finished dinner and went back to his dorm to study. I left the table—alone, and disappointed. But wait! The battle wasn't over yet! His friend wanted my phone number. Shameless, evil woman that I am, I gave it. "I will *hurdle* over Boring Friend," I thought, "straight to Fascinating Stranger."

The next night, I went to a horrible, three-hour, Japanese modern dance production with Boring Friend. I sat through the embarrassing question and answer period afterwards, dominated, naturally, by Boring Friend. Yet, I kept my Eyes on the Prize. Oh so casually, I asked how Boring Friend's friends were doing...like that Mike guy.

"He was funny," I continued. "Maybe we should get together, the three of us. The whole group. It would be fun."

Desperate, I would have suggested anything. But would Boring Friend get it?

**by
Christine Basham**

**Lexington Park,
Maryland**

**"Make him think he's kissing his sister,"
I plotted.
Just get that hall phone number and go!"**

Would he pass my number on? I wasn't sure. And the date had gone so badly, I couldn't even tell if Boring Friend would keep my number, anyway. So I took over. I asked for the number of his hall phone—the phone he shared with Mike, and leaned over for what I knew was the most important first-date kiss of my life. "Make him think he's kissing his sister," I plotted. Just get that hall phone number and go!"

Every few days, I'd call Boring Friend, just to chat. I was dull as dishwater, but persistent and talkative. I stretched out those conversations, until I finally heard Fascinating Stranger in the background, and got Boring Friend to hand over the phone for a quick "hello." We had such a great chat that days later, he called me. Would I come for coffee?

Now that was a roadblock. Coffee is disgusting. It smells. It makes me sick. I could endure modern Japanese dance. I could waste time talking on the phone with his friend, who clearly couldn't understand why I kept calling, since we had no chemistry whatever. I could be brazen and bold. But coffee? I hesitated for a fraction of a second, frantically looking for another way. Of course, I went.

Sitting around the coffeepot, I smiled and laughed, joked and flirted. I was on. I was irresistible. I was also faking sips of coffee every few minutes.

"Would you like some more?" he asked. "I grind my own beans."

No, no, I was OK for just then. I pretended to sip and made fake, slurpy noises as I batted my eyelashes and re-crossed my legs. Booyah! He headed for the men's room and I quickly dumped my coffee in the nearest potted plant.

"Isn't this great coffee? I get it downtown, at this little place that roasts on the spot."

"Oh, yeah, it's great. Can I have a second cup?"

I flirted. I smiled. I poured coffee into the dirt. A second cup, a third. The potting soil was eroding; a warm pool sloshed around the roots.

This summer, we will have been married eighteen years. I still hate coffee. But surprisingly enough, potted plants seem to love it.

Walkin' the Dog
—Aerosmith song

"Her life was okay. Sometimes she wished she were sleeping with the right man instead of with her dog, but she never felt she was sleeping with the wrong dog."
Change of Life by Judith Collas

As the owner of a fledgling pet-sitting business, I visited cats and dogs while their "parents" were away on vacation. During the day, while people were at work, I'd walk their dogs, an activity that wreaked havoc on the soles of my feet. Not wanting to lose my dog-walking jobs, I hired my unattached neighbor, Ray, to walk the dogs for me. He was between jobs and looking for something different to do—and it turned out he knew more about dogs than I did. Tall and burly, Ray had a salt and pepper beard, a sparkle in his eye and a very pleasant personality. He impressed me with his intelligence and good humor.

It wasn't long before I discovered that Ray had previously owned several businesses. I pondered proposing we become business partners; surely his diverse sales experience would be beneficial to the development of my business. For openers, I invited him to join me on an interview with a potential cat-sitting client. No sooner had we crossed the threshold of the client's home, than Ray nervously made a sexual joke, offending all ladies present, including me! While I was able to smooth things over and get the job, the client privately requested all cat visits be made by me, not Ray. I was perturbed that a potential business partner would demonstrate such poor judgment, but I decided to forgive him and give him another chance.

Our next interview was with a client who kept her dog in a crate all day. This bothered Ray, and he suggested the pooch get more than one

by
Brenda M. Haran

Portland, Oregon

Suddenly, he stopped calling. When I phoned him, he was too busy to talk.

---

visit per day. The owner was nearly convinced she should spend twice as much on pet care, but in the end, amicably settled on one visit per day. While I didn't care for the way Ray conducted the interview, the woman seemed to like him. Maybe there was hope for a business together, after all.

So after the busy holiday season, Ray and I spent a good deal of time at the local coffee shop strategizing about how we could build our clientele. Ray started using affectionate terms and 'making eyes' at me, but I couldn't have been less interested. Good heavens—he was twenty years older than I! Totally focused on the business, I found his advances annoying and firmly told him so. I didn't notice I had hurt both Ray's feelings and his pride. But despite my rejection of him as a suitor, he continued to walk the dogs and the business kept us in touch by phone, almost daily.

Then, Ray moved to another part of town where he'd found full-time work. Suddenly, he stopped calling. When I phoned him, he was too busy to talk. Now it was my turn to feel hurt, and I realized how acutely I missed my friend. After about three weeks of feeling abandoned, I finally called him up.

"I'm coming over—*now*," I said.

We talked for a while, and I found myself admitting he'd become more than a friend to me. Ray smiled and agreed that we might want to spend more time together. And so we did. We took a pair of poodles camping with us after that.

I know my direct approach would never have worked with the guys I'd previously dated—young men afraid of committed relationships. One minute, I was pretending I didn't care very much about them, the next, I was flattering them profusely to boost their egos. But none of that happened with Ray. Sharing our feelings honestly was natural for us, because we were already friends. Besides, Ray was too smart to fall for any "creative" line I might have given him.

Eventually I gave up the pet sitting business, but I didn't give up Ray. Nine months later we moved in together. Come February 2008, we'll have been happily married for five years.

18

by
Shashi Basu

Bangalore, India

It was a college fest night at our University way back in '99. I was an engineering student due to graduate in two more years. It was a wonderful life, full of lighthearted chatter, impromptu music soirees lasting far into the evening and little flirtations. I wasn't aware I would be happier still, and within the course of a few hours, when I settled into my seat in our college auditorium late one summer afternoon.

I was expected home for an early dinner, and planned to stay for only the first few songs of the evening's concert. I knew the members of the band vaguely, the lead singer, Sheila, a second year English Literature student, being the friend of a friend; and I was only there because the aforementioned friend had been very persuasive.

From the very first song, she caught my eye and held it. From one song to the next, Sheila very rarely broke eye contact with me. We'd had a few perfunctory conversations earlier, about the weather and such; nothing had prepared me for this sudden electricity that sprang up between us, separated as we were by the stage and half an auditorium.

Nothing had prepared me for this sudden electricity that sprang up between us.

Halfway through the fourth song, it occurred to me that I might be presuming too much, and looked around for confirmation. Sure enough, all my friends sat around me, without a smirk or a rolled eye in sight, listening intently to the music (which was pretty phenomenal I might add). Her diffidence while speaking with me, seemed to have fallen away on stage—her voice rang out like this was what she was born to do. I concluded it was just wishful thinking and almost physically shook myself out of it.

An hour had passed when I realized with a jolt that my mother would be breathing fire if I didn't get home in another fifteen minutes. Reluctantly, I left my seat and tried to ease out of the auditorium, apologizing as I trod heavily on toes along my path to the door. I looked up at her wistfully and paused for a minute. I felt like a bit of an idiot for having believed that this glorious, talented woman could be interested in me. She wasn't even looking in my direction anymore, even though I was much closer to the stage now. Perhaps her boyfriend was sitting right behind me and I, like a fool,…! I nearly laughed out loud.

Then, as I dithered by the door, she turned and looked straight at me in the crowd. After a few enthralled moments, while we looked at each other, I realized with a start that she was pointing at me as she sang her love song, and that more and more of the audience were craning their necks to see who I was.

Flushed with excitement and embarrassment, I groped my way back to an empty seat. My mother could wait. This couldn't.

It's six years later and we are still happily in love. In fact, we've been married for 10 months now. Sheila still pours herself into her music; a fact which might make me insanely jealous, had it not been the very thing that brought us together, that evening a million years ago.

19

by
Donna Yankay

**New Port Richey,
Florida**

Hi, my name is Donna and I have a true tale of how I grabbed my tiger. For the record, I am normally a very shy, soft-spoken person.

People often ask me why I packed up my ten-year-old daughter, a cat, a dog, some belongings and drove 3,000 miles from Southern California to the Gulf Coast of Florida, an alien land where I did not know a soul. I tell them what they want to hear, what sounds sensible—I was making a fresh start after a divorce. But that was only partly true. I mostly did it because I was called by The Dreams.

These Dreams were filled with clear blue seas, with palm trees fringing tropical beaches, and always, always, the man was there. Tall and tanned and incredibly sexy. When I frolicked with him, I felt safe and warm and 'home at last.'

As time went on, The Dreams became more specific; I saw the man standing on a peninsula shaped like Florida, beckoning to me. I saw him dressed in a blue t-shirt, grinning and waving to me from the driver's side window of a white pickup truck.

Although I enjoyed these nighttime escapades, I did not attribute any meaning to them, until everywhere I went, every book or magazine I opened, every conversation I had, and every time I turned on the TV or radio, there was a specific reference to Florida. Eventually I made the move to Florida—and once there, flourished like a philodendron in a greenhouse.

> **He asked for my phone number, but two weeks went by and he never called.**

Then one day, when rushing around a corner in the break room at work, I bumped smack into *him*: The man from The Dreams. He was Real. As our eyes met, I knew him and he knew me. I introduced myself, and David and I sat at a table to talk. It was all dreamlike, as I'm not normally assertive and had rarely dated since the divorce. He asked for my phone number, but two weeks went by and he never called.

I saw him occasionally, at a distance, at work, so when the Memorial Day company picnic was coming up, I made a point of approaching him and asking if he was going. He said he was, then asked if I would go to the fireworks in Tampa with him afterwards. My heart was racing!!

I went to the picnic with my daughter, and her friend, Michelle, but David never showed. On the way home, I told the girls about him and, as we had to drive right past work. Michelle said "Go see if he's working." Sure enough, his car was in the parking lot. People were just coming out of the building at the end of the shift and I started to drive away quickly, so as not to look like a stalker. But Michelle persisted. "Go ask him why he didn't show today."

"Isn't that too bold?"

Both girls said "No way!" Michelle added "He sounds like a babe!"

So we turned around as David came out of the building with a friend. Swallowing my fear, I pulled up next to his car and got out. The friend laughed and said "She hunted you down, man!" But by then it was too late for me to turn and run, so I walked right up to him and asked him why he stood me up. He explained he had to work, but asked if I still wanted to go to the fireworks. Of course I did. It was a night of pure magic, and we were inseparable afterwards. I still had a concern, because David drove a blue Chrysler and not the truck from The Dreams—a silly little detail, but nagging, nonetheless.

Then, the day he moved in with me, he borrowed a truck from his friend. I followed in my car. And as I pulled up next to him at a stoplight, the man of my dreams, wearing a blue t-shirt and driving a white pickup truck, turned to grin and wave at me from the driver's side window.

David and I were married in 1994. The "fireworks" are still there. And we frolic on beaches fringed with palm trees every chance we get.

20

by
Anonymous

Brisbane, Australia

I knew my tiger a while before I grabbed him. A passion for rock climbing brought us together. Climbing with him meant I got to stare at his hard, brown calves as he moved efficiently up the rock. Coming down, his harness would pull tight around his waist, emphasizing the power in his shoulders. There was warmth in his brown eyes and I liked the way the skin there crinkled when he laughed, which he did often.

Conversation was hard. We were both shy, but all that changed when he mentioned climbing at Brooyar State forest.

"Brooyar? Really? I love Brooyar! Hey, have you done 'Awesome Wells'? It's way cool. You have got to do it. We have got to go! This weekend? I'll pick you up." I'm not usually that pushy, but it was fine. After all, it's all about the climbing, right?

So we climbed, drank rum, chatted and gazed into the fire. In the morning, we groaned about sore heads and sore fingers, but did it all again anyway. Things were different after that. We saw more of each other: Friday night training sessions, weekend trips. Without even trying, we became friends.

Our favourite climbing spot was Frog Buttress. There is a camping ground on top of the mountain, and a pub at the bottom. We would have dinner and a few beers at the pub, drive up to camp and climb the next day. One night we had a few more beers, followed by some awful red wine and found ourselves on the lookout, watching a yellow moon sink behind the mountains.

Now would be the perfect time to kiss me, I thought. Instead, I sighed and said, "What a night. Couldn't be better."

"Mmm… Yeah it could."

Here we go. Any minute now…he's going to turn and…

"I can think of somewhere better than this."

What? That's not what you're supposed to say! Nooo… This is *not* how it's supposed to go!

What? That's not what you're supposed to say! Nooo… This is not how it's supposed to go! This is Frog Buttress! We've got climbing, dinner at the Dugandan, drunken shenanigans in the camping ground and tomorrow there will be more climbing. Where else could possibly be better?

"Moreton Island."

"What? There's no climbing on Moreton Island!"

"No. But… climbing isn't everything."

"Right…" But it wasn't right. I needed to think for a minute.

"So… When are we going to Moreton? How about Queen's Birthday weekend?" It was as simple as that.

Our first night didn't go according to plan. We lay on the sand, on opposite sides of the fire, not saying much. I got my swag out of the back of his truck and lay facing the fire. I was going for the 'seductive, but casual' look. He mumbled something like, too tired to get his swag out. I mumbled something back like, plenty of room in mine, and went off for a pee. I took longer than necessary. Instead of half-naked in my swag when I returned, he was fully clothed in his. Eyes closed. Bugger.

The next day I surfed until my arms went numb. My tongue felt like a fat piece of salami in my mouth. Oh well. It didn't look like I would be needing it for anything important anyway. I peered at the clock in the dash as I restocked the esky. Not quite twelve. Bugger it, I thought, and dug out a couple of cold cans left over from the night before.

We were back at camp early. Roast beef was his camping specialty, but we needed to get the fire going to make enough coals for the camp oven. I was back, digging in the esky, and he was digging around in the sand for the cigarette lighter.

"Why don't you smoke? If you smoked, we'd know where the lighter was." He was teasing. I hate smoking and he knew it.

"Okay. I'll take up smoking, if you take up sex." It was out of my mouth before I had finished thinking it.

Neither of us slept that night. Those broad shoulders took up a lot of space in my swag as we lay staring at stars. I grabbed his arm and rolled over, wrapping him around me like a kid with a favourite blanket. I could feel his heart beating against my back. Rather fast for such a fit guy, I thought. Nothing happened that night, but that's okay. I'm still a non-smoker, but eventually he did accept my challenge, and we've slept soundly together ever since.

21

by
Judy L. Adourian

Rhode Island

**So, if you'd
rather not
go to the movie,
I'll understand."
My heart
stops beating.
Did I just give him
a clear out?**

He strolls into the snack bar, surrounded by four or five other employees, obviously the center of their attention, definitely the focus of my lust. His impossibly perfect smile highlights his olive skin, chocolate brown eyes, and onyx black hair. Italian? Maybe. Certainly European with a muscular build that belies his 5'3" frame.

I must have him.

But how? It's my first day working at Wally-World (my nickname for the retail giant that employees me) and once this morning meeting is done, I'll be trapped behind a jewelry counter for eight excruciating hours. Besides, look at him: Laughing and chatting like a man running for mayor. He's probably a player, juggling three or four girlfriends already. Why get my hopes up and my heart broken again? But damn, look at that tight, little tush.

I must have him.

Later, sequestered in the jewelry department, the object of my desire stops by to say "Hi" to the girl training me.

"How's life among the diamonds?" he asks her.

Crap. With a line like that, he must be a player. A typical male. Another use 'em and lose 'em kind of guy. Why must I always fall for the bad boy? And yet, he looks so clean cut. Short hair with a little spike. Clean shaven. And he smells so damn good. Drakkar? Oh why must he wear that delicious scent?

Weak in the knees, I still have the presence of mind to check out his name tag: J-M.

"J-M?" I blurt out. "What the hell kind of name is J-M? Couldn't you afford to buy a vowel from Vanna White?"

"Not on this salary," he shoots back with a laugh. "And you are...?"

"Judy," I reply.

"Nice to meet you."

"Seriously, what's with the name tag?"

"It stands for Jean-Marc."

"You're French?"

"Only from the tongue down."

I must have him.

41

For weeks we play cat and mouse. He strides by. I stretch my paw with a sarcastic remark. He responds with a clever quip and slips through my claws.

"Cover your mouth," I insist as he walks by, coughing for the fourth day in a row. "I'd prefer not to get your cooties."

"Sorry, I just can't shake this cold. I need to take a vacation to Florida to get rid of it, but I can't travel alone in my condition. Know any good nursemaids?"

"My grandmother was a nurse." I lob a cough drop at him. "That makes me one by association."

"You want to go to Florida?"

"When do we leave?"

"Tonight."

Rumors spread through Wally-World. "Are you and J-M really going to Florida together?" J-M and I laugh over the gullibility of people. We keep leading them on. His wit drives me wild with desire. Then I begin to wonder, who's leading whom on?

I must have him now.

I am forced to go in for the kill. I set the bait.

On a Monday I say, "Hey, J-M, a bunch of us are going to see the opening of 'Wayne's World 2' Friday night. You're welcome to come, if you want."

"Sounds great."

As J-M walks away, my coworker looks confused. "I didn't hear anything about a group outing this Friday night."

"That's because there is no group outing."

"But you just told J-M..."

"I lied."

I will have him.

On Thursday I pull J-M aside. "Listen, we've got a little problem."

"What's wrong?"

"Well, you know how fickle people are. Back on Monday everyone was psyched to go out Friday night, now it looks like it'll be just you and me. So, if you'd rather not go to the movie, I'll understand."

My heart stops beating. Did I just give him a clear out? What the hell am I thinking? What kind of take-no-prisoners plan is this? And yet, if these past weeks have only been a mild flirtation on his part, I'd rather know now, before I get in any deeper.

"Perfect," he says, "and let's get some dinner too."

Holy crap, I got him!

Twelve years later, I still have him. And he has me. And we share a fabulous marriage and two adorable sons. And whenever anyone asks how we met, my husband beams with pride and says, "She found me in the clearance section of Wally-World and I let her trick me into a first date."

A Little Note Started It All

Eighteen years ago, I was a happy bachelor minding my own business. My Christian faith is very important to me, and I had decided I would just stay single, like the apostle Paul.

One day, though, a coworker asked me if I'd like to meet a female friend of hers. This young lady had been giving my coworker a ride back and forth from work, since they both lived in a nearby town. The girl sounded okay; I thought, sure, why not?

But, as fate would have it, our schedules changed, and the coworker was leaving work an hour earlier than I. The planned meeting didn't take place and I basically forgot all about it.

I had a couple of roommates at the time. One of them was getting serious about a certain girl. Unbeknownst to me, his girlfriend worked at the same place as Barbara, the girl I had been scheduled to meet. One evening she brought me a little note penned on yellow paper. It said something like this:

Hi, Bob! I don't know if you remember this, but about six months ago my friend, Mary, told you about me. I was supposed to meet you after work, but our schedules changed. Anyway, I was wondering if you'd still like to meet. Would you like to take me to your church's revival tonight? To refresh your memory, I'm a teacher. I'm twenty-nine (for one more week) and have a little boy who's five. Give me a call tonight after church if you are interested!

She ended the note with her phone number. Not being one to pass up a chance to take someone to church with me, I called Barbara that night, and we made plans to meet the next evening at six. That would give us a few minutes to visit, before we had to leave. Turns out she had a fresh baked pineapple upside down cake ready. She also turned out to be quite a talented singer and guitarist, entertaining me with a spiri-

22

by
Bob Wood

Missouri

What kind of girl was this that had two blind dates in two nights?

43

tual song she had written herself.

Needless to say, we hit it off really well. I wanted to pick her up the next night, too, but she said she had been forced into saying she'd meet another guy. Hmmm... What kind of girl was this that had two blind dates in two nights? She insisted that she had promised to meet the other guy, even though she wasn't really interested.

So imagine my surprise when she comes into church the next evening, about five minutes late. I was in the choir, but I sat with her when the singing was finished. Afterwards, at dinner, she told me how the blind date went. Turns out the other guy was at Barbara's house for about ten minutes, when she started wondering if he'd been there long enough to tell him to leave; seems like he was a real loser.

Anyway, she finally told him, "Hey, I met a really nice guy last night and he wanted me to go to revival with him tonight, but I couldn't because I had to meet you."

The 'loser' then said his first wise remark of the evening. "Do you still have time to make it?"

With that, the other guy left, and Barbara started getting herself and her little boy ready for church. She told me afterward that she wasn't real sure where the church was located, but she found it. That was one determined lady.

Three weeks later I asked her to marry me. We tied the knot six weeks from the day we met. Together, we have three children, including a set of twins, and have weathered a number of storms.

I've never regretted Barbara's boldness in getting things started or our hasty decision to get married. We are truly a match made in heaven!

I met the man of my dreams at a college alumni event: A wine-tasting, to be exact. It wasn't a singles-only thing, and I was talking to various people, wondering why I was there. I had signed up weeks earlier, then almost blew it off at the last minute to go to yoga, but I'm so glad I went.

I was talking to someone I knew from another alumni activity when "he" materialized from across the semi-crowded room. We started talking and realized that we had been college classmates, both English majors; we even had a class together, although we didn't remember ever meeting during college, more than a decade before.

We continued talking about all sorts of things, and suddenly the cleaning crew for the event was booting us out the door. I offered him a ride home, which he accepted, and we sat in the car talking for another hour or so. I knew I'd appear too forward if I turned off the engine and leaned over to kiss him, so I finally said "Drop me an e-mail." I gave him my online address and went home.

He wrote the next day and said that he enjoyed meeting and talking to me, so I took a shot and invited him to an exhibit at a local art gallery. At the time, being so aggressive felt out of character. I was worried he'd think I was too easy.

But he accepted, and we went to the gallery that Sunday. So I accepted his offer when he said, "I have a bottle of wine at home."

One thing led to another, and I ended up staying overnight, which in itself, was also out of character for me. I was falling for him, but I held off on sex, again, not wanting to seem like the type of woman who has sex on the first date. We spoke on the phone the next day, and two nights later he said, "when are you coming over?"

At that point, I decided I was the kind of woman who had sex on the second date, and hurried to get ready to walk to his apartment, which

by
Laura J. Colgate

Washington, D.C.

23

At the time, being so aggressive felt out of character. I was worried he'd think I was too easy.

was about a mile away from mine. Time permitting, I would have baked cookies, since I love to bake, but given the spur-of-the moment invitation, I showed up with a pint of Ben & Jerry's Oatmeal Cookie Chunk ice cream instead.

We became engaged seven months later, we were married in October 2004 and we still like to eat Ben & Jerry's ice cream in bed.

You Can Kiss Me

He was the reason I came to work every day—to hear his footsteps click across the kitchen tile; to smell his cologne drift over the scent of the food; to see his shining grin and hear, "Hello, how are you?" in that sweet Spanish accent.

But I didn't know it until he was gone—on vacation for a month. In his absence, I realized that what I felt for him was more than a ticklish infatuation; it was a surging desire, a need for something I didn't understand, like the need that all humans are said to have for the eternal. "As soon as he comes back," I told myself, "I'll tell him how I feel."

Almost a month passed, before I had the opportunity to keep that promise. I knew from the sound of the footsteps passing through the kitchen towards the dining room of the yacht club, where we worked, that he was finally here —but I didn't dare to believe it until I saw him. I took some drinks to a table and came back, and there he was, his black, curly hair now clipped close to his head, his body hidden by a sleek leather jacket.

"You made it back," I said. "I'm so happy."

"Oh, hello. How are you?"

"Fine. Did you miss me?"

Then, the smile came. "Miss you?" he laughed. "Yeah, of course I miss you." He went on about his business, punched his time card, took off his jacket, put his apron on.

I walked over to him. "You know, I had a dream about you last night."

He hesitated. "You dream of me?"

"Yeah. I dreamed that you came back, and I was so happy that I woke up crying."

Unsure whether I was telling the truth or joking with him, he smiled again—but with a curious expression in his eyes. "I don't know if I understand."

"You understand," I said. I glanced around

by
Meagan Bernabe

Los Angeles, California

How can I tell
you thank you?
Even I was
blushing now.
I looked straight into
his eyes and said,
"You can kiss me."

quickly to make sure that the other waitress was still keeping the manager occupied up at the hostess stand; she was. So I turned back to him. "I dreamed of you a lot while you were gone." I reached out and touched his hand—that smooth, brown skin.

The next night he was sick, stricken, perhaps, by the change in climate from some beach town, to our dim, wintry San Francisco, he'd come down with something like the flu. I sent him home with several packets of Echinacea tea, which had cured my most recent ills in only a few days.

Sure enough, he was back at work the following Thursday night. "Feeling better?" I asked him, as soon as he walked in.

"Hello, how are you?" he said as usual. Then: "Yes, thank you. I feel better. That tea was excellent."

"You liked it?"

"Oh, delicious. How can I tell you thank you?"

"With a kiss," I responded.

There was a moment's silence as he filled several carafes with ice. Finally, he said, "Sorry?"

Even I was blushing now, but there was no one around to see but him; so I looked straight into his eyes and said, "You can kiss me."

Nervously, he looked out into the dining room, which was practically empty. "Now?"

"Not right now," I said smiling. "After."

I could almost see his heart pounding through his shirt. "After?" he repeated. "Okay, after."

Then, as if a window had been raised between us and we could see each other clearly for the first time, our eyes met with sincere pleasure. "I kiss you after," he said again. The rest of the night passed like the action of a stage play; we were actors in it; but all we could think of was finishing the act and getting backstage, where we could be ourselves again.

Six months later, we were married, with several of the yacht club employees attending the reception.

25

by
Betti Mustang

Wailuku, Hawaii

"I think Tammi and I are going to work it out," James said flatly. We were sitting in his BMW, outside the Ale House in Kahului, Maui. James and I had been "friends"—you know, the kind of friends that push the definition of the word 'platonic,' for about three months. We met through my brother at a friendly card game and hit it off immediately. We both liked fast cars, a good game of billiards, imported beer, raunchy humor and dancing. We just never went dancing together because of her. Because of Tammi.

She and James had been on-again, off-again for about three years. They were just too different. He had a wild streak in him that couldn't be tamed and she was just plain dull. I couldn't see the connection between them. The only positive thing about their relationship was one-and-a-half year old Emma. She was the apple of her Daddy's eye.

Until now, James and Tammi had been off-again.

As soon as the words left his mouth, I felt a flash of cold. I was sure that James felt the same stirrings in his blood as I did when we were together. We were always touchy-feely in a "brush of the hand here" kind of way. More than that, I knew that we were compatible on a human-to-human level—we had the same passions.

When I didn't say anything in response, he said, "Bella, it's just that I figure I should try my best to be with Tammi for Emma's sake." "And have her grow up in a family where her parents resent each other? Oh, yeah. That seems really positive," I retorted.

We went back and forth about it for about half an hour. I had no doubt that our friends in the bar were wondering what-in-the-heck was taking us so long. Alex, James' best-friend, came up and slapped the hood of the car playfully. "Why don't you guys just do it and get it over with?" he joked, before walking off.

> **When he turned and looked at me, he had the look in his eye that men get only when they are thinking really naughty thoughts. Bingo!**

We both ignored him. Usually we'd both have witty comebacks, but not tonight. It seemed that the humor had been sucked from the night, leaving it dry and empty. I couldn't stand it. I made a decision.

When all else fails, resort to flat out seduction. A few days before, I had set out to Island Ink Tattoo in Paia town and had a little red rose tattooed below my hip bone. It was something that I had wanted to do for a while, and had finally mustered the courage to follow through with it.

James and I had talked about hidden, "secret area" tattoos when we met. As a teenager he had a panther tattooed to his shoulder and had wanted another ever since. He never followed through, because Tammi thought that tattoos looked 'dirty'. We agreed that ink that only a lover would see was completely tantalizing. The chemistry that flowed between us the night of the conversation was crazy-intense.

"I got a tattoo," I said into the silence.

Considering that it was a sudden declaration and completely off the subject, it was James' turn to be stunned. When he turned and looked at me, he had the look in his eye that men get only when they are thinking really naughty thoughts.

Bingo!

"You better let me see it," he said quietly. There was a demand and directness in his voice that I found overwhelmingly sexy. I pushed the band of my skirt down just enough to expose my new body-art. He turned on the cabin light and looked at me like he was studying me. He tentatively touched the surrounding area with a hesitant finger. I shuddered. He looked at me with darkness in his eyes and said, "You have no idea how much I want you. I want you so bad, Bella, so bad."

There were no words of tenderness or professions of love in the passion that happened between us in the car that night. Those things came in the weeks and months and years to come. My girlfriends still tease me about my "low-blow" attempt at snaring my man.

Hey, it worked. James and I are happily married (two years in April). His relationship with his daughter is flourishing, not to mention, Tammi even found someone new; James and I hope that it will be a positive relationship—for Emma's sake.

I still love my tattoo and it still brings out the tiger in James. Three weeks before our wedding, he came home with a little surprise of his own. He got another tattoo—this time in a secret place, just for me. It's a rose, covered in sharp, beautiful thorns. He said that he got it to represent the both of us. Needless to say, it was an exciting evening.

Now we really match—inside and out.

26

by
Brandon Abney

Lincolnville, Maine

"No!" That was the first thought that entered my head the moment my friend proposed the idea that I should date her friend. "She has three kids. I have none. I'm twenty-three, she's twenty-five. She's not really my type," and so on. I had taken my stand, regarding the woman who would someday capture every nuance of my heart.

But, truly, persistence does pay off. I remember quite vividly the first time I ever met my wife. It was in high school. She was an uppity junior who would never consider dating a freshman, and I was the geeky, fat, nerdy, freshman. I actually never talked to her in person during all our years of school together. Sadly, our first meeting came when I was flipping through a yearbook and pointed at her image and declared, "She's hot!"

Skip forward a few years and the tides had been utterly reversed. After high school, I lost seventy-five pounds and became rather fond of myself. Clearly, in my world anyway, there was none better than me. Arrogance was my demeanor, and a conceited heart, my forte. Funny, how a woman can bring all selfish thoughts to a crashing and victorious end.

Our first, true, meeting came after a church service. A mutual friend of ours introduced us and it was more of a "Hi-Bye" chat. My wife did not recognize me as the geek from school, and thought I had moved to the community from another state! After this, we would gather at our friend's house and play games, talk, but nothing serious. The state of mind I was in wouldn't allow her to get any closer than a simple friend.

While I tried not to let it show, at this time in my life, my heart had been shattered. I'd just coming out of a bad relationship. By bad, I mean atrocious. My heart was in no condition to love. I had put off such things for the rest of my life.

At that point, I truly believe it was God who spoke to my wife and told her to reach out to

> **My heart was in no condition to love. I had put off such things for the rest of my life.**

51

me. The beautiful woman, who had much of the same testimony as I had, became something I needed more than anything, and something that I had lacked all of my life. She completely supported me. During my moments of selfishness, disillusion and heartache, not once did she berate me or ask me to change. She saw past all of my flaws, which were many, and somehow found a spark of love that ignited to volcanic proportions.

There was some trickery involved with her goal to win me over. Those "meetings" at our friends were planned—something I was completely oblivious to. However, it was persistence, and a refusal to believe that my heart was untouchable, that caused a woman, to whom I hardly gave a second glance, to win me over. She used a tactic I had never before seen and it worked supremely.

Most guys fear marriage, but I honestly have to say it was the best decision I have ever made. If not for the boldness and persistence of my wife, God only knows where I would be. She took the first step and changed the miserable course I was on. Thanks to her, I don't have to reflect on what my life would have been like had she not come into it. What I *can* do, is look by my side and see a woman who will never forsake me, and who gives me hope for tomorrow. All because she wouldn't give up.

She Who Tells Porkies

by
Anna Maria Davis

Sailboat in Asia

When I met my future husband, Paul, I had three problems: First, I was sleeping with his neighbor; second, I had just bought a ticket to Alaska; third, he seemed to show no interest in me. Having spent a year in London, I put Paul's disinterest down to his being English, a people famous for their butt-clinching inhibitions. My relationship with Zev, the neighbor, reflected the emotional train wreck that was my life at that point. About six months earlier, I had been stalked by a crack-addicted psychopath who threatened to kill me and later set fire to my apartment. Zev's neurotic self-absorption mirrored my own. Escaping to Alaska was going to be my way of dealing with the trauma, basically, by running far, far away and sticking my head in the snow.

But meeting Paul stirred my heart and reinvigorated my curiosity. Interesting and intelligent, aware and witty, traveled and well-read, Paul made me feel a rush of excitement similar to what I experienced when landing in a new country. I knew I had to get to know this guy.

Meanwhile, I stopped sleeping with Zev and, instead, advocated the 'just friends' approach, which, while noble, was a mistake. The primitive reptilian part of my brain knew that the 'just friends' stuff was my pathetic and gutless way of trying to end our relationship, which in truth, had only been about sex. Without sex as a distraction, we were just two self-absorbed people with no audience. The 'just friends' policy resulted in our arguments getting stupider and more frequent. I gave into the wisdom of my primitive instinct and finally just came out with it—I fancy your neighbor.

So for the next couple of months, I concocted plausible and implausible schemes to spend time with Paul. At first I was subtle, camping out at his friend Lisa's place for hours. "Oh, it's you

> **When neither subtle nor overt advances work, a gal has to pull out her trump card: Bold-face lies.**

again," she'd say. I'd make excuses that my car was acting funny and I didn't want to risk it breaking down at night. When the subtle approach didn't work, I called him up and invited him to the movies, bars, and barbeques, but he never once flirted with me.

"Do you think he's gay?" I finally asked Lisa.

"Nah," she said, "look at the way he dresses."

True, gay men don't dress like slobs. So, in desperation, I showed up at his office and asked him if he had time for a coffee, as there was something important I had to tell him.

When neither subtle nor overt advances work, a gal has to pull out her trump card: Bold-face lies. I had run through my options: brain tumor, only a month to live. But I nixed this idea. Pity isn't conducive to romance. A dangerous job in Columbia… may never come back alive. But the problem was the job—what job? I delivered bean sprouts for a living. It's hard to imagine bean sprout delivery people getting caught in the crossfire between warring drug cartels. Plus, I'm a lousy liar—I easily forget the details of my lies. Thus, I had to stick close to the truth, so I decided to tell Paul that I was leaving for Alaska in two days time and I needed to know how he felt about me. It was a lie, as I had already decided to sell my ticket. Should the worst happen and he wish me bon voyage, I hadn't physically exchanged the ticket for cash; thus, I could still save myself from complete humiliation and split.

I couldn't look at him as I recited my monologue, but instead, stared into the steaming black coffee...so you see...two days...Alaska...may never return...need to know how you feel…

When I finally looked up, he was smiling, then leaned over and kissed me on the lips.

"You 'aven't cotton on yet?" he chided. "I would've thought it was obvious."

Beaming, I felt like the cat who'd found the cream.

"By the way," he started choking down a laugh, "Lisa asked me to pass on a message from a woman named Carole. She'd like to arrange a time and place to meet to pay you for the plane ticket to Alaska."

My face went beet red and my cheeks were on fire. I gave a stupid grin and he nearly wet himself laughing.

Today, fourteen years on, we live aboard a forty-two foot sailboat and cruise around Asia with our two cats.

28

"Ughhhhhh!" I groaned as I heard my exhaust amplify to a distracting series of loud, clanking noises. It was a hot, muggy day in August and I was driving home from work. This was all I needed, another car repair. I went to work the following day and my boss, hearing my arrival a mile away, suggested I go to a private exhaust shop about ten miles from there that did the work well and cheaply. I said "Nah, that's okay," figuring I would take it to one of the better-known muffler shops to get it fixed. He told me I would be paying more than double and he was right—I called both, compared quotes and made my appointment with the shop he suggested.

The next morning, I went. I was instantly captivated by a young man there. He was so handsome, and no, not a grease monkey like you may be thinking. He was one of the cleaner cut 'mechanics' you'll ever meet. He didn't fix my car, but boy, did we make eyes at each other. We exchanged smiles and glances. We were both smitten and there was undeniably something special between us, but I left.

For some reason, I could not get this guy out of my mind. Day after day, I thought about him, day dreamed about going back and meeting him and the feeling did not go away. Crazy as it sounds, I felt I had to pursue this—like it was fate or destiny. There came a point when I got such a strong urge to go back and meet this fellow, fate stepped in and had my muffler start making noise again. "Yeah!" I thought—"now I have a valid excuse to go back." I needed to get the car fixed anyway, but would I pursue this situation?

After getting my nerve up, debating whether this was a good idea or not, I called the shop the next afternoon and explained to the owner's mother that I'd my car repaired there a month ago and that it was making a noise again, like something was loose. I thought I was being clever when I said, "The guy who fixed it was slim

by
Natasha Nichols

New York

It was too late. The words had escaped my big mouth and they could not be taken back.

---

and had dark brown hair."

"That's Dave" she replied.

"Oh Dave," I said, "hmmmm, he was cute, probably has a girlfriend." It was too late. The words escaped my big mouth and they could not be taken back. What did I do?

She kind of chuckled and said in a drawn out tone "No... as a matter of fact he doesn't have a girlfriend. Why, are you interested in him?"

I quickly replied "Oh, I just thought he was cute is all." She made an appointment for me to come back on Friday at 9 am.

Friday morning came. I had butterflies in my stomach and I came close to saying "Forget it!" What was I doing? But I looked very pretty, my confidence kicked in and I figured I had nothing to lose. If I changed my mind, or I didn't like him for some reason, I could quickly just get my car fixed and get out of there.

I got there and I was nervous. I went into the office and gave them my keys. A moment later, Dave came into the office from the shop—he was smiling, but trying to look like he didn't know what was going on, but he knew. My phone call had been the topic of conversation for several days, and Dave was flattered I called and asked about him, especially if he had a girlfriend. He remembered me from my previous visit and he was glad I came back. We both tried pretending that I was there for the car, rather than for each other, but our efforts were flimsy.

A series of events ensued after that fateful morning when he invited me to look under my car and show me my loose clamp. I bought him a cup of coffee, we exchanged phone numbers and had our first date the following night. We declared our love for each other a week later, became almost inseparable and married less than two years after that. In twelve years of marriage, we have one adorable daughter who is six and are expecting our second child on our daughter's seventh birthday.

That first time we met, I had a strong feeling this was the man I was meant to share my life with. I know I went out on a limb and took my chances, but I listened to my heart, and I'm glad I did.

29

There were many reasons not to go, from things to do at home to people not to see at the party. I went, and of all mistakes, I went alone. The person who answered the door, was the one I didn't want to see—my ex-husband. I forced a smile, kissed his cheek and went inside. I greeted everyone and found a seat near the music. Soon, a couple sat beside me, and we settled into a comfortable conversation. I noticed that everyone present was a couple, including the ex. This made sense as the last time I attended, I was part of a couple too.

The doorbell rang, jerking me out of my thoughts. I looked up in time to see a 6'3" dark chocolate man dressed in a color-coordinated suit walk through the door. He greeted my ex-husband and was introduced to a few of the people present, before he went back to talk with him. I tried to follow the conversation of the couple I was next to, but I couldn't help but watch as the muscles in his face flexed with aggravation. I just knew the host would bring him to me, as he and I were the only two dateless people present.

Then, the doorbell rang again. My heart sank as I watched the man of my dreams kiss a tall striking female on the cheek and begin introducing her to the people he'd met when he arrived. Finally, he looked my way and our eyes locked. I could have sworn everyone in the room noticed, including his date. I had to meet this man. I had to meet him and make him mine.

There were a few problems. Not once—not ever—have I been the aggressor when it comes to men. No one introduced us and he may have been married. I tried asking our hostess, but she didn't know him; she'd been busy serving, so she hadn't been introduced. I spoke to my ex-husband, but his date pulled him away. I watched the time tick away until they were getting ready to leave.

He walked to the bathroom, and I followed. I picked up a pen and paper and wrote down my

by
Chris Cook

Birmingham, Alabama

**There were
a few problems.
Not once—not ever—
have I been
the aggressor
when it came to men.**

---

address and phone number, while I waited by the door. I tried to act as if I were waiting my turn. When he opened the door, I went inside before he could get out. I reached and grabbed his hand. The pit in my stomach turned into butterflies when I kept him in that bathroom with me. I put the paper in his hand, pulled his neck down and kissed him. Afterwards, I walked out of the bathroom, sat in my seat and watched him leave.

When I drove home, I had no idea if I would see him again. I thought I was an idiot for giving my information, and for being so brazen with a stranger. I realized I didn't give him my name or even ask for his. After I arrived home, someone knocked on my door.

"Tom? I don't know a Tom."

"We met tonight." This time, it was my turn to open the door. I found my dream man standing there.

"Come in." I invited him into my home and my life.

He later mentioned that he had been eyeing me as much as I him, but he wasn't going to speak to me because of my ex-husband. When I made the first move, he was intrigued, and two years later, he still is. Now when we pass in our bathroom, I don't hesitate to pull him in with me—and I don't have a pen or paper in hand!

Dakota From South Dakota

by
John W. Hursey, Jr.

Edwardsville, Illinois

Who really knows what women want? Movies tell you that you have to be handsome, books tell you that you have to be charming, and the little box under the nude pictures in "Swank" say that women like "funny guys, and tropical shirts." I'll admit, being a good-looking, suave, and devastatingly funny bartender at Friday's seems like an easy road to getting all the women you desire; unfortunately, though, the one requirement that acts as the great unsaid in all matters of love and the heart, is confidence. Yeah, it seems like the Fonz was right after all: Women dig guys who know what they want and aren't afraid to go after it.

So what's a gawky military brat to do when he's dying to ask out the hottie in Trigonometry? The answer is simple: Wait for her to do it for you.

My senior year at high school was the stuff zits were made of. First off, I was the new kid, which means that I was shut off from all the great experiences the rest of the class had lived through over the last four years. That summer between sophomore and junior year, last year's school play, and that fake bomb-threat were all things that I wasn't privy to, and they, therefore, cast me as an outsider.

Second, by senior year, all the cliques and gangs have closed their memberships, and everyone knows there's nothing dorkier than a senior hanging out with some stupid freshman. So if you think this is the stuff that a strong self-image is made of, then obviously you have never seen a film by John Hughes.

Enter Dakota: Pretty, nubile, and recently excommunicated from her own clique (which included the class president and the Homecoming Queen) for being too friendly with other friends'

> **I was such an unbelievable wuss, that she was going to have to do the actual "asking-out" for me.**

boyfriends. A class trip had forced her to share a seat with me on the bus, and soon I was in.

Now, I should mention at this point that, just because you don't specifically ask a girl out, it doesn't mean you don't do your best so that she will take the plunge for you. My modus operandi has always been to showcase what I believe are my talents, and then patiently wait for my prey to crawl into my web and then try and make out with me.

So, during the trip, I did my best to let Dakota know two things: One, that I was an incredibly smart, sensitive, and funny guy who would probably look better once his face cleared up; and two, that I was such an unbelievable wuss, that she was going to have to do the actual "asking-out" for me. Like stalagmite formations in underground caves, though, the process is a slow one. Gradually her interest in me built, which resulted in shared lunches and group work in classes. Finally, though, my patience paid off when my mother told me that I had a phone call, from "*a girl!*" (At this point I'm sure mom was just relieved to get confirmation that I wasn't gay.)

I picked up the phone and in the smoothest voice possible for a seventeen-year-old late bloomer, said, "Word up, dude?" I had not yet learned that girls don't like to be treated like Jeff Spicoli. Dakota, though, persevered, and in her own roundabout way asked if I was doing anything tomorrow night, because there was this, like, movie, she wanted to see with Mel Gibson, but, like, her friends totally didn't want to go, so she didn't want to, like, see the movie all by herself and thought maybe, like, I'd want to go with her.

Now, with hindsight, I realize that I should have just said yes right away and taken care of all the little details later, but I made the mistake of telling her that I had to ask my mom if it was okay first. This mistake was pointed out to me by my mother when I asked if it was okay to go to the movies with this girl; she told me that I should accept her offer, that is, if she hadn't already hung up by now. Luckily for me, she waited, and I was ready for my first real date.

Everything went well, the movie was good, and afterwards we sat in my bedroom (door open, feet on the ground, of course; thanks a lot mom and dad) and talked about all the stuff teenagers talk about. Finally, after an uncomfortable silence, she asked me, "Are you going to kiss me, or what?" I intended to respond to that with a well-reasoned answer that covered both the social and economic ramifications of such an act, but fortunately she leaned forward and took care of that herself.

Since then, Dakota was able to teach me a lot of things about women, men, and where I fit in to all this. We didn't last forever (ahh, the impermanence of young love), but I'll always remember what she did for me. It takes a lot of guts to walk up to a woman, no matter how well you know her, and risk rejection and abject humiliation to ask her out to dinner. It takes even more, though, for a woman to throw centuries of tradition and social etiquette to the wind and do the job herself. For that, I'll be eternally grateful.

Hooked

I found my soul mate at Radio Shack. It was during my lunch break—well deserved time off from an excruciatingly boring day working as a receptionist for a personnel agency. I needed some size "D" batteries for my boom box and off I went to Radio Shack in the mall. This was, however, not a chance encounter in the electronics store. It was part of a strategic campaign to lure my unsuspecting future husband into my trap. My plan worked, despite some unforeseen and unplanned maneuvers.

I was a lonely twenty-year-old girl, trying to make it on her own, living in a rented room, taking the bus to a dead end job. All I really wanted was to meet a nice guy who would fall madly in love with me and ask me to marry him. Time to wake up and smell the coffee! It was not so easy to meet a "nice guy," let alone a prince charming type, who would sweep me off my feet and carry me into the sunset. It was time to put down the romance novels and get serious, I figured.

A good friend of mine worked at Radio Shack and her manager was a divorced older guy who sounded like he had some potential. I'd caught a brief glimpse of him when I met her for lunch one day, and made the quick determination that he had 'possibilities.' The obvious solution was for my friend to set us up on a blind date. But he refused to take the bait and turned down the date. It was a setback, but not the end.

by
Patricia F. D'Ascoli

New Milford, Connecticut

Suddenly, he found himself the target of a headstrong, somewhat troubled, young woman, who had determined for some unknown reason that she must have him.

A little time passed before I made my surprise attack. I casually mentioned my friend's name during that first simple cash transaction. Being the brilliant man that my husband is, he put two and two together and figured out that I must be the rejected blind date. A connection was established, and the seeds of interest were planted. I was laying the groundwork for my future onslaught.

Giving him a few hours to recover from our lunchtime encounter, I reappeared after work, this time to buy double "A" batteries for my Walkman. It was merely another excuse. I definitely did not give him very much time to reflect on any future action he might take toward me. Like a dog on a bone I pounced a third time, on that very same day! Of course it took drinking a few glasses of wine to get up my courage to make the phone call that I felt would determine the direction we would go. There was no subtlety about me at all —just a plain unabashed desire to win him over. I made the fateful phone call to him while he was finishing up for the day at Radio Shack and asked him if he wanted to go out that night. Mercifully, he said yes. On the whole, our first date went very well, other than the fact that I drank too much. What was I thinking anyway? Our conversation was stimulating and we thoroughly enjoyed each other's company. Why on earth I couldn't leave well enough alone is beyond me. But my gut instinct told me to stick with this man, and stick with him I did. When that question "Want to come back to my place?" arose, there was no other answer but 'Yes'.

What ensued back at his place, was a mellow collaboration of innocent affection, which resulted in a sense of total comfort on my part. Feeling I was in the presence of someone completely trustworthy, I promptly fell fast asleep. He took off my cowboy boots and put a blanket over me, and I, a virtual stranger, proceeded to snore away the night in his bed.

The next morning dawned too bright for my taste, and there he was, the handsome man I sought to win over, smiling at me from across the pillow. The realization of my unconsciousness hit me like a cold shower, instantly sobering me in my hung-over state. The word "embarrassed" does not even begin to describe how I felt. I mumbled an apology and he drove me home to ponder my fate. He did kiss me good-bye, however.

All that day and the next, I strategized some maneuver that could offset any damage my errant behavior had caused. What could he possibly think of me now? I knew that the heroine in a romance novel definitely did not pass out on her lover on any date, let alone their first date! But this was reality, and I was a girl with a mission to be completed, even if it turned out to be Mission Impossible.

And so it was that I found myself returning to Radio Shack, not to plead my case in any way, but to face the truth at all costs. If I had crossed the line, I wanted to know. If he no longer found me desirable, then so be it. I figured I had nothing to lose and everything to gain. The direct approach was the only approach I knew. There was no sense in waiting for him to call me (only a rational, patient person would do that, after all).

Looking back, I realize how very awkward the situation might have been. There he was, a nice guy who was just minding his own business, trying to get his life back to normal after a messy divorce. Suddenly, he found himself the target of a headstrong, somewhat troubled, young woman, who had determined for some unknown reason, that she must have him. And this woman had already made a very strange first impression on him. Why did he not see a red flag or a "Wrong way—go back" sign when I came into his store? Why did he not run away, or better yet, bar me from the premises?

It never occurred to me in my zealous quest that I should not continue to pursue this man. There is no explanation for why I blindly forged ahead in my campaign. I only know that when I returned, like a moth to the light, he warmly welcomed me and made no mention of my inappropriate behavior. He must have realized that I was much more than the narcoleptic fool he had unwittingly shared the night with.

More than twenty years have passed since that spring day when I first staked my claim for the man with the golden eyes. We've been married for nineteen of them. Who can say what forces conspire in the universe to bring two people together? When someone is right, you just know it and there's no turning back.

32

by
Joy D. Voltz

Omaha, Nebraska

When he walked in the room, I was immediately attracted to him. I felt weird, having just had my heart broken by my high school sweetheart of five years. What's worse is that I found out about his new girlfriend when she sent me an e-mail. Ouch!

I was rarely physically attracted to men, however, I found myself in friendships with men very easily. They often took me the wrong way, wanting more than I wanted to give. Men often suffocated me. I guess it was unusual for them to encounter a strong young woman who had goals besides wearing a white dress and a veil.

I went to college three states away from my high school boyfriend and saw him only on vacations. I encountered a lot of guys. I just never felt chemistry with a single one of them. So I stuck with my high school sweetie, because I had not found anyone else as interesting. Plus, men never understood that I needed my own time to do my own thing. I was not ready to share every waking moment with one person. I wanted to be independent and was determined to live on my own without needing a man.

I never planned on Mike. I always tell him, he threw me off course.

One of the people in the room shouted, "Come on, game time. We need to divide up girl, guy, girl, guy in a circle." I was seated next to a friend I had dragged with me to the party, as I needed to get out and see something other than my teary face in the mirror. I decided to make my move. I walked over to sit by him, making the room even for the game.

> In that same evening of our first meeting, I insisted he dance with me— which he did *not* want to do.
> I was so confused the next day. Why did I act like that?

The first words out my mouth would be the beginning of a night that just went horribly wrong, even though I was attempting to make a good first impression.

"So, do you enjoy being an Engineer?" I asked.

He barely looked at me and said, "Well, I am not an Engineer, so I would not know. I am a

Drafter. I work for the Engineers."

I had one of those moments where I wished I had been swallowed by a giant hole in the floor. The guy throwing the party had introduced Mike as a coworker, and I just assumed he was an Engineer. The voice in my head was screaming in agony at my mistake. I focused on the game. I do not remember what the game was, but I do remember I stank at it. He was on my team and we lost, big time.

Later that night, we all went to a club and I proceeded to get a little drunk. In that same evening of our first meeting, I insisted he dance with me—which he did *not* want to do. I told him to buy my friend a drink and I confessed that I was twenty-three-year-old virgin (yes, it's true, I was picky).

I was so confused the next day. Why had I acted like that? The behavior was not like me. I tried to let it go, and to let go how attracted I was to him. I realized that I was so rarely attracted to a man like that, I'd lost control of myself. I'd never done that in my life. I was always so confident, so cool and got what I wanted.

By happenstance, he showed up at dinner a couple of weeks later with those same friends. I was both humiliated and excited to see him. I got over my behavior and began to talk to him; from that point on, we'd talk on the phone for hours, we had so much in common.

Yet, weeks passed and he never asked me on a date. We'd see each other only when our other friends got together.

One night on the phone I said, "You know, if you asked me on a date, I would say yes."

He then invited me to his house the next day. He showed me his place, and on our first date, we were so comfortable, we fell asleep in each other's arms. We've been together for three years (and I'm no longer a virgin).

Mike has taught me a lot about life. But the biggest lesson is that there are times when making a fool of yourself is worth it. The true love of your life will look past foolish parts and see the real you.

33

At twenty-four I decided to stay single the rest of my life. I spent time with my friends, male and female, and much more time with myself. I read alone, wrote alone, rode my motorcycle alone. I dated here and there, mostly women from the college campus nearby, or the church I went to. I never went on a second date, however, because I knew in the first twenty minutes of a first date whether I wanted to know this person more. It was something in the eyes or the way the eyes looked when she smiled. Most women didn't have it.

I also tired of initiating. The attitude among most women, it seemed, was that the man should initiate a date, a meeting, a cup of coffee: Show no interest until he does. I grew sick of calling, inviting and asking out women who, for whatever reason, maybe the Midwestern upbringing, didn't know how to show their interest.

I drove my motorcycle to Daytona Beach for spring break with a college group from the church. Again, I was still alone, having remained aloof from the group because I preferred to explore Daytona all day than lay on the beach.

I was on my way out, the second afternoon, when Nicole, a girl I had only commented with in the past, approached just before the elevator arrived and said, "Hey, you're about to go out on your bike, aren't you? Can you wait? Just wait, lemme get my jacket and I'll come with you. Just wait."

We spent the day cruising down Highway One, watching for alligators when we passed over low bridges and stopping to see a plane take off from some no-name municipal airport. That night we ate in a Mexican place with some other people from the trip. I don't remember what she said, or even how she said it, but as I sat there beside her, I thought, "I think I could marry this woman." I forgot the thought within the next few minutes.

by
D.A. Holroyd

Bloomington, Indiana

> **I grew sick of calling, inviting and asking out women, who, for whatever reason, didn't know how to show an interest.**

Summer came. She went to California to perform with the Disney All-College Band. I went to Australia with my brother. When I returned, college was back in session, as were the Sunday night church sessions for twenty-somethings. I had shaved my beard off to a goatee for no reason at all, but that first night back, Nicole, who I now barely remembered, had me stand to pose for her camera phone. She said she was going to call sometime. I said, "Sure. Why not?"

My phone rang the next Saturday. "Do you feel like watching some jazz tonight?" she said.

"Just watching some jazz?"

"Yeah, well…watching jazz and buying me dinner. It'll be fun."

"I'm gonna have to pick you up on the bike, though."

"Well, of course! You think I called you just because I needed somebody to go with?"

She came out of her building wearing a skirt, black tank top and a green windbreaker (to this day I love that jacket). She had straightened her long hair, adding a curve around her cheeks. Slight make-up. Tinker Bell earrings. She spoke about jazz in a certain way that made me want to know more. Halfway through the evening she made a point of letting the jacket fall off her shoulders onto the back of her chair.

I knew then that I'd marry her. I didn't suspect. I knew.

I proposed two months later. Five months after that we stood for the vows. A month after that she bought her own motorcycle.

She keeps pace with me every mile, and I always thank her for calling me that Saturday.

I wasn't planning on any of it.

My friend Karla is an incredibly talented, confident young woman. After a string of bad relationships, she had almost written off men for good when Keith came into our workplace, or as Karla puts it into her life. One look at Keith had her floored, and more than anything, she was completely sure that he was "the one."

After snooping around a bit for information about her dream guy, my friend realized that wooing him would be no easy task, because unlike her previous conquests, this one was quite different. Keith was much more career-oriented, and on the surface, showed very little involvement with the opposite sex. His aloof, arrogant behavior had made it all the more challenging for her, especially since he hardly evinced any interest in her.

My friend wasn't going to give up without giving it her best shot. First of all, she knew that she had to make a wonderful impression, and a lasting one at that, to make him notice her.

Lately things had become very hectic in Keith's project, and he was inundated with lots of critical work which required some creative ideas. A couple of days before the main presentation, Keith held an informal department meeting for a brainstorming session.

After hearing his team out, he still wasn't satisfied and Karla knew that something was bothering him. She befriended his best pal and realized that Keith was still waiting for some ingenious method to solve a difficult task.

Karla was quick on the uptake and didn't waste a moment. She poured over scores of relevant material in order to get all the background information about the project, as well as some creative ideas. She researched extensively, read up as much as she could and even asked all her friends for their input.

At the final team meet, not only did she blow him over with her resourcefulness, she was also completely nonchalant about all her efforts.

34

by
Beryl Kunjavu

Mumbai, India

Karla knew she had to do *something* to make him take the plunge.

Keith was very impressed by her intellectual antics, but he still wasn't ready to open up completely.

A very persistent Karla made sure that she landed herself enough work to spend the evenings working in close proximity with the object of her affection. Initiating a coffee date wasn't easy, and it required all of her wit and charm to ask him out for a cappuccino. Over lots and lots of coffee, she got to learn about his not-so- pleasant, romantic past, and it wasn't long before they were sharing things about each other's backgrounds. As the days passed, the friendship gradually deepened, and she knew that he had fallen for her somewhere along the line.

Although Keith was smitten, he still had issues taking their relationship to the next level. Karla knew she had to do *something* to make him take the plunge. On Valentine's Day, she discreetly ordered herself a large bouquet of very expensive flow-ers to reach her workplace, with a strategic "Your secret admirer" note attached. It worked. Keith and Karla are going steady now and plan on tying the knot early next year.

As she told me her story, Karla had some advice for all women. She told me, "If you find your soul mate, or someone you know you should be with, don't waste a mo-ment. Be secure in the knowledge that there is some arcane way to reach your man's heart and never stop trying till you find out what it is. Seize the day and give it all that you've got! It's your love story, and only you can create a beautiful one."

I had already been playing in the orchestra for several years when our concertmaster decided to retire and we had to find someone new to fill his spot (which happened to be the seat right next to mine, in front of the first violin section). It's not a terribly big or posh orchestra, but, along with the bit of teaching I do on the side, it's enough to cover most of my bills, and it is a pleasant, if not terribly exciting existence. Or was, at least, until our new concertmaster showed up.

He was my age, or maybe just a bit younger, a really brilliant player with soft brown hair and eyes. I fell for him almost instantly. However, even though his violin spoke volumes, the man, himself, was painfully shy and hardly ever spoke to me, even when we were sitting side-by-side for week after week of rehearsals and concerts.

I tried everything I could. I arrived at rehearsals early and left late, just hoping to squeeze something resembling a conversation out of the man, but it was no use. He kept strictly to himself, warming up and cooling down alone with his instrument in a back corner of the hall. Something drastic had to be done.

I enlisted friends and family, everyone I could muster, (even some of the other members of the orchestra), and had them all do one small favour for me. (A favour is small if one person does it, but if dozens of people help you out, miracles can happen...) You see, there is a small Suggestions Box in the lobby area of our concert hall where patrons can write down any comments or suggestions they might have for the orchestra. I had as many people as I could write down the same suggestion and toss it into the box: Bach's Concerto for Two Violins in D minor.

Our musical director was blown over by this sudden and overwhelming demand for the piece and hurried to schedule it into a concert a few months down the road. Wouldn't you know

35

by
E. Hooper

Canada

I enlisted friends and family, everyone I could muster, and had them all do one small favour for me.

---

it, since the concertmaster and I are (respectively) the first and second chair players in the orchestra, we would be the ones playing the duet. Private rehearsals were scheduled and at last the man and I were forced to interact.

Three months and one concert later, he finally opened up and we were officially together, making beautiful music in more ways than one.

I Knew Jacob Was The One

Every day he walked into the office and back into my life. Jacob knew me as Ester, but he never considered me more than a coworker.

The office clique laughed at his square black glasses, nerdy appearance, and his lack of socialization; he neither spoke to anyone, nor did he eat anywhere but in his office. But there was more to him they couldn't see. It was a persona of confidence, stability, and true self, which I saw in him. It was rumored that he did not have a girlfriend and probably never would.

I decided to make the move to let him see me in a different light, anonymously, at first. I wrote a letter to him, telling him of the person I saw him as and what was within. I went on to explain that I worked in the same office and understood, as well as respected, his privacy.

Then I wrote about me, quiet, plain looks, the books I read and the music I cherished. I told him I liked him and hoped that he would take a chance and meet with me. I ended by saying that I would be watching as he read my letter.

If he smiled, it meant he would take a chance and if he turned away, he just might miss out opening up to something that would change both our lives. And then I sent it via an interoffice envelope.

I watched as his mail was delivered to him. He opened and read each one, never smiling nor turning away. There was one more left to open. I watched as he opened the envelope and read my words.

Jacob looked up and out to the surrounding desks. I averted my eyes. He reread my letter. I waited for his response. He read the letter again, I'm sure, hoping it wasn't some cruel trick life or the clique was playing on him. Then he stood up and smiled. I had to turn away to hide my joy. I typed another letter, telling him I was happy to see he had decided to take a chance;

36

by
Deborah L. Mireles

Fort Worth, Texas

Would there be acceptance when he saw me? Or would he see me, then turn and walk away?

I would be waiting at the coffee shop three doors down after work, and once he walked through the door, he would recognize me.

I watched the clock that afternoon waiting nervously for what would be a pivotal moment in my life. The clock finally moved to five. I calmly finished shutting down and glanced into Jacob's office. He, for the first time was closing down early…to meet me. I gathered my things and left.

I walked to the coffee shop, ordered a coffee, and waited. I watched Jacob through the window as he entered, holding my breath as he came through the door. Would there be acceptance when he saw me? Or would he see me then turn and walk away? I smiled nervously, ready to greet his acceptance.

Jacob stopped and scanned the room for a familiar face. Then his eyes fell upon me. Oh, God, please let him smile, I thought. And then it came. He smiled.

Jacob, at that moment, walked into my life. He sat down across from me. We shyly began talking about my letter, then moved to our liking one another and to having dinner together that night to continue talking.

By day, we were coworkers, never speaking, just like before. The only difference now were the slight smiles whenever there was eye contact. By night, we continued to be together over dinner, a concert or a game of chess. Our weekends were spent going to museums, visiting exhibits or just relaxing, enjoying each other's company.

As time went by, Jacob slowly began to want to change his appearance. He threw away his square black glasses and bought contact lenses. Then we went shopping for clothes that were more in style and fitting for his position.

As we expected, the change was quickly noticed and rumors spread around the water cooler. I sat back and watched, as the single women suddenly became interested and began flirting, which embarrassed Jacob; he did not return the flirtation. Little did they know, we had kept a great secret: Jacob had asked me to marry him and we'd eloped. Our ceremony was intimate with only our two closest friends sworn to secrecy, which added a dash of excitement to our day.

That was forty-five years, three children, and seven grandchildren ago—years before it was proper for a woman to do such a thing.

Our first meeting was of no consequence. I was just interning at the ambulance company while training to be an EMT. It was early in the morning and he was grouchy from just waking up after the night shift.

After I'd worked for the ambulance company for a few months, John and I became partners on a sixteen-hour shift. We had to travel to Cape Cod to return a patient to his home. John made me laugh, and at that time I needed a good friend. After spending that sixteen hours with each other, we began to work more shifts together. Because of the stressful nature of our job, at the end of our shift, we'd all go down to the wharf for a few beers to blow off some steam.

As time went on, I began to believe there could be something between us. It didn't help matters that another partner and mutual friend was playing matchmaker—but only one sided. He would tell me John was a nice guy and loved kids (I had two preteens) and I'd say "Okay, tell John I'm interested," but according to John, he never relayed my messages.

One night after a few beers, John gave me a ride back to the lot to pick up my car. I was totally sick of waiting for him to make a move, so I grabbed him and kissed him hard. The kiss was heartily returned and the intentions were clear, or so I thought. My love interest was slow when it came to women. He didn't totally get it, even after the kiss! It took a few more kisses like that to get him to realize I wasn't playing. He didn't believe a woman like me would be interested in him. Silly boy!

Things between us were really never awkward throughout that four-month period before we consummated our love. Oh, and what an interesting scene that was: We had a Paramedic test to take, so I stayed at his parents' house overnight so we could get on the road early. It just made everything easier, because I was riding to the test with John and another fellow EMT. The

by
Elizabeth A. Gaughen

Bridgton, Maine

My love interest was slow when it came to women He didn't totally get it, even after the kiss!

73

night started out normally enough, but when it came on time to go to bed I was offered the twin bed next to John with his younger brother on the other side. Talk about tension...Yikes!! We were so nervous about the test in Harwich—and then to find out we were sleeping right next to one another! The electricity between us was palpable.

We watched VH-1 for a while then decided we'd better get some sleep. We both got into our beds, which felt really weird, and the next thing I knew we were having a pillow fight. It was difficult trying to be quiet, so as not to wake his young brother, not to mention his parents, downstairs. One thing led to another and we were in each others arms, awkwardly trying to make love in a twin bed, with his brother only twenty feet away. It was wonderful, clumsy and certainly not perfect, but who cared? We didn't. We had grins a mile wide and it felt like we were floating on air all that day at the test. I passed but he didn't. None of that mattered.

That was the beginning of a fairytale love that no one could destroy. Its been seventeen years since that April 29th and we are happily married.

The story doesn't end there though. John was born with a heart defect that has since caused major damage to his liver. I saw the man I wanted and got him. I have never been so happy, and now to lose him is tearing me apart.

Since I wrote this tale, John's condition has improved and we are enjoying each day one day at a time. Go out there and grab what you want and cherish it, because it doesn't last forever!

Making the First Move 101

My first year of university was drawing to a close, and I had much more on my mind than studying for final exams. The previous September, I had met Mark, who lived one floor above me in our student residence. Despite our many differences, with him being from a small town and me being from the big city, we became incredibly close and spent virtually every weekend enjoying the freshman life with our lively group of friends.

Little did he know that I had a major crush on him. He was the life of every party, played the guitar, and was incredibly intelligent. He was in the Science program, planning to become a physician. His concentration in his studies was inspiring, but not inspiring enough for me; his constant presence, along with my growing affection for him, proved to be a major distraction from my Humanities courses. I hardly noticed that my grades were plummeting; all I could think about was how I might go about acting on my feelings for Mark.

Great accomplishments, however, often come with great obstacles. The biggest one standing in my way, was the fact that Mark had broken up with his previous girlfriend just before leaving for university. The break up had been unwanted; both were leaving home to attend schools that were several hours apart, and neither was keen on the idea of a long-distance relationship. The situation, of course, was heart-breaking for him. For me, it meant that any chance I might have had with Mark would be jeopardized by bad timing.

For the majority of the school year, I struggled with the realization that this person who had become my best friend might never be anything more. As summer approached, the tension between us became unbearable. I knew that Mark had feelings for me, but his rational, scientific

by
Emily Dontsos

**Toronto, Ontario,
Canada**

**I struggled with
the realization that
this person,
who had become
my best friend,
might never
be anything more.**

---

brain told him it was too late; we'd soon be back at home, two hours apart, and there would be no point in taking such an enormous risk on our amazing friendship, when things were so uncertain.

Two weeks before we were to move out of residence, I decided that things had to change. It was painfully obvious that we had deep feelings for each other, and the idea of leaving him for four months without knowing if we could have shared something more, was overwhelming. If I wanted to find out, I knew I had to make the first move.

It was Easter weekend, 2004. Most of the students in our residence had gone home for the holiday, but Mark and I both stayed to study for final exams. This meant that none of our roommates were around, which presented a rare opportunity. On the first night that we were alone, the two of us spent the night in my dorm room listening to music and talking until the wee hours of the morning like we always did. Again, nothing happened. Around 2 a.m., Mark left my room to go to bed.

After I closed the door behind him, I stood with my hand on the knob for several minutes, telling myself that this was probably the last chance that I would ever have to make something happen between us. After lecturing myself about the need for a backbone and some confidence, I marched up the stairs to confront him. I caught him as he was coming out of the washroom, clad in pyjamas with toothbrush in hand. I was speechless, and my hands were shaking. Mark asked me several times if I was okay, and I finally managed to stutter: "I am going insane. I can't take this. Would you kill me if…?"

He knew what I meant. He nodded his head slowly, now equally speechless, and I walked over and kissed him. Finally. Despite the fact that we were both suffering from head colds, we kissed a lot that night, there in the hallway of our residence. I had taken an enormous gamble on our friendship, not knowing if we were cut out for a relationship, and it has proved to be the most life-altering choice I have ever made.

Today, Mark and I are still together, and our relationship, as well as our friendship, seems to get stronger with every passing day.

Don't be afraid to take chances; they make the world go round.

39

by
Dragana Zanko

Velika Gorica, Croatia

The story I'm about to tell you happened more than half a century ago in Yugoslavia (former Yugoslavia, in today's area of Croatia and Serbia). A young girl named Milica lived in a small village Pirot, in southern Serbia. She had a stable and loving family. Her brother and sister were always considered to be far more restless than she. She was her father's daughter, a favorite child, you might say, always fulfilling her parents' wishes, with no complaints.

Back in those days, and even today, it was extremely important in the village that people, young women especially, keep their good reputations, which actually meant that they had to stay under their parents' roofs up until the day the parents arranged engagements and a wedding. Milica was obedient in every way, so naturally she expected her parents to find her a decent husband, to whom she would dedicate the rest of her life.

> **She had no choice but to forget him, but that was not as easy as she thought it would be.**

At the same time, in a nearby village, stayed a young man named Dragomir. Dragomir actually moved away from that village when he was a very young. As a boy, he had a strong will to study, and not guard sheep for the rest of his life, so he moved to his cousins' in Zagreb, capital of Croatia, to go to school. Every summer, though, he came to Pirot to visit his family.

One day, he saw a girl riding a bike. He was so fascinated by her at that moment, that he ran through a couple of fields of corn, just so he could see her passing by the road again. Soon Milica got a secret love letter from Dragomir, who was utterly in love with her from the moment he saw her for the first time. Opposite to what anybody would expect, and considering the way Milica was brought up, she replied to that letter and to many more that came in the following two years.

Letters were always coming to her friends' addresses and not to her own. In those two years Dragomir and Milica did not see each other at all.

They did, however, know they were in love. Two summers later, Dragomir came to Pirot and straight away asked for Milica, but as scared as she was, she did not want to see him. Summer passed and Dragomir realized that his love was in vain. Milica was devastated; she knew her parents would never grant her permission to marry Dragomir. She had no choice but to forget him, but that was not as easy as she thought it would be.

On the day of his departure, she realized she could no longer live without him. While her parents were away, she packed one shirt, one skirt, one pair of shoes and some underwear in a plastic bag and ran. She ran towards the train station, as fast as she could, running away from the family she loved, from parents who might never forgive her, from the only life she knew, into the unknown world, towards a person she hardly knew. She made it to the train station in time. They made it to Zagreb, fearing at every station that police would come after them, considering Milica's father was a police officer and she was under age. They did, however, make the trip safely.

Later on, they learned that her father shot all the bullets from a pistol the day she ran away. He did it, not in anger, but crying, at the sidewalk of their family home and wishing them best of luck. In Zagreb, it was hard for Dragomir and Milica at first, but they made it. Their life was a true fairy tale. He treated her as a drop of water in the palm of his hand.

They spent twenty beautiful years by each other's side. Unfortunately he got sick; he had an ulcer and ended up in hospital in 1983, and doctors could not save his life. He left Milica devastated. It took her a really long time just to get used to the idea that he was not around anymore. Years passed, she was still young and beautiful, but no man could ever be her Dragomir. No one could ever make her run away, and leave all she ever knew, for love. So she never got married after him.

Today, she is still single, surrounded by her two daughters and three grandchildren. I was born one month after Dragomir died, so naturally, my mother called me Dragana in memory of him.

Now, when Milica, my grandma, tells me the story of their love, and of her sacrifice, I can still see the sparkle in her eyes. That is, my dear readers, what I call bravery. That is what I call taking the important, crucial step to earn and keep the one you love. Milica says she would do it again if she had to. She liked spending twenty happy years with that man, more than a whole life with someone else.

My Perfect Man…

Backstage, at a charity fashion show, he looks at me. Shyly I look down at the floor and wonder if I have imagined the whole thing. There he is standing at the other side of the room and I cannot stop the numerous thoughts that are running through my head at that very moment. Could he be the one who will gaze deep into my eyes and make me want to melt? Could he be the one who will stand by my side, no matter which decision I make? The man who will be proud to look up to his wonderful, ambitious woman without bringing her down in any way to make himself feel better? I wonder.

Timidly, I look up again, and this time, surprisingly, a pleasant smile greets me back. All of a sudden I speculate if my many thoughts have been heard out loud. Those eyes! His eyes are sending a message. I cannot exactly set my finger on which message he is sending. I don't know and I don't care. All I know is that I want him and I want him badly. For the first time in my life I feel dumbfounded, out of control and suddenly I start hearing the loud, rhythmic pound of my heart in my chest. He's the one who is meant for me. I feel it, I know it and he has to know it or else I will never be able to calm the ferocious beast inside me that yearns for his taste, his touch, his presence. Dressed in my skimpy leopard stage outfit, I feel out of place. I am afraid to approach him. Will he find me trashy? Grrrr... Again, I hear the beast groaning and I desperately need to satisfy its appetite. The hard throbbing in my upper body is creating such unutterable pain that I can slowly feel the suffocating sentiment in my throat.

Out of nowhere, I find myself nearing him, my feet leading the way. "Hi, I'm Nicola. What's your name?" I ask. "Sean, my name is Sean," he replies with a smile. His voice is deep, sensual. It reminds of me of chocolate ice-cream with a

40

by
Annie Vanessa Myrén

Copenhagen, Denmark

For the first time in my life, I feel dumbfounded, out of control... He's the one who is meant for me.

79

cherry on top. Delicious!

"In all honesty, Sean, I would really like to have some one-on-one time with you," I tell him while licking my lips and sending him my sexiest glance.

"You sure know what you want, don't you?" he asks, with a gentle smile.

"Follow me," I say, as I take his hand and hear him mumble a quick apology to his friends standing nearby.

As I lead the way, I see the glances they are sending at me and they can stare all they want. As I turn around to lead him outside, I feel the weight of my body change and my back tilt backwards. What's going on? Within seconds, I'm on the floor with champagne spilled on my leopard outfit. Great! This could not have been more embarrassing.

"Are you all right? Here, let me help you up." I take Sean's hand as he pulls me up.

"I'm sorry for the scene," I try to explain.

"Oh, I didn't see that piece of leftover cake laying on the floor either," he replies.

As I stand there across from him, I don't care how I look, and out of nowhere, I reach over and kiss him. He sure does look surprised, but I don't care. I can feel the beast in me calming down. It has what it wants now, the touch of Sean. Finally, I apologize for the awkwardness of the whole situation, and as I say my good-byes, I ask for his phone number. He gives it to me, and as I turn to leave, he grabs my arm and whispers that he'll be waiting for my call. And so he was…

We are now engaged to be married after dating for three years.

Disco Inferno

I couldn't stand it anymore—it was torture living next door to him. I made myself a deal: Friday night was the deadline. He and I had been friends for two years and I couldn't take it a second longer. I was going to tell Sky that I had a crush on him, no matter what.

That Friday, his house threw a dinner party, as a warm-up to Disco Inferno, a renowned disco party held at one of the co-ed frats on campus. I never really went to frat parties, and I probably wouldn't have gone, except that I knew Sky was going.

After dinner, someone decided we should play a game. Everyone sat in a circle on the floor. I, of course, made a point of sitting next to Sky, not knowing what the game was all about. The point is to pass a playing card around the circle, without using your hands. The first person puts the card up to her mouth and sucks so that it stays in place. Then she leans over to the next person and blows the card, while the second person starts to suck the card from her so it doesn't drop.

The card made it halfway around the circle to me, and I then had to pass it to Sky. I held it on my lips and leaned over to Sky, but our timing was off. The card fell, leaving us leaning toward one another with our lips thrust outwards. Everyone laughed. I could feel my face turning red. We started up again and the same thing happened! Sky and I were left lip to lip. I was so embarrassed, I didn't know if I could carry through with my plan.

We all drove over to the disco party, but we split up as soon as we arrived. I saw my friends, Liz and Josh, and decided to hang out with them upstairs; after an hour or so, they wanted to go somewhere else. As we walked down the stairs, I saw Sky sitting by himself on a couch and I decided to reactivate my plan. I said good-bye to my friends and sat down next to Sky.

41

by
Kara Shane Colley

Voorheesville, New York

"I've had a big crush on you for a while, and I don't want it to ruin our friendship, but I just had to tell you."

Immediately, I declared, "I have something to tell you!" I wasn't quite ready yet, but I didn't want to give myself a chance to chicken out. He said, "OK, go ahead." I don't remember what I said next, but just as I was beginning to work up my courage, my friend Chris walked over and sat down next to me. I also don't remember how I got rid of him, but when I did, I turned back to Sky and said, "I have a crush on you. I've had a big crush on you for awhile and I don't want it to ruin our friendship, but I just had to tell you. So, what do you think?" He paused for a second or two and then said, "I think it would have been better if you had just kissed me." We leaned in towards each other and kissed for a while.

That night, we started dating. A few weeks ago, we celebrated our fifth wedding anniversary.

For the past ten years, I considered him "fine," and watched him from the sidelines. For some reason, he never quite left my mind.

More than eye candy, he was spiritual food— a kindred spirit. Both poets and writers, we met at a popular hangout for creative artists. An upbeat, eclectic place, we "free spirits" came to connect, kick back, share poetry and mellow moods.

When we met, we exchanged pleasantries, contact info, and then proceeded to mingle with the crowd. As I remember, nothing earth-shattering, nothing worth penning a diary page for. But impressionable just the same, though initially, I didn't really consider him my type.

Over the years, we would occasionally bump into one another in mutual circles. I was recovering from a divorce, and he was coping with a career transition and his own relationship woes.

Through shared experiences and common interests, we gradually became good friends. And that was okay for me—or so I thought. But the more I got to know him, the more I wanted to learn about this gallant guy. His favorite color, what made him laugh, cry, and more importantly—what made him tick.

Somehow, the time and circumstances just never seemed quite right. Eventually, we both became engaged to other people, and went our separate ways. Through technology, and by divine plan, more years went by and we would periodically connect and keep in touch through e-mail.

One day, he sent me a brief e-mail asking me to accompany him to a poetry event. I declined, but asked for a raincheck to dine at my place, and he accepted. By this time, we were both single and available again (both engagements had failed). Not to mention, we were no longer "spring chickens!" So I made up my mind that time was of the essence. If we were to have a future together, it would have to begin the night of this reunion.

I would need a sure sign of the possibilities. No more of this crazy back and forth, speculations and flirtations that kept me frustrated. Shy and old-fashioned by nature, I didn't want to come off as being brazen, or desperate. I figured I would devise a way to put out some bait, see if he would bite, and snag what many women considered the "ultimate catch."

I prepared weeks in advance for his visit, to create the right ambiance, eye-appeal and chemistry, counting the days to our coming together. Realizing that my "Tina Turner legs" were legendary with men, I put on a very short-to the-point-long-on-expectations, blue skirt! To add a little more arsenal, there was wine and romantic music to

42

by
Jennifer Brown-Banks

Chicago, Illinois

I would need a sure sign of the possibilities. No more of this crazy back and forth, speculations and flirtations that kept me frustrated.

---

set the mood.

I longed to know what it was like to be held in his arms, so, nonchalantly, that evening, I asked him to slow dance. And as they say, there is definitely magic in music! When he held me, I melted. He confessed that he had been wanting to embrace me for years. He gently kissed me, and when he did, he made my heart dance too!

This beautiful beginning ended in a committed relationship. Three weeks after that first dance, he wrote me this beautiful poem that defines his depth and the magnitude of our meeting. With his permission, I share it with you.

NO ONE CAN LEAD ME
Like You Do　　© 2005 Sporty King

Better put… I won't follow them…
For you are where I want to end up.
(Can you forgive me for being this subtle?)

You see, I've been down this road before
yet never on this side…
By your side…
So my feelings I might seem to hide
Are no more than blushing from my pride
Which I'm happy to put aside because it's you I want
to be inside…
Inside your head, your heart, your every body part
beckons my visit
And invites me on a tour
Destination: More!

More understanding… more time… more laughs… more
happiness…
more walks in the Garden of Eden,

You are the breath I most enjoy taking
The love I look forward to making
The habit I seek to justify… the drug who keeps
getting me high
When I'm with you I can relax
(I'd love to flatter you, but these are the facts)

Let me massage your toes and fingers, for your
presence comforts my heart
Let me somehow find a way to confess my feelings
And let you know that you're my "Jones" when we're
apart.

You're the grip that won't release… my salvation… my peace.
You are the drink I want in my cup.
Better put… I won't follow them…
For you are where I want to end up.

by
Tanja Meece

Richland, Washington

Sometimes, a woman has to do what a woman has to do, just because the man won't do it. My husband, Jim, forced me into just that sort of position, and, fifteen years later, I'm glad he did.

When I met him I just knew that he was going to be mine, even though the man I'd been seeing on and off, a former coworker of his, told me he was 'trouble.' We lived in a little hotel/apartment complex, and I invited him to a party. He didn't want to come; he'd just lost the job he'd been dreaming of since childhood—union sheet metal worker—and he was just generally antisocial. For some reason, probably the loud music and laughing, he and his buddy came to the party, anyway. That was the beginning of the end.

I spent the night talking to him, and when one of my female friends flirted with him, I actually got jealous. He came over a couple of nights later, and then the next night, and so on. By the third night I'd proposed to him and he turned me down, not because we were moving too fast, but because he couldn't support my son and me. I didn't care whether he could or not. We were already at poverty level; how much worse could it get?

> **By the third night, I'd proposed to him, and he turned me down.**

When his best friend got him a job working with him, I took it as a sign that this was meant to be. So while they were out of town setting up a mobile home, I did two things. One, I moved to a one-bedroom apartment, right next door to his best friend, and asked my six-year-old if he liked Jim enough to let him move in, to which he said, "Cool." We'd been living in a studio prior to that. And, two, I went over to his friend's place and moved Jim's single box of clothes and backpack into my place.

I spent hours trying to decide if I should move them back before Jim got home that night, but I figured the worst thing that could happen would be he'd get angry and stop talking to me. He took it like a man, and he never went back to the neighbor's couch.

He's been a sheet metal worker for the last six years, he's been my husband almost four, and a father to my son. We got married on Friday December 13th, for luck. We are making mortgage payments on our first house, one we all like, three years prior to our having the credit to buy it. Over the intervening years, we've managed apartments together, been homeless together, and dealt with my son's and my mental illness together. Even when I threw him out, he wouldn't go away. I guess I'm stuck with him; but whose fault it that, I wonder? I caught my tiger by the tail. Now we're joined at the hip and I like it that way.

Friday Night Blind Date

At forty-two, I knew very little about blind dates. I guess you could say I followed protocol when listening to my single girlfriend recount her Friday night fiascoes over lunch on Monday —you know, roll my eyes, giggle, and yet listen intently to her horrific story. I was very thankful and prayed that I would never be one of those women who would tell someone about her blind date experience.

But, one Monday morning I woke up to get ready for work, and my husband of twelve years didn't. I was widowed, and my world was suddenly very strange. I was as awkward in it as a new born giraffe standing up for the first time.

I remember thinking about what my next step was going to be or if anyone would share it with me. My children were seventeen and nineteen. With one in college and the other a senior in high school, I thought the empty nest was the next life altering experience I'd have to face. You see, I'd been married from age eighteen to thirty. Then divorced, and boom—married again. I'd never experienced having to actively look for a mate. They, all two of them, had found me and married me. Now both had gone away.

But there I was, all dressed up on a Friday night, at the insistence of—you guessed it—that single girlfriend. "Too soon," I mumbled; "I shouldn't do this, especially at a bar." But, in a moment of weakness, a moment of real loneliness, wanting someone to hold *me* and appreciate *me*, I went. I didn't want any more of those looks; you know the ones when you tell someone your husband died in his sleep. Wait, of course you don't! Well, let me tell you. Women always became visibly shaken. I think they were hoping my "karma" didn't rub off on them. Men really didn't know what to say or do. They'd either hit on me most inappropriately, or smile and walk away, one step at a time. "Hey, I'm not a piece of

by
Margo Hetrick

Englewood, Colorado

So, I gathered my courage and walked in... Well, guess what? I was stood up on my first blind date!

---

meat," I'd hiss. Nor was I a black widow spider with the kiss of death, "It wasn't my fault," I'd whisper to myself.

That night was supposed to be different, my girlfriend assured me; "It'll be fun." So, I gathered my courage and walked in behind her and her boyfriend. Well, guess what? I was stood up on my first blind date! Wow! I laughed, they laughed and we ordered dinner. With the entrees on the table and a toast to life, I looked up to see a tall, very good looking, younger man standing next to me. Did I say he was younger? "Haven't I seen you in here," he asked as he grabbed a chair and took a sip of his beer.

I couldn't believe it. My first time in that establishment had been two nights earlier. I had gone to the circus with another friend and my girlfriend had been there arranging my "blind date" for Friday night. He just happened to be sitting at the bar.

I learned that he worked in HVAC, which was great; I just happened to have a furnace/thermostat problem. I know what you're thinking, but I really did. That night, we played pool, and I asked *him* for his number. Two days later I called him— he was watching the Penn State game with a group of friends—and I asked if he could look at my furnace. He did, that night. Turned out I did need a new furnace.

Well, he and I have been together for six years. We married in a beautiful, mountain setting a year ago and my furnace has never worked better! Our age difference is fifteen years, but who's counting! He is the love of my life, the most adorable, frustrating male I have ever met, and he loves me, really loves me with all of his heart. We met because our paths crossed and I took control for the first time in my life.

By the way, if you ask him, he has a different perspective on our first meeting. He and his buddies frequented that place often, and all night they sat around commiserating on their lackluster dating experiences. He told his friends "the next woman that walks through that door, I am going to talk to." Guess what, it was me! And as they say, "The rest is history."

45

by
Heather M. Orr

Rogers, Arkansas

I met Joe completely by accident, through a mutual friend. He was already there visiting, when I decided to drop in for an unexpected visit. Immediately, I thought he was gorgeous, and I knew he was going to be mine. After initial introductions it became clear that he was timid and didn't talk much, but I saw something special, a twinkle in his eyes. I was extremely outgoing, so I just went ahead and took a seat next to him.

I tried to engage him in conversation, but he just kept answering me with short "Yes or No" type answers. So I just went for it! I looked into his eyes, smiled, and said very matter-of-factly, "What are you doing the rest of my life?" He just looked at me wide-eyed and shocked. Then I laughed and said, "OK, then what are you doing for the rest of the afternoon?" He smiled and said, "Well, I guess I'm doing whatever you are doing."

From there, we went on a picnic and a nature hike at a local state park; we had an amazing date. It was fun and romantic, with absolutely no pretensions. I had never felt so relaxed on a first date before; in fact, we ended up spending almost every day together for the next week. He asked me to move in with him after only three short months, and we were engaged on our one year anniversary. We have now been extremely happily married for five years.

He told me later that he'd wanted to ask me out for dinner and a movie, but he thought I was out of his league. Too intimidated and too shy to have ever asked me out, he was waiting for a woman who was confident, spontaneous, and fearless: I was that woman. I just laid all my cards on the table and went for broke. He says he couldn't be happier that I made the first move.

Turns out it was the boldest move I have ever made, but it was also the most rewarding. It just goes to show that you never know what can happen when you look beyond traditional views about dating and the roles of men and women.

> **He told me later that he had wanted to ask me out for dinner and a movie, but he thought I was out of his league.**

Grab Your Tiger

Throw caution to the wind and go after what you want!

46

When I met Michael at work in January of 2004, I was not looking for a lover. I was miserably married, and didn't see an end in sight. My husband handled all the finances. I didn't even have my own checkbook or credit card. In short, I was codependent on my husband. I would fantasize about different men I met at work or online, but I didn't think it would go anywhere.

I'd been married for three years when I met Michael. He and I worked the night shift for the offline division of T-Mobile. I actually had a crush on a guy named Arthur, another coworker. Arthur vaguely reminded me of an ex-boyfriend. Michael didn't appeal to me, because he was extremely extroverted and had a manic Woody Woodpecker laugh.

One night I was packing bills into manila envelopes across the table from Arthur and Michael. Michael was telling Arthur about his ideas for a cable access show. I had always kept to myself at work but I was curious, so I asked questions and told Michael I'd love to participate if he ever actually put a show together. I was thinking that would get me closer to Arthur.

So Michael showed me some of his scripts for skits that parodied the Bush administration. He suggested I write a few and he'd look them over. Turns out he was impressed with my scripts; Arthur decided he also wanted to participate.

Soon, I was hanging out on lunch breaks with Michael, Arthur and a coworker named Flavia who did some freelance work for different magazines. I was elated to have friends. For three years it had just been me and my husband. I'd felt like the proverbial caged bird.

The more I hung out with Michael and Arthur the more I realized that Arthur wasn't my type at all. I was becoming more and more attracted to Michael. At work we were allowed to listen to the radio or CD players at our desks. I noticed that Michael never had any decent CD's

by
Misti Rainwater-Lites

Albuquerque, New Mexico

The attraction hit me full-force. I decided to be naughty.

91

to listen to, so I started lending Michael some of my eclectic mix tapes. By 'eclectic,' I mean that I'd have "Chinese Rock" by the Ramones, followed by "Pancho and Lefty" by Willie Nelson and Merle Haggard. Michael started seeking me out to ask for more tapes.

One night at work, he handed me "The Rocky Horror Punk Rock Show" CD. He had borrowed it from a friend and wondered if I would dub it onto a tape for him. When Michael handed me that CD, I felt a sudden animal attraction, a chemistry, that I'd only faintly felt before. The attraction hit me full-force. I decided to be naughty. I dubbed the CD onto one side of a cassette. On the other side I put a variety of flirtatious songs, the clincher being "Let's Get it On" by Marvin Gaye.

I gave the cassette to Michael the next day. I was a nervous wreck, wondering what he would think. Arthur caught up with me on a smoke break and told me that Michael was elated. So after work, I met Arthur and Michael at a local hangout called Burt's Tiki Lounge. I knew I was going to get together with Michael and there would be no turning back. I knew my marriage was over that night.

I slammed tequila shots and drank beer and got very drunk. When Burt's closed, we hung out at the Frontier, a popular twenty-four-hour-diner across from the University of New Mexico. Michael sat beside me in a booth across from Arthur. We were all talking, and I don't remember much of the conversation, just Michael telling me that he'd heard I wasn't happy in my marriage, and me telling Michael that I was miserable and was going to get a divorce. Then at one point, I turned to Michael and said,"Aren't you ever going to kiss me?" And he did, and it was magical. And that was that.

I moved out of my apartment that weekend with the clothes on my back and not much else. Michael was living with his grandmother, so I had to sleep on the floor in Arthur's apartment until I got some money from my husband and I could move into my own studio apartment in Arthur's complex. I got a divorce two months later.

I've been married to Michael since April 22nd of this year. I have never been happier or more in love. Michael says it all began with my mix tapes.

I guess I should have seen it coming. I always thought that the man was supposed to track down the woman, and that is what I thought I did, until years later.

I was a senior at Crescent High School in Iva, South Carolina. She was a freshman. I was standing in the chemistry room looking out the window watching other students walk by on their way to homeroom. She walked by, and I noticed her from behind.

A few days later she and her friend Holly popped up outside the window. Holly did all the talking. She asked me if I wanted to feel how cold Suzanne's hands were. I figured, "Why not?" so I held her hand for a minute. They were cold, as it was already fall and getting cool outside.

It seemed that I saw her almost everywhere I went. And friends would tell me they ran into her too. She never said much, just kind of smiled and looked very beautiful.

Finally I asked her out. We went on several dates and then things happened and I decided we should break up, so we did. Then I was not able to get a date at all. I had one date with a girl named Cindy all lined up and suddenly she canceled it. It was odd. Cindy used every cliché line for canceling a date I had ever heard.

As it happens, before Suzanne and I broke up, I had promised Suzanne that I would take her to the highway department to try for her driver's license. I figured that since we were broken up, all promises were null and void. Suzanne did not see it that way. She wrote me a letter reminding me of my promise, and telling me that if I did not keep my promise that I was a liar. As a Southern man, I would have punched out a man for saying that about me, but I could not do such to a female. So, I did the next best thing. I took her to get her license.

The day that I took her, just happened to be the day that I was supposed to go out with Cindy, the girl who gave me every excuse in the book

47

by
David E. McClendon, Sr.

Wharton, Texas

I knew I was licked. I asked Suzanne to go with me again and we have been together ever since.

93

for breaking a date. She had to wash her hair. She had to go out of town. She had a sick aunt. She had to study. Well, on the way back from taking Suzanne to try for her license, she asked me how my plans for my date with Cindy were going. First of all, I had not told Suzanne about the date. Second, I was not aware that she even knew Cindy, and third, as far as I knew, only Cindy and I had any idea that there had been plans for a date. I was puzzled.

Years later, I learned that the "Sisterhood" had banded together, as females often do, and decided that if I was not going to date Suzanne, then I was not going to date anyone in the county. Girls I knew as friends would not even talk to me, except to ask me how Suzanne was doing. Girls would not return my phone calls, and they would act like they didn't see me, if I said hello to them on the street.

As it turns out, one of Suzanne's friends had heard that I had a date with Cindy. She told Suzanne and the two of them told several other girls, and then the group collectively went to Cindy to "encourage her to find other things to do that evening."

Finally, one night, I was sitting at home watching TV, when the phone rang. When I answered, a girl was on the phone who I did not remember knowing. It was Suzanne's cousin, Tammy. She started making small talk and then said, "Someone here wants to talk to you." That someone was Suzanne.

Suzanne started playing records over the phone and one of them was Elvis singing "Are You Lonesome Tonight?" I knew I was licked. I asked Suzanne to go with me again and we have been together ever since. This coming November we will celebrate our twenty-first wedding anniversary.

Eight children later, I learned that I had been the hunted instead of the hunter.

48

by
Anonymous

Leominster, Massachusetts

My friend Craig was tall, sweet, and gentle. He had messy dark brown hair with a permanent cowlick, and the worst taste in clothes I'd ever seen. I was eighteen years old when we met, and starting my second semester at the University of Connecticut. Although we'd been in the same class for weeks, we didn't notice each other until we got assigned to do a group project.

Craig and I became friends quickly, but since I was nine years younger, he only saw me as a friend. For a long time, the feeling was mutual. I was in the midst of an abusive relationship and the last thing I needed was more complication in my life.

But one day, a few months after we met, he gave me a hug. Eight years later, I can still remember exactly how wonderful that hug felt. I can still smell his aftershave, and feel his warm arms around me. I'm very petite, and being hugged by my tall friend made me feel so safe and completely wrapped up in his arms. The next day, I ended my abusive relationship, despite my boyfriend's threats and pleas.

But nothing worthwhile is easy. It took a long time for me to recover from the past, and by that time I didn't want to be in a relationship, because I couldn't deal with any more pain. So when Craig asked me out, I said no. It impressed me that he didn't resent me for rejecting me and still wanted to be my friend.

A few months later, I'd healed enough to notice men again. Being in college, I was surrounded by hot and flirtatious guys. But the only one I cared about was Craig, the one who respected me enough to be my friend, if that's all I wanted. By that time, Craig had accepted my rejection and was trying to move on. Now I was the one with the crush, and he had no idea how I felt.

Finally, I took him out to dinner for his birthday. I wrote, "I love you," on my napkin, and put it on his plate when he got up to use the

> **By that time, Craig had accepted my rejection and was trying to move on. Now, I was the one with the crush, and he had no idea how I felt.**

95

bathroom. Naturally, he thought I meant I loved him as a friend. I finally realized that men don't get hints, or at least this one didn't. But how could I ask him out now? If he rejected me, I couldn't handle it as well as he had. I was so afraid to risk losing my best friend.

That night, I walked him back to his room and we sat down on his bed. Putting my arms around him, I leaned over and whispered, "Happy Birthday" in his ear. He looked at me with the sweetest smile. Still holding him, I leaned towards his other ear and whispered, "I want to be your girlfriend." Then I stopped breathing, and looked into his eyes as I waited for his response.

A few days ago, we celebrated our fourth wedding anniversary. It's been eight years since our first date. And what does Craig think about all this? He told me that I was the best birthday gift he's ever had. I will never forget the way I felt when he said yes. It was his birthday, but I'm the one who got the gift.

An International Pursuit

How many people have traveled across the world to track down the man of their dreams?

My friends often teased me throughout college for refusing to find a committed relationship with an American guy. From having dated a German boy in high school, to one Spanish, two French and a melange of other individuals during and after college, I had duly made my international dating rounds.

Filled as they were with romance and amusing flirtations, these relationships were not enough to hold my interest. Something was missing. I knew what I needed and I was not ready to settle for less: A challenge that presented itself in the form of language barriers, cultural misunderstandings and a very appealing accent. So I traveled the world to pursue the one I knew was out there, waiting for me.

Pursue him I did, despite the important detail of not having a face or a name. Nonetheless, I knew I would eventually find him. I have never renounced the power of creating my own destiny. With that faith as my buttress, I crafted the journey of a lifetime to the one European country that I had not yet experienced.

After arranging for a brief interlude from my job in New York City, I juggled the logistics of my trip to Rome with responses from dozens of Italian e-mail pals I'd contacted; I kept the details of my trip private.

Upon my arrival in Rome, I was shuttled Roman-style (i.e. perilously) to my new monolocale (studio) in Campo de' Fiori. Flopping down on the studio's century-old bed after the most reckless ride of my life, I smiled with more gratification than I had in months. Neither speaking the language, nor having any friends or family in Italy, my only connection to my future was via these recent Italian e-mail pals.

I met with several of my new friends and

by
Katie Doling-Bastianelli

Rome, Italy

> **So I traveled the world to pursue the one I knew was out there, waiting for me.**

enjoyed my interaction with this new culture. Although some of the Italian men lived up to the typical Italian stereotype, I managed to fend off any promiscuous propositions.

When I had almost exhausted my list of new friends, I got a phone call from the one person that I had sent a message to, but from whom I had not heard back. As fate would have it, Stefano had never pursued a girl in his life, and my attempts to pursue *him* were thwarted, because I'd entered his number incorrectly into my cell phone. Despite his broken English and my mispronunciation of his name, we set a time to meet, both of us strangely aware of the electric tension sparking from the other's voice.

From the very first moment we saw each other, our eyes knowingly sparkled. As he crossed the piazza wearing gray slacks and a black overcoat, I crossed to meet him in my black chinos and gray sweater set. Our instantaneous recognition proved to me that I knew all along what I was doing in Italy: I was pursuing my destiny. I was pursuing the one.

Nearly three years later, I am still in Rome, completing my Master's Degree. My monolocale in Campo de' Fiori was replaced by a terraced apartment fifty feet from Fontana dei Trevi, where my coin-toss wish in the fountain led to the new home that I share with my new husband Stefano, three kittens, and a myriad of ornate plants.

If You Want It, Go Get It

I was in St. Simon's Island, GA for a girls weekend, when I locked eyes with the man I knew I would love the rest of my life. Luckily, he was on his way to our table when our eyes met. Between dances, we chatted about baseball, booze, TV, movies, golf, nothing and everything.

Three a.m., final call, and we were shooed out of the club with the rest of the die-hards. We meandered to the pier, with a couple of our friends in tow, and watched the faithful fisher-folk dotted along the edge with huge rods planted like great oaks in between the boards of the pier. These dedicated fishermen found it necessary to defend themselves and their catches from Mary the Fish 'Free-er', who found great fun frolicking up and down the pier, kicking fish back into the water yelling, 'Free the Fish!! Free the Fish!!'

Luckily, the fishermen found Mary's antics almost as amusing as we did, although, not quite as amusing as she. But, before they could revolt and throw Mary into the rising tide, we all took off to our respective sleeping locations for some much needed rest.

Jimmy and I enjoyed a very leisurely drive to where he was staying, while my friend, Kris accused him of being an axe murderer, because he 'couldn't remember exactly' how to get there, although things were 'beginning to look familiar.' I received a hand squeeze and smile, and joined his ruse of not knowing how to get to his place, while we continued our conversation about movies and music.

At the intended destination, after whispering our good-nights behind a latticed porch dripping with red, climbing roses, we ran into a man in tight, black, cotton boxers, who just happened to be on his way for some 5:00 a.m. milk out of the jug in the fridge. Jimmy introduced me as his 'future ex-wife.'

The next evening, after the girls and I enjoyed an extremely amusing dinner, and collected

50

by
Gina Webb Sutherland

Black Creek, Georgia

I was distraught, to say the very least—sick to my stomach for days, thinking I'd never see him again.

---

more than a few "what's so funny?" stares from the other patrons, we laughed our way back to our suite, where I was pleasantly surprised to hear Jimmy's voice on the message line. We'd spoken of dinner and cocktails, but I have to admit that I had prepared myself for him to not call, while secretly hoping for the best. I was far from being a schoolgirl, but my heart was racing like it didn't know the difference. We connected by telephone (the old fashioned way, before cell phones) and he came to visit our slice of the island. We managed front row seats to a cat fight on the back deck, watched a tussle in the bar between a glass door and a rouge cue ball (cue ball won), and did the Macarana for what felt like hours.

At 5:30 a.m., I forced myself to do the respectable thing and booted him out of our suite, where the rest had all fallen asleep watching a movie. I walked him out to the parking lot; we exchanged DNA and e-mail addresses, and made plans to meet after we both napped, but before I had to head back. Those plans fell apart and we neither saw each other, nor spoke, before I left.

I was distraught, to say the very least—sick to my stomach for days, thinking I'd never see him again. He didn't respond to the e-mails that I began sending as soon as I returned home, so armed only with what I knew—name, general profession and where I took him the first night—I began my reconnaissance mission—via telephone operator—to try to locate his place of employment. But, as everyone knows, fate can have a wicked sense of humor; dozens of long distance phone calls yielded absolutely nothing. Butterflies formed a conga line in my spleen, as I thought over and over, 'I will never see this man again!' So I clocked out 'sick' at work, jumped behind the wheel of my white mustang, and hit GA Interstate 95 South doing 100, back to St. Simon's to track him down.

It only took an hour to get there. I started at the house where I had dropped him off, looking for people with information. When that failed, I went to the airplane hangar just down the street (he fixed big planes), told them who I was looking for and what he did for a living. They didn't know him, but were kind enough to direct me to another location. I finally reached it, only to find that they'd never heard of him either. At their suggestion, I went to another site. I was prepared to drive through the state until I found him.

Then all of a sudden—Jackpot!

Pay dirt!

My gold at the end of the rainbow!

They knew Jimmy!! Not only that, but the nice lady at the entry desk called the hangar and let me talk to him on the phone. I still don't know if he was picturing boiling rabbits or ice-picks when I told him I was standing in the lobby, only a few hundred yards away, but he said he was about to take a break and asked me to stick around so we could talk. Turns out, his computer had crashed, and he was pulling double shifts, which left him with no time to call and no way to communicate.

Within one month he quit his job and moved to be near me.

We've been married for eight years.

We have three children.

We live happily ever after.

I Took Life With A Bucket Of Salt

If I have learned anything in this life, it is that "good things may come to those who wait" but better things come to those who go after them.

Four steps into the diner, I saw him: My tiger on the prowl. Pacing behind the restaurant grill, he resembled a caged beast. He stood six-feet-two-inches with dark brown hair that nearly hid his hazel green eyes. I tried not to stare, but my eyes always found their way back to him. A playful grin quickly spread across his lips and that was it—I knew I had to have him.

I didn't know how I was going to do it, only that it had to be done. That's when I saw it. Out of the corner of my eye, the bright red "Help Wanted" sign. Admittedly, this was a little spontaneous. But for me, there was no other choice. I had to get a job at that restaurant. (What? People have gotten jobs for lesser reasons... well okay, maybe not.)

I eagerly filled out an application and waited dutifully by the phone for a call that might not come. Two agonizing days later, I called to follow up. I was asked to come in the following afternoon for an interview.

The first question was blunt and took me by surprise. "Why should we hire you?" my prospective manager asked. Two thoughts raced through my mind "Because you have a sign in your window, and your cook is hot!" I took a drink of water to buy some time. I hadn't really been prepared. I just figured I'd get the job no questions asked. (Yes, I know. I live in la-la land.)

After clearing my throat, I said what I felt. I am good with people. Waiting tables for me is a rewarding job. People want something, I go get it for them; they are happy, so I am happy. He looked at me a long while, and I was sure I'd blown it. "Well, I gave it my best," I thought. The man across the table extended his hand and said

by
Melanie Brening

Minneapolis, Minnesota

**Not to be deterred,
I would
make the first move.
I had to.
I'd already come
this far.**

"Welcome to the Convention Grill."

I started my new job the following week and soon found out that while he exuded confidence from afar, Don, the object of my affection, was actually quite shy. Not to be deterred, I would make the first move. I had to. I'd already come this far.

Sometime into my first week, I decided this was it. I walked up boldly to the counter, batted my eyelashes and asked the tall, dark and handsome cook to …"please pass the ketchup." Smooth. It's okay that I didn't have him, I had ketchup! No, no, this would not do.

Back at the drawing board, I tried to imagine a first date. Dinner and a movie? No, too ordinary. A walk through the park? No, it was February. Much too cold.

It was February. I had it!

My idea firmly planted, I strolled up to the counter and told Don we needed more fries from the basement. As soon as he left, I got behind the grill and with a bucket of salt, I spilled out the grains onto the flattop.

"Be mine".

I had almost made a clean get away … but as soon as I turned to go, there he was. That breath stopping, heart pounding, knee bending smile…

We have now been together for seven years, (married for four of them) and we have a beautiful daughter together. Not only did I grab my tiger, but I trained him too!

I want to tell you how I got My Man! The funny thing is, he had heard my voice long before he met me in person. It was 1999 and I was in London doing press for my film festival. My first interview was at a radio station. It was taped and would air that Friday, and that's when The Man tuned in, while he was driving, and heard my interview. Remember, he had no idea who I was.

A few months later, I was throwing a launch party at a bar in Manhattan. My friend Brendan brought along The Man, who was in town, visiting. We chatted for a few minutes and he joked that he could recite my telephone number backwards.

I didn't see The Man again until March when I was in Miami attending a music conference. The Man said, "You're the film festival girl." I nodded and he got in a cab with me to go to a party at a club called Space. Well, there no space to stand, because there were zillions of people there. Within five minutes I'd lost The Man in the crowd.

That June, The Man came to New York again. He, Brendan, other friends and I hung out regularly that month. Then we clicked. We had a long distance relationship for months. Then… Bing!! I told my friends I was leaving New York to move to London to be with The Man. Everyone asked if he had proposed, and I said, "Not yet, don't worry…we will get married!" Taking the initiative, I packed my two suitcases and didn't even think about what I was leaving in New York, which was pretty crazy, since I loved being in the city and my life there.

A few months went by and I took action. I told The Man we were getting married and picked the wedding date, which I'd kept ever since I was a little girl. I made all the arrangements. We would be married in Maine, standing next to the ocean.

In June 2002 we stood on the rocks in Maine and exchanged vows. Our original witnesses were supposed to be the people in the gift shop, but since they forgot to look, the guy who married

by
Lisa Estall

London, England

Everyone asked
if he had proposed
and I said,
"Not yet.
Don't worry…"

---

us asked two onlookers to substitute. (To this day I have no idea who these people were, but their signatures are on our marriage certificate.) A crowd gathered around us. Some ate their ice creams, some sat on the rocks and smiled, and others videotaped the ceremony. I made him My Man!

It was only last year that My Man confessed that he almost jumped off the rocks and swam away. Also, for some reason, in that same conversation, the radio interview came up. We both realized that he had heard my voice that Friday night, before even meeting me!

So I guess it was fate, combined with my 'go get him' attitude, that won me The Man Of My Dreams!

53

It's been said that opposites attract. I really don't know if that's true or not, but it's the only rationale I can come up with, for going to the hassle of trying to become better acquainted with a man who intrigued me.

I wasn't looking for a relationship. I wasn't even desperate for dates. However, he exercised in the same health club as I did, and the contrast of his persona to mine was more than I could resist. He was a man of few words. I was loquacious. He was European. I was homegrown. He seemed very intellectual. I probably seemed very silly. I had to learn more about him.

In the few conversations I had with him, while going about our respective exercise routines, I managed to learn that he was here on an extended Visa to work on his Doctorate in our local university. He didn't own a vehicle, and for the most part, walked everywhere he went. I also learned that he was an opera fan and had a respectable knowledge about the genre. Armed with this information, and the fact that my neighbor was an Artist-in-Residence in the music department and was encouraging me to see him perform in Verdi's La Traviata that month, I set my plan in motion.

I purchased two tickets to see my neighbor perform, and I bought a cassette of the opera to play in my car. Then I waited for it to rain. When the rains came, I headed for the gym at about the time that my dashing European usually appeared. I knew that he was quite faithful to his exercise regimen. I admired that. I must have walked countless more miles on the treadmill than I normally did, waiting for him to finish his leisurely workout. When I sensed he was about to finish, I offered to drive him home, so that he wouldn't have to hoof it through the deluge. I was just being a good Samaritan, after all!

Since he always changed clothes in the gym, and I always changed and showered at home, I told him that I would just wait in the car until he

by
Cam Ridenour

Morgantown, West Virginia

Armed with this information... I set my plan in motion. Then I waited for it to rain.

105

was done. I already had La Traviata playing in the car when he got in. My ruse was that I was trying to learn more about it before going to see my neighbor perform. Before reaching our destination, I invited him to see the opera with me, on the premise that he could help me understand what I was seeing and hearing. He was happy to oblige.

Unlike La Traviata's lovers-unto-death, Alfredo and Violetta, my European and I weren't even destined for a second date. I decided that, since I had purchased the opera tickets, and the après-opera drinks ended up being Dutch treat, he was either far too poor, or far too cheap for my taste. As for the opera—that was two hours of my life that I would never get back.

54

by
A. Moreno

Fresno, California

Four years ago, I was a recently-divorced, working mother, dedicated to her child and career. Working in the medical field meant having a demanding schedule, especially because I worked the graveyard shift. I had just enough time to care for my child, and, on rare occasions, to socialize, but I was pretty limited in my social interactions outside my career. For that reason, I chose to accept an invitation by my mother.

She told me she was going to my uncle's to visit with a friend from Central America and thought it would be nice if I joined them. So, I took some time off, and my daughter and I got in the car and went to visit my uncle. On the way, my cell phone rang with an unidentified number. I answered, and was greeted by a rich Latin voice. To my surprise it was an old childhood friend, who was waiting to see me at my destination. My first thought was that my mother was somehow involved.

When we arrived, the Latino gentleman with the rich voice escorted my daughter and me inside. I became nervous and aware of my inhibitions, as I recalled that as children, this man and I used to date. I later found out that he, too, was divorced and that he was actively dating.

> **I wanted him to kiss me, but feared he wouldn't make the move. I knew chances like this were rare, and decided to make the move, myself.**

As the weekend progressed, and we had time to catch up, I forgot all about the stress associated with work. It was nice to talk with an old friend, especially since we both had similar backgrounds. Being a romantic, I dreamed of reconnecting with him; I knew I had only one opportunity, since he would soon be returning to his home in Central America. But, I had already embraced a 'can-do' attitude: I knew I had nothing to lose.

The following day, I decided to make my move and confront my old lover. I asked him if he would accompany me to dinner, just the two of us, and perhaps, dancing. Being a gentleman, he kindly accepted my invitation. I hadn't packed any nice clothes, since I wasn't expecting to attract a mate, so I took off and bought shoes and a dress. After so many years as a working professional and mother, I deserved to treat myself like a princess.

I hurried home and carefully dressed to impress: I did my hair, makeup, and reminded myself that fairytales can come true. We left for dinner, and had a wonderful evening. I felt so special in his arms. I told him more about my past, and he, about his. He hinted some interest by stating that it would be nice if he could come and visit me—but I didn't want him to leave.

As the night closed, I began having teenage butterflies in my stomach. I wanted him to kiss me, but feared he wouldn't make the move. I knew chances like this were rare, so I decided to make the move, myself. As we exited the car, I stood outside for a moment; when he asked if I was ready to come in, I convinced him to come look at the stars with me. As we gazed at the heavens, I took his hand, looked into his eyes, then, lowering my lids, I kissed him. We spent the rest of that evening together, romantically.

Not wanting any awkwardness, I asked him to keep the night a secret between us. I knew he had to go home, so the day before he left, I just came out and asked him if he would be interested in getting to know me better.

Four years later, I'm happily married. I'm glad I did.

I'd like to tell you how a wonderful woman grabbed my attention and stole my heart. Call me gutless, but there was no way I could have approached her first.; perhaps my horrible break-up five months earlier had made me gun shy.

On the Tuesday morning in question, I was at the Chicago Hyatt, having breakfast with a potential client, whose account I'd hoped to win. After my presentation, I sat back to gauge his response and field questions. In walks a lovely lady in her mid-thirties, wearing a tailored pantsuit, her auburn hair draped softly across her shoulders. She had a well-scrubbed look and almond-shaped eyes. The minute her coffee arrived, she proceeded to bury herself in her notes.

I went back to focusing on the business at hand, periodically shifting my eyes over to where she sat; fortunately, she was in my direct line of vision, and I, in hers, so we locked eyes more than once. She was bewitching, and if my weary heart were in better shape, I'd like to think I'd have had the nerve to walk over and introduce myself. When my client got up to make a private call, she held her coffee cup to her lips, and as she lowered it, offered what I thought was a smile. In an instant I was trapped in her gaze and imagining the possibilities.

When my client returned, I slipped on my glasses so as not to miss even the slightest tilt of her head. I spotted what I thought was another smile, as she applied her lipstick and prepared to leave, but I quickly decided she was checking her teeth. She and I have since discussed this episode, and she claims she must have smiled at me at least a dozen times before I finally returned the gesture. Clearly, I'd developed some sort of mental block. As a single man of thirty-eight, I'd approached scores of what I thought were flirting females, only to have them look at me as if I had two heads when I'd walk over and say hello. Like many guys, I'd learned to second guess even the most blatant signals, figuring they

55

by
Mitchell S. Davenport

Atlanta, Georgia

Like many guys, I'd learned to second guess even the most blatant signals; the subtle ones, I missed altogether.

were just another tease, grooming behavior or meant for the guy next to me; the subtle ones, I missed altogether. Having sworn off romance for a while, I was certainly not up to taking another shot.

As she gathered her material and got up to leave, she lifted her left hand, offering what appeared to be a shy wave. Just then, the waiter handed me a folded note. It said, *Hi, I'm Beth, the smiling redhead. It appears we keep looking at each other and I feel like I know you from somewhere. Anyway, if you're not seriously involved with anyone, and have some time later today, perhaps you'd like to meet for a cup of coffee.* Her number followed.

This, I wasn't imagining. As soon as my meeting ended, I called her, both excited and flattered by her initiative. We met for more coffee, and the rest is history. She admitted she'd made up the line about knowing me from somewhere. Beautiful and clever. I proposed in February and we will be married at the end of the year.

To all you ladies out there: Trust me, we men don't always get it. Sometimes, we need you to spell it out.

He Jump Started My Heart...

I had seen Pat around my apartment building, but in the five years we lived there, we hadn't said more than hello to one another. Pat also attends my church, and I would see him at evening mass, sometimes at an early morning service. Spirituality is very important to me, and for Pat to have the same faith as I did, was, and continues to be, a bonus. I asked my next door neighbor if she knew anything about him, and she said, "Nothing except that he plays his music really loud." (And he still does.) Then I asked my apartment manager if she knew if he was single or not, and she said that he was. That was all the invitation I needed to attempt to "jump start" a relationship with him.

My car didn't start one morning (really, it didn't) and he was the only one home to help. I decided to let the little vixen inside of me out to play, so I knocked on his door and asked, with a smile on my face, "Will you jump start me?"

Paying Pat was not an option. He insisted that was what neighbors do for each other, so I offered to bake him a pan of brownies. I gave him the brownies on a plate he had to return, with a note that read:

I am much better at my conversational skills than I am at my baking skills. How about a beer sometime?

"Yes, I would love a beer sometime," he said to me, as he was jump starting my car for a second time. (Really, it didn't start again!) Of all the great luck.

The second time I said to him, "I baked you brownies the last time how about a cheesecake?"

"Cheesecake, I could do," he said.

I baked him a cheesecake the second time; again, I had it in a pan he had to return, with another note that read

56

by
Michele Klecker

River Falls, Wisconsin

I decided to let the little vixen inside of me out to play, so I knocked on his door and asked, with a smile on my face, "Will you jump start me?"

Roses Are Red Violets Are Blue, How About Some Beer, Brats And Brownies For Two?

"Yes " was the answer to that.

Our first date was May 29, 2004 on my birthday.

He said "I love you," on December 12, 2004, and we are now planning our wedding.

Shall We Dance?

57

by
Julia Joy

Colombo, Sri Lanka

I saw him for the first time at the student union meeting in my first year at college. He was tall, tan, handsome and vivacious, in a weirdly enchanting way. His name was Jason. He was exactly what I was looking for. The moment I saw him, I knew I wanted him.

I also knew I had to take action if I wanted him to be my man. First, I made sure to become friends with Winnie, who went to the same high school as Jason. She told me that Jason was a ballroom dancer. That was the opening I was looking for; dancing was something I could use to get closer to him. As luck would have it, the annual college dance was coming up and my group was organizing it. The evening was to include a special ballroom dance performance by the students, so I volunteered immediately

There was a slight problem; I was rusty with my dancing. I started taking dance lessons immediately, and practiced until my moves were perfect. One fine morning I went up to him with a bright and chirpy smile and said "Hi! I hear you were a dancer." We started chatting about our shared passion and he agreed to help me with the college dance. He even agreed to meet me that evening at the studio to see if we could get our moves right. We danced for hours. I was over the moon.

"Julia, you move really well," Jason whispered into my ear during a waltz.

"So do you," I replied.

We kept at it until late evening and he offered me a ride to my flat. Just as I was going to bid him good-night, he said "Julia, I don't even have your number." He wanted my number! Clearly, my efforts had paid off.

That night he called me with an idea for the special performance by the students. Meeting the next day, we created a medley and called for auditions.

> **I knew dancing was something I could use to get closer to him.**

Since we'd be participating, we spent a lot of time practicing and getting to know each other very well over casual dinners. Suddenly, after months of work, the big day arrived. When we came together on the dance floor, we couldn't take our eyes off each other.

Jason leaned in and whispered, "Julia, I love you."

My heart leapt and I managed to say "Jason I love you, too."

We kissed underneath the stars that night. It was the most perfect kiss I had ever experienced. That moment, I knew I had found the place where I belonged—on the dance floor and off.

58

My lady grabbed me by first straightening my tie, then straightening my life.

As I walked in a London park, my future wife gave me a strange look from across the commons, strode across the park and straightened out my tie. She then said, "There, you look much better."

Being a bachelor, I could have cared less about my appearance, or about folding my clothes and putting them into a proper drawer. Every morning, I carelessly ironed and looked for my clothing in the dark, which was an adventure at 5:00 a.m. My life was adrift, out of control. I mean, sometimes I'd even eat cookies for dinner.

We sat nervously next to each other on the park bench. I couldn't help but notice that a piece of the chocolate biscuit I had eaten for breakfast had stained my white shirt. After shyly looking away, I noticed she was looking at it too. Strangely, these motherly actions attracted me to her even more.

We laughed, chatted and exchanged phone numbers. I lumbered on my way, but accidentally stepped into a mud puddle. She couldn't help but laugh again. I couldn't believe I forgot to wear socks, again.

Some time after our first meeting, my lady showed me that it doesn't make any sense to keep dirty running shoes on the mantle piece, as it may put off invited guests. She showed me that a woman is not impressed with dirty shoes lying anywhere in the living room. After a thought, her words also made me realize that cleanliness makes a man. After all those dull years, some etiquette was bubbling in my brain, or maybe, it was the boiling water I'd failed to turn off in the kitchen.

One of her first wise teachings was the importance of keeping a clean kitchen. In a young man's world, a rotting tomato and moldy cheese are viewed with a blind eye. When rushing to

by
Robert Hanshew

Washington, D.C.

**She showed me
that a woman
is not impressed
with dirty shoes
lying anywhere
in the living room.**

115

catch a good TV show, it's hard to appreciate the impact of falling potato chips lodged behind kitchen counters. After that second visit, the fresh smells around me while I cleaned were invigorating. I also discovered that my counter was not yellow, but white.

With a lot of guidance on the third visit, my lady showed me the advantages of folding and sorting clothes within the various dressers. At that point, I realized that having a beautiful girlfriend, who also organized, can be a wonderful thing. Her beauty then became irresistible. Gone were the funny stares; colleagues looked at me in awe because my clothes actually matched. I started to feel good about myself.

Her golden ways taught me about the importance of using a napkin while eating out. My days of leaving the restaurant with a huge dash of ketchup marking my khaki pants were over. My heart warmed with her knowledge and class. How could I not fall in love with someone who would protect me in any of life's circumstances? She was my angel against life's demons.

On the occasions that this girlfriend, who is now my wife, happens to be out of town, I find myself slipping back into my old ways. I've learned that a t-shirt left by the oven will only catch on fire, it's not wise to place a roll of paper towels on a toilet seat or to leave meat out for more than an afternoon in summer. In those moments, I realize that I miss her, not only because she is my love, but that my life is a complete mess without her.

by
Katie B.

Arlington, Texas

I was relatively young, by today's standards. At twenty-four, I had lived a, shall we say, provocative life. Zillions of boyfriends, two cross-country moves, and several fiancés later, I found myself back home in Texas, looking for the "quintessential life." I landed a job at a local non-profit, which satiated my desire to assist the forces of good in saving the world. My boss was also a young woman, who, unlike me, had married young and had begun a family. We became friends instantly.

One day during our closing paperwork, I was rambling about the dearth of decent, date-worthy guys in the area, when Debbie perked up and looked over in my direction. I only caught her out of the corner of my eye, and as the momentum of my ranting had increased, I didn't really pay attention to her.

Thirty minutes later, Debbie snuck into my office and pulled from her pocket a tiny piece of paper that looked as though it had been folded several times and possibly crumpled up and thrown away once or twice.

She stammered, "I promised Tim (her husband) I wouldn't do this again, but we were talking…and it got me to thinking…and you don't have to do anything you don't want to…but if you want to…"

"Debbie! What is it?" I interrupted.

She hesitated and then handed me the wrinkled parchment. I opened it to find a name and number on it.

Debbie stammered, "It's my brother-in-law. I just thought, if you were interested, you two might get together sometime."

I, of course, being the wallflower I am, went home that night and called him immediately. I believe the first words I ever spoke to him were "Hi, Ed? This is Katie. I work with your sister-in-law, Debbie. She said you were a great guy, and I figured since I was a great girl, we should get together. How about Saturday night?" After four

> **I started
> the engine
> and watched him
> get into his truck.
> My mind raced;
> this is ridiculous!**

or five seconds of stunned silence, he agreed and we had our first date.

We met at a club in Dallas, had a few beers, danced a couple of two-steps and ended the night at a local breakfast joint. When it was time for us to head to our respective houses, we said good-bye, he leaned in to hug me, opened my car door and told me to be careful. I started the engine and watched him get into his truck. My mind raced; this is ridiculous! We're grown people who just had a great date! I got out of my car and ran to the driver's side of his truck.

He rolled down the window, looking a little sheepish. "Are you okay?" he asked.

Without saying a word, I grabbed his shirt with both hands, pulled him to me and kissed him. When we parted, I smiled and whispered, "I'm fine now. Talk to you tomorrow?"

He mumbled something like, "Yeah, I'll call you." I could tell he was taken aback. It was kind of cute.

We went on a several other dates, did the dinner date that ended with both of us confessing I love you, but the one that hooked him for good was on a Friday night. After that, he was all mine. I knew he was working late because I had called earlier in the day with the specific intention of finding out when he was getting home. I got off work early, grabbed my sexiest teddy, my favorite sex music, two dozen candles, a bottle of champagne, and headed over to his place.

On the tree he had to pass from the driveway to the door, I nailed a love note telling him there was a surprise inside for him. Five feet from the tree, I placed my red high heels in the grass. Five feet from there, I draped my blouse on the shrubs and five feet from the shrubs, I dropped my skirt on the porch. Inside, I had placed candles absolutely everywhere, and hit the repeat button on the CD player. I pilfered every pillow and blanket in the house and made a palette in the middle of the living room, strategically placed my scantily clad body in the middle of the billowy mound, and waited.

It was all over from there. He asked me to marry him shortly thereafter.

When my boyfriend and I first met each other, we were both in relationships with other people. We had spoken to one another, but we never showed an interest in dating, since we were both taken. Time passed, and when we met again, we were both single. I knew from that moment, that I just had to be with him—almost as if it were love at second sight.

He was the man I had wished for all my life. I didn't want to seem too eager, so I sat back and felt out the situation. I had mostly dated shy guys before, but he was definitely not shy. In fact, he was very open about his opinions and acted cocky and arrogant. When we were around his friends, he found it necessary to show off. I could tell that he was interested in me, but I didn't buy into his false bravado. So I decided to fight fire with fire and show him how much of a turnoff it was.

When he'd say "I can walk into any room and take home any girl I want," I'd respond with "Yeah, any room at a woman's prison." He'd say "Girl, I could take you home if I wanted to," and I'd say "Yeah, okay, call me when you wake up from that dream." Ever time he mouthed off, I acted disinterested and refused to give him the much-needed approval he sought.

Soon, he started calling me nonstop and insisted I go on a date with him. At first, I turned him down. I made him think I was too good for him. Then I made every effort to show him I was unlike any other girl he had ever known.

I deliberately got under his skin and drove him crazy. I was going to make sure I was all he could think about, because he had to figure me out. I went head to head with him: When he insisted girls didn't know anything about cars, I took him up on the challenge and fixed my own car right there in front of him. I even dragged him with me to the junk yard with him and pulled my own parts. My hands were greasy and my hair

60

by
Connie Apruzzese

Beach Haven, Pennsylvania

...it was at that precise moment he realized I was different from all of the other girls.

---

was a mess—we won't even talk about how dirty my clothes got—but I know it was at that precise moment he realized I was different from all of the other girls.

I finally accepted his offer, and went out with him on the date of my dreams. We have been completely inseparable ever since. We lived in Florida when we met and we have recently moved to Pennsylvania together.

He tells me every day that he wants to marry me.

And I always tell him that maybe one day I just might let him.

In early 2005, I ventured to an international meeting in Orlando, Florida. A stranger I spoke to on an empty Disneyworld bus caught my eye. I discovered we lived 17,318 km apart, yet I wasn't discouraged. Over the next seven months, I learned to make sacrifices and redefine how I took risks as I traveled throughout five countries to get to know him better. Then, I made the biggest move of my life.

Our story began one rainy morning…

"That's some lens! Aren't you afraid rain will wreck the camera?" I remarked.

"It's not afraid of getting wet," he replied.

After talking a bit, I sensed I'd met a fellow thrill-seeker. He wasn't easily deterred from capturing what he wished out of life. As I got up to leave, he impulsively asked,

"Doing anything for dinner?"

As it happened, I was not.

Turned out his hotel was located close to mine. I knew a quiet, Italian restaurant. He liked my choice of artichoke-eggplant pizza. I decided to open up completely and share my passions with this virtual stranger. initiating a four-hour discussion about cemeteries, unexplained phenomena, outer space issues, travel and spirituality. He seemed truly engrossed and the conversation flowed.

Afterwards, as we strolled, I asked to see some of his animal photos, so we innocently returned to his hotel. Like Cinderella before midnight, I interrupted our photo show, figuring he'd want to pack for his departure.

When morning came, I felt compelled to leave a bon voyage card for this charming stranger, but just before I was to deliver it, he phoned to invite me to breakfast. We spent two hours at a café, and then parted.

From the moment I returned home, I began to write him letters. Each card contained a story or reflection wax sealed in an envelope and

61

by
L.C.

Melbourne, Australia

Our first night together was memorable. We'd discussed sleeping arrangements, but didn't foresee what ensued...

---

placed inside another card. Up to nine cards would arrive inside a card. Sometimes, they formed connected stories. I occasionally placed a book or confetti inside. He never knew what to expect. Within a few months, he had received over five-hundred cards.

All the while, we exchanged hundreds of e-mails which led to phone calls that lasted for hours. In one of my e-mails, I challenged him with a 'choose-your-own adventure' story. We each wrote chapters, incorporating images, music videos, or interactive clips, then, swapped to inspire the next fantasy. All the while, we were unfolding our hearts and dreams to one another.

Around the time I met him, I'd also partly completed an inspirational manu-script; this lovely man answered a long questionnaire, suggested additional questions and kindly read the entire book. Since meeting me, he said, he had never written so much in his entire life.

A while into our correspondence, he asked, "Would you like to meet for coffee in Paris?" I suggested some key stops and we collaborated on creating a romantic, eight-day train trip through France, Switzerland and Italy.

Our first night together was memorable. We'd discussed sleeping arrangements, but didn't foresee what ensued: A double room at a historic jailhouse hotel! I recall the moment when we unlatched a heavy cell door and found a single bed on either side of a small room with bars on the windows.

"Hmm…I'll just use the toilet," was his immediate reaction (clearly, he was in a quandary about what to do). So I quickly pushed the beds together and suggested it would be easier to listen to music that way.

In Paris, the Jardin de Luxembourg inspired us to completely lose our inhibi-tions.

"You can do anything here and blend in with the scenery," I offered, as we nes-tled down on steel chairs to share intimate moments. After Europe, our phone calls reached a record four and a half hours… Our souls had blended.

Fascinated by him—and by the continent of Australia—I decided to pick up and move to Melbourne. The land Down Under became our new playground. We found ourselves hiking in mountains and deep caves, immersing ourselves in waterfalls and discovering remote parks and venues along the scenic Great Ocean Road. Our explo-rations even took us to the most remote parts of Indonesia where together we shared the cultural and spiritual nuances.

By May 2006, I had been living with my tiger for eight months.

My experiences in Australia encouraged me to finish my first book, secure a new job and take new initiatives to develop myself. Trusting my intuition in this relation-ship has truly reinforced my confidence. I am devoting more time than ever to my passion for writing and public speaking, as I aim to empower people to recognize, and follow, their own inner voices.

It has certainly worked for me.

"Don't touch him; he's mine!" That's how my future wife fended off her roommates after she first met me. A senior in college at the time, she knew that if she didn't stake her claim, her roomies—experts in the fine art of hooking up—could potentially ruin her shot at someone in whom she had a strong interest.

I was the new guy in town. I'd graduated from college, and spent a few months traveling the U.S., before I ended up in Dover, NH. My roommates were known quantities to my wife and her friends: two guys from her university, and a friend of mine from school, who the girls had met before. If nothing else, Beth told her roommates, she had dibs on me because we were the same height: 5 feet 11 inches. They honored her request.

I met the girls at a party shortly after I moved to town. I noticed Beth right away, out of all the girls there: She was pretty, easy to talk to, smart and liked a lot of the same music I did. But there was a problem.

One of my roommates liked her. I didn't know him well; he was burlier than I, so I didn't get in his way. For the first two months after I met Beth, I played it cool. We talked a lot, and even stayed up all night once hanging out with a few other people. But I made no advances.

She, of course, was confused. Was I aloof? Was I an idiot? Why didn't I ask her out? Finally, she delegated one of her roommates to find out what was going on.

"You should ask Beth out," her roommate Cathy told me at a party.

"But Joe likes her," I said.

"She doesn't like him like that," she drunkenly told me. "Ask her out."

We had that same conversation at a few more parties, before I realized I had to make my move.

Gathering my courage, I approached Joe one evening in our apartment.

"Hey, Joe," I said. "How's it going?"

62

by
Dave Brigham

Newton, Massachusetts

I played it cool. She, of course, was confused. Was I aloof? Was I an idiot? Why didn't I ask her out?

"Good, man. What's up?"

"I gotta talk to you about something," I said, my heart beating fast like the punk rock he and I loved.

"OK," he said, looking concerned.

"I was talking to Cathy a few days ago…."

"Yeah," he said, suspecting something unfavorable.

"And she said that Beth wanted me to ask her out." A blank stare.

"And I know that you like her, so I just wanted to, you know, see what you thought about that."

"Yeah, I don't think it's gonna work between me and her," he said, somewhat dejected. "Go for it, if that's what she said."

And that was it. I had learned in two months of living with Joe that he was a good guy, and that while his size was a little intimidating, he was as gentle as a lamb. But I was surprised at his willingness to step aside for me.

Being a dork, I didn't race to the phone to call Beth and ask her out. I waited a day or two and called her, just to chat and see how she was. And, after a half hour or so of small talk about parties, music, politics, whatever, I…hung up after saying good-bye. Just a test run, I told myself.

The next day I called and chatted nervously for a while, before finally asking her to a movie. Even though I knew she wanted me to ask her out, I was incredibly nervous. She said yes. I was so relieved after hanging up; I'd never been good at asking girls out, and therefore hadn't gone on many dates.

On the big night, I drove my van around the corner to pick her up, and then the three blocks to the movie theater. Did I pick something romantic, like "Bull Durham" or, hell, even "Who Framed Roger Rabbit?" No. Something funny, like "A Fish Called Wanda"? No, I selected "Betrayed," a movie in which Tom Berenger plays a neo-Nazi, and Debra Winger's undercover FBI character falls for him.

As if that heartwarming movie wasn't enough to win Beth over, I managed to elbow her in the head while trying to put my arm around her in the theater. I also spilled my peanut M&M's and thought for sure I'd blown my chance.

Despite that first date, we have been together for seventeen years, eight of those as a married couple.

The real mystery was that I was in the pub at all. Having been rendered something of a recluse through a combination of a personality prone to aloneness and a recent bout of depression, the chances of my leaving the house were small, never mind that I would leave the house and change my life on the same evening. Getting dressed for outdoors had been stressful enough on its own.

As anyone who has suffered with it will understand all too well, depression is a dirty foe, but it's no match for the determination of a stubborn friend. A combination of guilt and quiet awe at her persistence made me decide to venture out in the company of my friend, though a part of me was sure that I might once and for all prove to her how miserable I was to be around, and she might finally give up on me.

But she has always been far wiser than I. I don't think she ever planned on it, but her determination changed my life. Because it was that evening that she introduced me to the only man lunatic enough to put up with me without going quietly mad himself.

It was a few days after Christmas, and convenience brought us to the local pub. We found a table easily, and we sat, drank, and talked, interrupted only on occasion by her younger brother and his friends; seated not far from us, they would come over on their way to the bar or to the bathroom to say hello. Or rather, one of them did.

Blinded by a lingering lack of self-esteem, and by the ridiculousness of the apparent size of this man's bladder, I chatted with him without putting up my guard, as I would have had I had even a tiny notion that he liked me.

My friend and I drank and talked until we were tired and we went to leave. But we were stopped at the door by the tiny-bladdered man, who said that it was early yet, and that we should sit with him and his friends for a while. And then

63

by
Fiona Condron

Dublin, Ireland

**For one brief moment,
a light switched on
within me,
and I believed
that I might
possibly be happy.**

it hit me like a ton of bricks. The strange boy likes me.

Having had only limited exposure to positive experiences during my period of depression, I was unsure of how to deal with one. I looked to my wiser friend for guidance. And once again, she refused to let me down. She shrugged her shoulders and said casually, "I don't mind. It's up to you."

For the first time in many months, I realised that I did, in fact, have power over my own destiny. With her simple words, my friend had held a mirror to my face and said, look. You can go home and be alone and safe forever, or you can take a chance. Not everything that happens is bad.

In retrospect, my world stopped at that moment, though I'm told I carried on as normal. We sat down with strangers, something I hadn't done in such a long time, and I talked to them as though it were something I could do—something that didn't scare me and something that I didn't dream about as I drifted into a dark sleep each night. For one brief moment, a light switched on within me, and I believed that I might possibly be happy.

We sat together, and before I knew it, we were holding hands. I don't remember what we talked about, but I know that it was the best conversation I've ever had. He offered to walk me home, and I said yes, because there was nothing else to say. One week after we met, he told me that he loved me. I was relieved, because I loved him too, and was scared that I would blurt it out and terrify him. But this man is not easily scared, and that is partly why I love him.

There are so many reasons that cover some part of that, of why I love him, but there is nothing that can cover it entirely. I love him because of everything, because of nothing. I love him because he is himself; I love him despite that sometimes. But mostly, I just don't think about it anymore. He is here now, and that is all I want.

64

by
Melanie

Calgary, Alberta,
Canada

In May of last year, I met a good friend for dinner. Several months had passed, and we were both about to move away. Though we had not worked together for two years, we still kept in touch. At the time, he was focused on his new job and rather discontented with relationships; I was contentedly single, dreaming up ways to help the world. Our relationship had always been platonic. At ten years my senior, he had far more life experience. It was never a consideration.

Over dinner, we chatted about past events and aspirations for the future. The more we spoke, the more I longed to mend his perspective. With ten years of steady work history, he had no promise of a visa. Previous relationships had left him jaded. Life had not turned out like he envisioned and he was leaving the country, disenchanted. Although I could not change the government, I knew that before me sat a man who—if he could only find someone with similar ideals—would be a supportive, loving partner. He was a successful man, with a great sense of humor, gorgeous smile, and a big heart, and I was surprised no one had 'staked their claim.'

While dining, I discovered that no woman had ever bought him a drink—not even past girlfriends! So, I asked if he would like to go for a drink, afterwards, on me. After a couple beers, he drove me home. Not wanting to overstep my bounds, I asked if I could kiss him. He complied. It was late, so I offered for him to stay. He declined.

Over the next couple weeks, I spent whatever time I could with him. When he returned from a business trip, I showed up with massage lotion and a book on self-cultivation. I also screen printed a t-shirt for him, camouflaging the message "Fear is Ignorant." I managed to stay the night a couple times—and work in a massage—before time ran out.

We met for breakfast, before I hit the road. Not wanting to wonder 'what if,' I told him I had

Not wanting to wonder 'what if,' I told him I had feelings for him. Unbeknownst to me, he didn't comprehend.

127

feelings for him. Unbeknownst to me, he didn't comprehend. The first week, I called every morning, just to wish him a good day. By week's end, he had booked a day-trip to visit me before leaving the country. Again, my affections went undetected; we remained friends. He asked me to visit in the fall. Meanwhile, I phoned often, and sent homemade inspirational cards and a journal for contemplation. By fall, he had a better understanding.

I can't be sure what made him realize I wanted to spend my life with him—perhaps it was when I told him so, but I doubt it. Nevertheless, he responded. He visited often throughout the winter. In March, he moved in with me, and when he received a job offer in his home country shortly thereafter, he asked if I would join him. We now reside in Canada, exploring life and pursuing our dreams—together!

65

My quest for a good man of my choice began in 1989. I tried bars and laundromats and grocery stores. I found nothing that fit what I wanted, however, and would quickly brush off would-be suitors after discovering they were as shallow as a crack in the sidewalk.

So, I thought it over, and decided to run an ad in the personals. It described what I was looking for, and sounded more like an employment ad, than a call for romance. I was all business. In spite of that, I got call after call. I interviewed each man the same way. Of the thirty or so calls that came in, I decided to meet with only three of the applicants.

The third, is the one I chose; he called one evening when my eleven-year-old son was acting a fool for no reason. Since the gentleman in question would have to be able to deal with him if this worked out, I asked him if I could put my son on the phone. In short order, my son, John was laughing and smiling; he told me he was sorry, handed the phone back to me, went off to his room and turned on his TV, leaving me in peace to talk to my new hero, Brian.

We met about two weeks later, and have been together ever since. We have a thirteen-year-old daughter and life has been very good. Brian has never told me what he said to John that night and I don't really care. My son grew into a fine young man who has children of his own. I see Brian in him as he deals with his children in the same quiet caring way.

People don't believe me when I tell them we met through an ad, because that doesn't work for most people. But it's true. And I got what the ad described:

Seeking a hard working, caring man to help me raise my son and have a child of our own. Must be willing to relocate, must be willing to share responsibility. Looks, age, ethnicity unimportant, but must have good heart.

by
Maureen Skaar

Las Vegas, Nevada

**I decided to
run an ad
in the personals.
It sounded
more like
an employment ad
than a call for
romance.
I was all business.**

Brian came in to our lives and took over in a mild-mannered way, and he supported us financially and emotionally. It was a risk, to be sure, and I can't recommend it to everyone. But it worked for me.

66

by
Graciela Sholander

Fort Collins, Colorado

I was working as an Electrical Engineer for a large company, surrounded by men, so you'd think it'd be a piece of cake to get hitched. Not so. More than half were already married, and of the singles, most were too into their careers—or themselves—to settle down with a nice, smart girl like me.

Enter Kevin. I first saw him when a co-worker interviewed him for a job at the company. Right away I noticed that he was very cute, very sweet. He had that old-fashioned charm about him, a politeness hard to find these days.

Plus he looked mighty nice in his gray suit.

A few months later, he was back—they had hired him! He moved into a cubicle one aisle over, and became friends with a married woman engineer I knew, who worked at the end of my aisle.

Kevin and I smiled at each other in the hallways, but never really exchanged words. We worked on different projects, so we never interacted beyond the occasional passing smile. Finally, I asked my colleague if Kevin had a girlfriend. She said she didn't think he did.

So a couple of days later, I took a deep breath and scribbled a note on a sheet of puppy-motif stationary. It read, "Hi, I'm Grace and I work one aisle over from you. If you don't have a girlfriend, would you like to go out to lunch with me sometime?"

I waited until he went home for the day, then left the sealed note on his chair.

> The next day
> I had butterflies
> in my stomach
> as I arrived to work.
> Feeling kind
> of stupid
> for having
> written that note,
> I was ready for
> rejection.

The next day I had butterflies in my stomach as I arrived to work. Feeling kind of stupid for having written that note, I was ready for rejection. Instead, a smiling Kevin stepped into my office and introduced himself. He thanked me for the note, and said he'd love to have lunch with me.

We were married a year and a half later. We'll be celebrating our seventeenth anniversary this year. Our kids, now fourteen and eleven, think this is the goofiest story!

67

by
Whitney Acke

Lexington, Kentucky

Finding a quality man can be next to impossible these days. My biggest fear as a single, childless woman, was growing old alone. I could see myself lying in bed with my emergency necklace around my neck so someone would come if I fell and couldn't get back up. I just knew I was on the path to my 'Old Maid' destiny. I had decided to accept my fate, and to ignore the questions about my single status from family at holiday dinners.

That's when my luck changed. It was a cold Friday night in December and a friend and I decided to drown our depression in a late night visit to the local pancake house. We sat and analyzed our lives, and our boring romantic situations, for a few hours. The conversation inspired me, and knowing we were not on our way home, I joked, "Tonight I will find the man I will marry." Of course, I was not serious and my friend laughed at my insane comment. After forcing our stomachs to hold more than they were intended for, we got on the road.

We jumped into my friend's car and headed through the center of town, which gets rather busy late on a Friday night. The town is shaped in a circle and we decided to drive around the circle until we could think of something more exciting to do. It amazed me that my life had come down to driving around in circles out of boredom and hopelessness.

We pulled up at a stoplight on a three-lane road. I glanced over and there was a car full of younger and more beautiful girls next to me. I glanced another lane over, and saw this huge new blue truck with two men laughing inside. Blue is my favorite color, and being a country girl, I do have a place in my heart for big trucks as well. I commented on the truck to my friend and smiled at its driver. Immediately he smiled back and I was excited. He was hot!

Without thinking, I rolled down my window, ignoring the confused protests of my pal. I

> **It amazed me that my life had come down to driving around in circles out of boredom and hopelessness.**

leaned into the driver's view and shouted loudly across the car of beauties. "Hey, pull over," I instructed. At this point my friend was panicking. She immediately began lecturing me on how axe murderers live in the city and it was not safe to ask two unknown men to pull over with us in some deserted downtown alley. Shutting out her attempts to keep me safe, I told her not to worry.

The light turned green and the guys raced ahead to get in our lane. In all of the traffic, however, we lost them. As soon as they were out of our sight, my friend decided all hope was lost and turned onto the road out of town. I was furious. I had this strange feeling that I should fight to get this one. I started yelling at her to turn around. After ten miles and what seemed like a lifetime, she turned the car around, probably just to get me to shut my mouth.

My protests were not in vain, however. We found the mystery men, who turned out to be normal non-axe carrying people. I began dating the driver, fell deeply in love, and nine months later we were married. I will never regret embarrassing myself by screaming over lanes of traffic to fulfill my fate. After all, sometimes you have to reach out and make it your own.

Two-thousand-four was a very hectic year for me. I was a junior in college and in the middle of trying to get my life together. I was majoring in Animation and my relaxation time was scarce. I rarely had time for myself, yet, I always seemed to make it. I look back on it now, two years later, and still don't see how I managed to go to school at eight-thirty in the morning until almost ten at night, return to my apartment, shower, do my makeup and be out till four in the morning.

Yeah, I was a party girl and I had my fair share of boyfriends through out college. It was never anything too serious, because my taste always screwed me over in the end. For some reason I was always attracted to the heartbreakers. You know the type, the "bad boy image" guys who didn't have a care in the world. I loved it, too, because it fit right into my lifestyle. I thought nothing could be more perfect, everything was just the way I wanted it to be…Or so I thought.

The beginning of junior year started out just like the previous two years in college, boring and uneventful. I was dating a guy named Rob at the time, but he was away at boot camp (a marine in training). I kept partying and having fun. He trusted me (I have never been the cheating type).

Everything was the same old, same old, until I met Kevin. Kevin had graduated the year before, and I had only talked to him once or twice, nothing special. I was attracted to him, but then again so were all the girls. He was definitely the "ladies man." We bumped into each other at a party, and I found out he was staying in Philadelphia to work.

We hit it off instantly and talked for most of the night. Through one of my friends, I found out where he worked. The next night I just *happened* to bump into him again and we exchanged phone numbers and screen names. We began talking online and quickly moved to the phone. We became best friends instantly. I talked to him everyday, at least six or eight phone calls, sometimes for two

68

by
A. Camilli

West Chester,
Pennsylvania

I had actually fallen in love with my best friend and I couldn't have him.

or more hours at a time. I wouldn't go out anymore, and if I did, it was to his house for the night. Our friendship grew and grew, and this went on for several months. I had broken up with Rob by then and had a few boyfriends, on and off. Kevin had a girlfriend as well, one who was not too keen on his and my friendship.

Finally one day midyear, I realized I had all these feelings for Kevin. He was so much more than any guy I had ever met. I had actually fallen in love with my best friend and I couldn't have him. To hell with that I told myself. I began making my moves, slowly but surely. To make a long story short, after a few months, the girlfriend was out of the picture because, as we all know, *she just wasn't right for him*.

Then, one night, Kevin and I were hanging out as usual, and we both started to drink. Well, he started to drink. See, I kept the same beer with me the entire night. He would be pounding them, thinking I was doing the same, when in reality, I would go down to the fridge and just bring up a new beer for him and my old beer with me. Yes, you are right; I was taking advantage.

When I knew he was a little tipsy, I made my move. I asked him for a hug and pulled him close to me. We embraced for a good three minutes. I slowly ran my hand up and down his back and around his neck. Then I kissed him on the cheek and slowly pulled away. Well, that was all I needed to do, because as I pulled away he leaned in further and ended up landing right on top of me on the floor. As I laughed he looked down at me and said, "You know you really are so beautiful..." and then kissed me.

The next day I explained what I did, and he actually laughed and thanked me because he had felt the same way, but didn't want to make the first move for fear of losing our friendship. A few months later I moved in with him and now, after two-and-a-half years we are planning our future together.

Call me evil, but I got my man!

As a Dog Obedience Trainer, I have the opportunity to meet many folks who share my love of animals. And when I met the gorgeous owner of a cute little Lab mix, it was no exception. Clare fawned all over her new puppy Daisy, and lovingly talked about her two cats. I was smitten. She was graceful, sweet, funny, but much to my disappointment, she wore a huge wedding ring. We hit it off great and I solved her dog's leash-pulling problem.

Seeing an opportunity to make a little money and at the same time gaze upon a beautiful woman, I sold her on the idea that her puppy needed a series of obedience training sessions. Clare agreed and I whistled all the way home.

The next week I met with her and her puppy again. While teaching the 'sit' and 'down' commands, we chatted with a little more familiarity, and I was happy to see that she easily laughed at all my jokes.

Soon the conversation rolled around to how hard it is to meet compatible people. I half-jokingly said "too bad you're married" which she quickly followed with "oh, I'm flattered but no thank you, I am really happy" which itself was followed by the inevitable awkwardness that usually accompanies my bold missteps. Having thought that I had made a fool of myself, I resigned myself to sticking only to dog-related topics the following week.

We met several more times, and I stuck to my normal dog obedience routine, reviewed what we had previously discussed and shared other basic tips that make living with a dog easier, healthier and more rewarding. At the last meeting, I noticed she was not wearing her wedding ring, but thought better of going down that road again.

As we wrapped up, Clare reminded me of our conversation a few weeks earlier, about how hard it is to meet compatible people; then, with incredibly cute awkwardness, she mentioned she

by
M.E. Kingman

Seattle, Washington

She had stopped wearing her "stay away from me ring" after our first meeting, but I did not notice it, or her advances.

had a girlfriend with whom she thought I would get along great. I was caught off guard, to say the least, but accepted her offer to set us up. She told me where to go and when, and what to look for. I was to meet this girlfriend outside a neighborhood coffee shop, with our dogs, the following Saturday. That made sense to me...public, safe and easy exit strategies for both of us, if we did not hit it off well.

At the prescribed time, I sat there, all polished and sipping my coffee with my own trusty Gus sitting loyally by my chair. And, as luck would have it, my 'date' was a no-show. I finished my coffee and was about to leave when up walks Clare and her little Daisy. Naturally, I was happy to see her, but pointed out the obvious fact that her friend had stood me up. As our dogs began to exchange scents, in that wonderful way dogs do, she apologized and sat down. I asked her what she was doing here. I assumed that her friend had asked Clare to join us in case she needed her own exit strategy. Clare did not answer, and instead fussed with our dogs, which, by now, had gotten their leashes all tangled. We chatted about our pets for a minute or so when I said, "So, where is your husband?"

Turns out she was not married at all, and never had been. She said it had been so awkward for her from the beginning, with the false pretense that she was married, that she never saw a graceful way to suddenly say she was not. Apparently, she had stopped wearing her 'stay away from me ring' after our first meeting, but I did not notice it, or her advances, because I was so focused on the dog. I said, even if I had noticed, I was not going to make a fool of myself again. She said "Why do you think I kept taking all this dog training with you?" She'd been waiting weeks for me to 'make a fool of myself' so she finally came up with this 'clever plan' and hoped the change of scenery would make it easy for her to start anew.

She was right. We did start over. The rest is, as they say, history. Clare and I have been married for three years now and we are very happy. And it seems I was not the only one smitten...Gus is fairly enamored with his new babe, Daisy, too... but they've not yet set a date!

by
Neha Girotra

Mumbai, India

What my wife wants, my wife gets. So when she set her heart on marrying me, a die-hard bachelor, I didn't stand a chance. She reappeared in my world, one cold, slushy, rainy Sunday. I cannot imagine what my life would have been if I hadn't ventured out of my suburban haven and into the big, bad city that horrible rainy day, to meet an old acquaintance whom I hadn't been able to shake off my mind for the last eight years. But before I tell you how my charming wife snagged my unsuspecting heart, let me tell you a little about how we initially met.

I saw her for the first time when I was seventeen. I was visiting my parents on a vacation when I first laid my eyes on this exquisite creature, never realising that one day we would be bound together for life. She was introduced to me by common friends and we forged a strong alliance in the few days I was there. We would go for long walks, play tennis, wonder what life had in store for us.

When I met her for the last time, just before I was leaving, I wanted to hold her in my arms and tell her that she was one of the most special people I'd ever met. Instead, all I did was stand there and watch her walk away until she disappeared into the distance. I never saw her again for the next eight years, but thought of her constantly. I compared every woman I met to that memory of the perfect woman, whom I'd just known so briefly, which may have been the reason for my short-lived relationships and fear of commitment.

And then one day, just like that, I was given an opportunity to know her again. My kid brother mentioned that he had stumbled upon on her phone number through an old acquaintance, and remembered how dreamy I got whenever someone mentioned her name. So, armed with her phone number, I sat by the phone and contemplated for days if I should call her. I mean what if she was busy, or worse, did not remember me! I finally mustered the courage and called her a few

She meant business this time, so I did what any smart man would: I tried to bribe her.

days later, and as the phone on her end rang, my heartbeat quickened. By the time she picked up the phone, my heart was beating so fast, I was sure she could hear it on the other end. She answered and I thought I'd just had an attack, but I found my voice, and surprise, surprise, she remembered me.

We arranged to meet the next week. And so dressed in my Sunday best, unaware of the heavy rain, I set out to meet the love of my life. We met, and a few days later we were seeing each other. A few days passed into a few months and soon we'd been together three years. As each year passed, her determination to move things to the next level became more and more persistent. The final straw was when her best friend decided to get married. That day that will be written in history as my doom date. She raised hell with me for hours about my fear of commitment and lack of maturity. But even though I loved her more than my life, my bachelorhood was far too important to give up without a fight, and I was unmovable in my decision to let things be as they were for a wee while more… an indefinite while more.

So she packed her bags and left our little love nest. I let her go knowing full well she'd be back in a few days and we'd both be better off then. But as days passed, it was becoming clearer to me that she meant business this time, so I did what any smart man would: I tried to bribe her. I sent her flowers at work every single day, called her machine and left loving messages, but in vain.

Then one day, a month later, I was sitting at my desk, daydreaming about happier times, when I was rudely interrupted by a loud beep from my computer announcing the arrival of an e-mail. I clicked on the mouse with irritation and was delighted to see an e-mail from my love. I opened the e-mail with excitement; I hadn't heard from her all this time and was desperate for word from her. And there it was in big bold capital letters:

I am delighted to inform you all, that after years of wasting time on a lost cause, I've decided to give in to an old pursuer and will walk the altar with him this Valentines Day.

And just like that she handed me my life sentence. I was shattered, and then it hit me. My life as I knew it would be over if I let her marry that jerk. It was like a light bulb went off in my head. I rushed out of my office, mumbling something about a headache, stopped off and picked up the biggest bunch of white roses, her favourites, and headed towards her work place. I marched up to her desk and there in front of everybody got down on my knees and begged for her forgiveness. Then I said the four words I didn't think I would ever hear myself say 'Will you marry me?' and without a fuss and a sly smile she said 'Yes'.

It was later that I realised that I had been duped by the most beautiful girl in the world. We still laugh about the e-mail that changed my life; she'd gotten the idea from a popular women's magazine.

71

It was a cool October evening in 1983. I was thirteen years old and in the eighth grade. My friend, a freshman in high school, had been invited to a party and asked if I would like to go with her, so we hopped on a bus and headed out. When we got to the party, my eyes were instantly drawn to a table where a bunch of people were playing a game of quarters.

Normally, I'm a pretty shy person, but for some reason I made a beeline for that table and sat right down next to 'him.' I introduced myself and he said his name was Bill. He had thick, jet black hair, and these intense green eyes. I had butterflies in my stomach, and although I was un-aware, it was love at first sight. We started see-ing each other, but I was feeling guilty, because I already had a boyfriend; so I broke it off with Bill after a couple of weeks, but I never stopped thinking about him.

The following spring, after I had broken up with the boyfriend, I ran into Bill again. The butterflies returned, and happily, we got back to-gether. Things were going wonderfully; he came to my eighth grade graduation and we hung out all summer; we walked around holding hands, went to the movies, and were said to be locked at the lips; it was the best summer of my life.

Then, one night, out of the blue, the phone rang; it was one of Bill's friends. He was calling to tell me that Bill no longer wanted to see me. I had this terrible lump in my throat and I started to cry hysterically. Is this what it feels like to have your heart broken? I didn't like it, but what was I to do, beg him to take me back?

Over the years, Bill and I would run into each other, get together for a day or two, and just as quickly, it would be over. Once, when I was in my early twenties, we ran into one another again, but he was with someone. He tried to leave her to be with me, but she would find him and beg him to take her back.

by
Karen Gibson

Absecon, New Jersey

I didn't like it, but what was I to do, beg him to take me back?

Turns out, this other girl and I had gone to high school together; she was in my homeroom and something in my gut gave me a bad feeling about her, but I couldn't put my finger on it. Anyway, she told him she was pregnant and he believed her, without asking for proof. So that was it. He was gone again, and the butterflies were replaced by a lump.

A few years later, I was working as a food server at TGI Friday's, and one afternoon I looked over and there he was, sitting at a table, having lunch with a friend. I didn't know what to do; should I go over and say hello, or should I just pretend I didn't see him? Something in my gut (butterflies?) propelled me over to him. He told me his girlfriend had lied about being pregnant (big surprise; I knew there was something about her I didn't like) and he asked me for my phone number. But, I was wary. My heart had been broken by him so many times before, but the butterflies would always convince me to go for it, once again.

That night, he told me that he was in love with me and always had been. He left her, but this time was for good. Wouldn't you know it, she tried the same trick again—only this time it didn't work.

To make sure I didn't lose him forever, I decided to heed the butterflies and I asked him to marry me. So here we are, eleven years and three kids later.

If you love someone, set them free…Well, you know the rest.

The Golden Rules Of Dating Are For Goldilocks

by
Debra E. Powell

Los Angeles, California

My entire twenties had been spent in a relationship that had ended suddenly over the phone, with him saying that he "loved me like his sister". So two years ago, at the age of thirty, I entered the dating scene for the first time as an adult. Luckily for me, I worked as a nurse at one of Los Angeles' prestigious hospitals and had eight experienced single female coworkers to give me dating advice.

**He was about
to skate away
when I grabbed
his arm...**

The one thing they all swore by, was a set of do's and don'ts they had come up with one day over lunch while trying to help me. Their 'Golden Rules,' as they liked to call them, were mostly made up of commonsense things, like meet at a neutral location, so if he turns out to be a weirdo he won't know where you live.

The two rules that I knew I would have the hardest time complying with were

1) If a guy calls after Wednesday, wanting to see you that weekend, say you're busy even if you're not and

2) don't—no matter what—have sex with a guy before you've dated him for at least three months.

Nonetheless, I stuck to their 'Golden Rules' for the next six months. During that time, I went out on a lot of dates with guys I met at work or through friends setting me up on blind dates; they would all try to have sex with me after three or four dates, if not the first. Surprisingly, I stayed on course, and politely let them know I thought we should wait. That was usually the last time I would see or hear from them.

So when the winter holiday season rolled around, and the realization hit me that I was going to be spending the holidays alone, for the first time in my life, I decided to take matters into my own hands. I didn't just go out and grab the first guy I saw and have a wild bedroom romp, but, I did grab the first hottie I saw.

It was Christmas Day. I decided it would lift my spirits to get out of my tiny studio and go for a walk around Venice Beach. It was a bright, sunny afternoon and Venice, despite the holiday, was packed. After taking in some of the street performances, I decided to check out the concrete circle that was designated for roller skating. That is when I saw a tall muscular Greek god. The sun shimmered off his shirtless bronze chest and glistened from a light dew of sweat. I caught my breath, and with a do-or-die attitude, I leaped out in front of him when he skated by. He crashed into me and we both fell to the ground. As I returned from my momentary loss of consciousness, I realized he had landed on top of me.

As I lay there, taking in the sexy, musky cologne he was wearing, I mentally gave myself a pep talk. I didn't want to play games any longer; I wanted what I wanted and that was him. I opened my mouth and forced out a, "Hi, I'm Debbie. Sorry about that. Are you okay?" He spoke with an accent and had an enduring smile. We got up and went and sat together in the grass.

I came to find out that he was Greek and had moved here nine years ago with his family. The conversation flowed easily and continued for some time—at least until the setting sun forced us to say goodbye. He was about to skate away when I grabbed his arm and asked him if he would like to come over to my place for dinner the following night. He smiled a flirtatious smile and said yes.

The following night's dinner went perfectly and I didn't want it to end, so, when it came time to say good night, I asked him to stay. The sex was hot and passionate between us. It not only felt incredible; it also felt right. He must have felt the same way, because we spent every single day together for the next month.

After we had been dating for a month, we talked and decided to live together. Well, that was a year and half ago and we are still passionately together. As a matter of a fact, eight months ago while on holiday in Hawaii, I proposed to him and he accepted. We got married two days later on the beach at sunset.

When someone asks him what it was that attracted him most to me when we first met, he tells them it was my confidence and that I didn't play mind games. So my advice is to stop playing Goldilocks and go after your Big Bad Wolf.

My wife, partner, and best friend, Sue Ann, is a TV Producer and Director. Our story is an example of successful internet dating, and so much more. About five years ago, I was in the midst of a divorce and went to an online daring service to find women who shared my interests. Sue Ann had never been married, due to her busy, twenty-five-year-plus television career in the D.C. area.

At about midnight on a Friday evening, she saw my profile and was interested (my photo was of me in RenFest attire—a man in tights). Even though I had two strikes against me (smoker and not divorced yet), she saw I was online and e-mailed me to check out her profile. I liked what I read, so I wrote back to her. After several e-mails, Sue Ann gave me her cell phone number so we could talk faster (typing is not her favorite activity). We chatted for almost two hours about life, the Renaissance Festival (I worked there as the village deputy), our likes and dislikes, etc.

She said she was scheduled to go to Bosnia for a couple weeks, but would like to meet me first. As I was working at the Maryland RenFest, Saturday and Sunday, she agreed to come Sunday afternoon, after she was done directing a talk show for CBS.

Well, Sue Ann and I hit it off right away. I escorted her around the village while staying in character. Lot's of flirting and eye contact made the day pass quickly for me. Sue Ann asked when I finished. I told her that I would be off the clock at the end of the Pub Sing, usually 7:00 p.m. when they sound the cannon. At 7:00:01, she pulled me close for a "soft, slow, wet kiss that lasts forever" (see the movie Bull Durham if you don't recognize the quote). I was hooked.

Then she left for her two-week trip to Bosnia. While she was gone, I accepted a one-year tech writing contract in Florida, and she returned to find out that I was leaving the state in a few weeks (right after Thanksgiving). We dated pas-

73

by
Gary Wayne

Kensington, Maryland

I was unaware of Sue Ann's love and determination to win my reluctant heart.

---

sionately and often, those two weeks, but I had been burned by a couple of other relationships, so I was hesitant to make any long-term commitment. When I left for Florida, we were "just dating" and I was determined to keep her at a distance until I saw what Florida had to offer. Being a typical man, I was unaware of Sue Ann's love and determination to win my reluctant heart.

A few weeks after I settled into life near Fort Lauderdale, Florida, I joined the cast of their Renaissance Festival as Richard Rich, a historical character from King Henry the Eighth's time period. During this period, Sue Ann and I talked often, and sent romantic Christmas Cards to each other. She sent me a small Christmas tree to decorate my apartment and a basket of goodies to help me through that Christmas far from home, and flew down to spend a few days with me around New Year's Day. The romance grew, but I was still gun shy.

Sue Ann flew down, again, to celebrate Valentine's Day with me. That week-end we went to the Florida RenFest with me in costume and her in street clothes. We separated for a couple of hours, so I could check in at cast call, appear at the opening gate ceremony and perform the first act of our two-act play. Our plan was to meet at eleven.

When I stepped out from backstage, I saw a vision of Renaissance beauty waiting for me. Sue Ann had used those two hours to completely clothe herself in a period costume with gown, underskirt, hat, jewelry, belt with pouches, feathered fan with mirror built in, and shoes. At that moment, she must have known that she'd won my heart. It was clear that she not only loved the Renaissance Festival as much as I did, but that she was the perfect Renaissance lady.

I moved back to D.C. to live with her after only seven months in Florida. A year and a half later, I asked her to marry me during a special Roguing Ceremony at the Maryland RenFest in front of about fifty witnesses, including Sue Ann's mom, her brother and his wife, and one of my daughters.

A little over a year later, we married on board a cruise ship in Fort Lauderdale, where this remarkable lady captured my love.

P.S. I quit smoking, too.

Acapulco Dearest

Some call me a risk taker; others think I'm plain crazy. On the eve of the new millennium, weary of unhappy love affairs, I knew it was time for a radical change. I decided to look for a man I had not seen for over a decade, and who lived three thousand miles away.

It all started when I landed in Acapulco on a December afternoon in 1983. Being a French-Canadian, I welcomed the warm sun, a nice contrast from the harsh winters I was accustomed to. So, the second I stepped in my hotel room, I jumped into the smallest bathing suit I'd packed and headed to explore my new surroundings. I wasn't looking for a man; I already had one, though I shared him with his wife and four children. I simply embraced being away from the heartbreak of a relationship where I was the "other" woman. All I was looking for was peace and perspective.

Clad in my blue-striped bikini and a pair of high heels, I crossed the hotel lobby, on my way to the pool area. While I luxuriated, a shadow suddenly covered my book. "Sorry to bother you, but ever since I saw you in the lobby earlier, I've been dying to say hello," a deep voice said. That kind of statement can pretty much knock a girl down. Since my English, at the time, was comprised of no more than a hundred words, I sat there, frozen, my translating gear seriously lacking juice.

"Hi," I mumbled, trying to stay calm at the sight offered to me: A six-foot frame, penetrating green eyes, thick luscious lips, wavy salt and pepper hair and a body that would make Adonis jealous. We managed to exchange a few words, despite his French being no better than my English. For the next three days, Thomas and I spent a lot of time together, ignoring this communication problem. We figured that flirting was as good a way as any to get acquainted.

74

by
Odile Leclerc

Sparks, Nevada

I was still looking for a fulfilling relationship that never came, forcing me into deep soul searching.

"I love you," he confessed, eyes filled with tears, a few hours before I was due back at the airport. His pain was palpable. Unable to find soothing words, I said nothing. A week later, my phone in Quebec City rang. It was Thomas. Despite my joy to speak with him, I simply apologized for having misled him. My trip to Acapulco had not cured my sorry love life, nor had it brought the perspective I was looking for. I had gone back to my married boyfriend.

Yet, Thomas became my confidant of both the good and bad happening in my life. I never cared that he was sixteen years older than me; I prized his charm and savoir-faire. For years, weekly letters filled my mailbox, all carrying a subtle "Say Yes!" message. But I did not. Admirably, he persevered for five years before giving up.

Long after Thomas and I stopped communicating, I was still looking for a fulfilling relationship that never came, forcing me into deep soul searching. The soft memories of Acapulco and Thomas' romantic words haunted me. Ultimately, I decided to search for him. Forty-eight hours after sending an e-mail to the company he worked for, I received a response: "We will see each other again."

We did. We met in San Francisco the following week. In my chest, a pounding hammer had replaced my heart. At the airport, I was glancing around quickly like a nervous sparrow on a branch, trying to spot through the thick crowd a man I had not seen for a dozen years.

I had only two nights and three days to make an impression on Thomas. Fortunately, it turned out his love for me had not dimmed, although he admitted that he had given up any hope of us ever being together. Yet, he did not let the setbacks of the last decade deter him. On our second night, while we dined in a cozy bistro, Thomas looked at me with a mix of hope and determination. "Will you marry me?"

He was true to his word and a year later, we were married. He may not have offered me a diamond ring when he proposed—he bought me one later—but he gave me back my life. "You warm my heart; every day, I fall in love with you again," he told me recently. Likewise, darling!

75

Something is different today. Something is special about today.

Maybe it's the scent in the air; the parched eucalyptus outside, leaves throwing off their subtle aroma, carried though the ceiling-to-floor window by the desert breeze. The dry air swirls between our bodies, lifting the perfume from her neck to me. I nuzzle into her silky red hair; the smell of her shampoo fires my senses. It all smells wonderful, but it isn't different today. That's not it.

Our situation was a strange one—she lived next door to my ex, and my best friend really liked her. As is its way, love somehow managed to negotiate a course between all of that and to find us lying there together, happy and excited as to what the future would hold.

Is it the light? The withdrawing sun, shedding its last rays of this day, the harsh yellow of a midday Australian sun softened to a vibrant orange. Those oversized windows filling the room with an amber glow, light reflecting off pale yellow walls until finally catching in her hair, crimson red in this sunburnt room. No, that's not it either.

We met at college, as many do. After a particularly messy breakup, I was in no mood for love. My heart had been shattered, and setting myself up for that again was the last thing I planned to do.

As the months passed and my room became the most popular drop-in centre on campus, I found myself clearing one person, more than any other, from my bed at the end of the day. The sexy redhead would visit at all times of day and night, which didn't bother me one bit. I found my mood brightened considerably whenever I saw her smile as she glided into the room.

Maybe the heat? The brittle air that swirled over her skin carried the cracks of the trees outside, the branches finally cooling after a day of baking in the hot southern sun. The amber light

by
Geoffrey Campey

Newcastle, Australia

**There were
so many reasons
it wouldn't work,
not the least of which,
was that my heart
was Artic stone.**

---

glints off the thin film of moisture on her skin; cheek, neck, arm, waist, thigh and calve. It is hot. I had lain behind her, a hint of cooling air between our spooning figures. She obviously wasn't too hot. My hand rests lightly against the soft skin of her waist. Hers found mine, and she pulled it gently around her. Fingers interlocked and spread apart, two spiders dancing together across her stomach. Slight pressure from above as the soft ridges on her stomach pressed against my palm. She nestled back against me, the curve of her buttocks pressed into my loins, her shoulder finding space beneath my chin.

Although we were just good friends, even this was not different. We had lain together like this before; intimate, caring and sensuous, friends, enjoying each other, comfortable in the knowledge that nothing more would come of it.

There were so many reasons it wouldn't work, not least of which, was that my heart was Arctic stone. She was the perpetual tomboy, twenty-two and never been kissed. I was the perpetual playboy, sampling all the delights that college life had to offer. She was a committed Christian, me a confirmed hedonist. We had a great time together, but it just couldn't be.

That's it! The feeling that it could be. That something more could come of it. But why today? Why the spark of electricity as she placed my hand upon her stomach? Why did it feel like her buttocks were pressed just a little firmer against me than before? Why can I tell that her eyes are smiling behind their closed lids? Why that sigh of contentment that just whispered past her moist, pink lips?

Those eyes! Those lips! Yes, of course. Today was different. The "nothing more will come of it" had lost its "nothing."

She, lounging on the bed, me, behind the desk; glowing, dry air separating us. She looked across the room, wanting to say something. Her eyes pleading for me to understand without a voice required. The room, like her words, stifled. Then courage returned to her eyes, her lips willed into moving, throwing herself open to the hurt and rejection that she believed was about to befall her. But hurt and rejection did not appear. In their place was I, joyful to fulfill her command, moving with haste to join her.

Happiness filled me at the realisation that she wanted my affection and love, and that she had the courage to make her feelings known to me. I will always love her for those words. Whether it was question or command, I was ready to answer. Her words?

'Geoffrey, when you are ready, will you come and join me.'

I met Aaron in middle school, but didn't set my sights on him until our junior year. He was shy, but incredibly adventurous and very smart. He didn't have a lot of free time, and he had never had a girlfriend. If I wanted him, it was going to be up to me to get him. First, I had to get his attention.

"Hey Aaron, I'm planning my wedding. Do you want to help? So far I have everything picked out but the groom. Of course I'm too young to get married yet, so will you just pretend for now?"

"What do I have to do?"

"Well, I'll just tell you about it, and you, as a guy, can tell me if it's okay."

He gave me a skeptical look, but I had a plan. Based on our school cafeteria experience together, I thought I could draw him into the make-believe plan. I was right.

"...and for the dessert, you know before the cake, I thought we'd serve Jell-O with, like, oranges, cherries..."

"There will be no fruit in the Jell-O." It was uncharacteristic of him at the time to be so bold. But gelatin dessert was something he felt strongly about. I was thrilled. He had now imagined us getting married. I was in his head.

"Oh yeah, and since you're the groom, you need to plan the honeymoon."

That was an easy pitch. Planning travel was something he loved to do anyway. Now, he was planning to travel with me.

We never did end up dating in high school. I moved out of the state at the end of that school year and my hopes began to dim. I went to his graduation and we kept in touch while we were at different colleges. He told me that he would not date while he was at college because he could not give enough of himself to a girl to be fair to her. It broke my heart, but I tried to subtly remind him that I was still interested, by sending him things in the mail. I sent a letter covered in

76

by
Mary Hudlemeyer

Laramie, Wyoming

**My head
was spinning
with things
I wanted to tell him.
I wanted to hold
his hand, to tell him
I loved him...**

---

stickers and bright pink feathers, a few different kinds of homemade cookies and one box of limited edition Power Puff Girl cereal.

After two years, I went to visit him. My head was spinning with things I wanted to tell him. I hardly heard what he said as he showed me around his campus. I wanted to hold his hand, to tell him I loved him, to explain that I was willing to give him anything. Then, he said something I couldn't ignore. He wanted to transfer schools.

Back at home, I researched the schools he had mentioned, which included mine, and did my best to skew the statistics in my favor. I prayed that God would either give him to me or take away my feelings. He came that summer.

After several nights in a row of sitting very close to each other, watching movies and talking until morning, I pushed again.

"You know, I don't think that anyone would believe us if we told them we weren't a couple." He put his arm around me and squeezed a little. "I suppose not."

Two weeks of dating may not seem like very long, but I had loved this guy for five years. One late night, two weeks after we were official, I asked him, "What do you think the chances are that we'll get married?"

"Really?"

"Yeah."

"Well, I guess...between ninety-eight and one hundred percent."

I begged and pleaded with him over the next year and a half to marry me. I even wrote some poetic proposals, but he had taken control. He finally asked me under the starlight if it would be all right if he loved me for the rest of his life.

77

by
Mariska Plavin

Eugene, Oregon

By all accounts, I should not have had to make the first move. But I blew it. I told Mike I would never date him. Told him he was like a brother. And damn him, he took me at my word. Mike dropped the idea of dating me and we spent our college years becoming the very best of friends.

So, three years later, like an experiment from the movies, where a kid releases a ball down a ramp and into a bucket to set off a chain of events—I had to start my own chain reaction.

It was my roommate, in fact, who started me thinking.

"You *do* realize," she said one night, "that you've changed clothes twice just to watch a movie with Mike Plavin."

I snorted, "Ooookay, Jenn. Whatever." Mike's roommate was a little less subtle later that night as he observed one of our usual wrestling/tickling matches.

"Geez, will you two just get it on and get it over with!"

Even our parents had said something similar, after seeing us together.

We laughed like it was the funniest idea we'd ever heard. We weren't attracted to each other! We were like brother and sister. But it wasn't funny to me anymore. After four years of friendship, I needed to make a careful first move. I needed a plan.

"We should bet on grades," I suggested a few days later, my plan taking shape.

"Okay, what's the bet?"

"Loser takes the winner to dinner."

He smiled, "You've got a bet!"

He's too easy, I thought. Mike was a decent student, but I had an "A" average and was an admitted nerd. He would never beat me. Eight weeks later, my ball dropped.

"Four-point-Oh!" I shouted triumphantly when I called him.

"Dammit! Three-point-eight. Where do you

> We should
> make it a date!"
> I laughed.
> Long pause.
> "What?"
> "Why not?" I tried,
> "How come we
> never went on one
> anyway?"

want to go to dinner?"

"We should make it a date!" I laughed. Long pause.

"What?"

I could hear my ball screeching to a stop. My ramp had changed directions too quickly and the ball was not going to make it to the bucket.

"Why not?" I tried, "How come we never went on one anyway?"

"Uh. Hmmm. Let's see." Mike was great with sarcasm. "You said you'd never date me."

"Well… screw it! We've both just been through bad breakups and I'm moving home soon. Let's get dressed up and go out. It'll cheer us up. You could take me to Ambrosia."

Ambrosia was a very nice Italian restaurant with a very cozy atmosphere—dim lighting, small tables, creaky wood floors and wine. I changed clothes four times that night (Jenn pointed that out too) and was too nervous to eat all day. The wait was long so we walked around downtown and I spent the walk wanting to take his hand. I chickened out and felt like a kid again.

After dinner was an exercise in frustration. Back at his place, we spent hours flirting with the idea of kissing, but we were both too afraid that the other wasn't serious about this "date." I stayed up the whole night with what felt more like bats than butterflies slamming around in my stomach. My ball was not dropping in the bucket and I was becoming impatient. Two days later I became exasperated and slammed the ball in the bucket myself.

"Mike, I find you frustrating," I was saying on the phone. Poor guy had been up nearly forty-eight hours after shepherding three girls, high on ecstasy, safely home from a rave. He had called me to thank me for being so sane and drug-free and I was calling him frustrating.

"Why?"

"I'm finding myself attracted to you."

Really long pause. I was convinced I had just screwed up the best friendship I ever had. Little did I know he was lying on his bed, fists raised in a victory salute.

"Mariska, I've been up for forty-eight hours and I just took a pill to go to sleep. Otherwise, I'd be over there right now."

Twenty-four hours later, I kissed my best friend for the first time (after many laughing tries I might add) and the chain reaction hit full speed. The next day I told my mother I would marry Mike Plavin. Seven months later, he proposed, and eleven months after that, we married.

He's still my best friend. I still get excited when he asks me out on a date. And nine years later…we still love to tell our story.

From A Vision Of Life

I've had them before, maybe two or three times in my life but never as vivid. This one happened on a steamy August evening in the large clubhouse at the Aliso Creek Tennis Club.

I sat on a white leather sofa beside Bruce, a guy that I'd met a few times at club functions. We were casually discussing the upcoming Labor Day weekend. His head was turned toward me, his long legs stretched out of faded red shorts, hair still damp from his tennis match.

Instantly, my vision of Bruce changed from a sweaty guy in tennis shorts to someone, well, let's just say, in this vision, we were not at the club. In this vision, I lay on my stomach on a navy blue bedspread, and just above my head I saw the wispy, gray ocean through a small porthole. The ship rocked, and we laughed together over a silly make-believe story, like two lovers who shared secrets that no one else could understand.

Just as quickly, I returned to the scene at the present moment at the club. My expression must have changed because Bruce stopped talking and stared at me.

"Everything okay?" he asked.

"Sure, I'm fine," I said quickly, trying to hide my confusion. I was stunned. How could this easygoing, personable every-day-kind of-guy turn into the person in the tiny ship's cabin who made me feel delirious? I felt flushed.

"Hey, excuse me for a minute please, I need to go check the board to see if I'm up for another match," he said and left the room.

My friend Heidi, who had given me a ride to the party, walked over to the sofa and said, "Let's go now. I promised JoAnn that we'd meet her for a drink."

It had been a long day. In the car on the way to the restaurant I said to my friend, "Hey, I forgot to say goodbye to Bruce."

78

by
Kathryn Hedderig

**Arroyo Grande,
California**

I was raised in a conservative home and learned quickly that women did not call men. Period.

155

"Who is Bruce?" she asked, obviously uninterested.

"You know, the tall guy in the red shorts. What would you think about me calling him and apologizing for not saying goodbye?"

"That sounds a little lame to me, but whatever," she replied.

I was raised in a conservative home and learned quickly that women did not call men. Period. It was okay to wait by the phone for them to call you and then act surprised when they did. But never would you make the first move. So I felt intimidated by the idea of locating Bruce's phone number and uneasy about what I would say.

But I couldn't get the dark wood paneled walls, the small porthole, our laughter, and his smile out of my mind. When I thought about him, I felt a warm feeling of contentment. That powerful sense of intuition couldn't be ignored.

I tried to sound casual and hide my nervousness. "Hi Bruce, it's Kathryn Robinson. I didn't get to say good-bye to you at the last party and we were having such a great time talking. I thought maybe you'd like to get together for coffee sometime." I left my number and hung up. Maybe I was glad that he wasn't there, it's much easier to make a quick call and hang up, than stumble through an embarrassing silence. Or what if he had been busy—busy with someone else. I could feel myself cringing from humiliation.

The next day I came home from work and found his message and the next week we had our first date. One year later we married.

I'm thankful that I acknowledged the premonition that told me, "Go after that man!" I now know that Bruce is grateful also; he tells me all the time. He thinks it's cute that I called him first and says he'd have called me eventually; I'd like to think so.

We will celebrate our fifth anniversary this year. We've spent much of our time together traveling and have even taken some cruises. I haven't found that small cabin with the brass porthole window. But it may happen someday; probably not.

What I did see that night at the clubhouse was an unfolding of my life to be. And every day we wake up together slowly, with time to talk, sharing our make-believe stories.

Just Who Do You Think You Are?

"Either you sign the dotted line or I go to another accountant," I told her firmly. She had just started practicing as a certified accountant, while I used to work for a mid-sized textile company in the office next door. I wanted her to certify a statement for my company; she was asking for some details.

My arrogant stand resulted in a long, dismayed look from her. For about a minute that appeared to be an eternity, we both were silent. She slowly picked up the pen and signed the certificate.

We were together in the lift the next morning, but she turned her face away. I, too, decided to play it cool. But I did look at her every now and then, and most of the time, I saw her glaring at me in a manner that was hard to interpret. I concluded that she probably despised me because I had been rough to her. Being short of work, she had no alternative but to sign on the dotted line.

Several weeks passed. We ran into each other every now and then, mostly in the lift, where we were forced to stand next to each other for a few minutes.

I didn't know she wanted me. But she got me a few weeks later.

It was a Friday evening and. I was working late. At around 8.00 p.m., I came out of the office. The corridor was deserted. While I was walking towards the elevator, a soft voice came from behind.

"Excuse me."

I turned to look at the caller. It was she.

"Just who do you think you are?" she asked, softly.

Unable to understand what she meant, I looked at her questioningly. She looked back defiantly. I knew in an instant that she was in love with me. It took, maybe, thirty seconds for me to

by
Surendra

India

I saw her glaring at me in a manner that was hard to interpret.

---

realize that I, too, loved her.

Without uttering a word, I took her in my arms and held her tight. She returned the hug and started sobbing. I took her face in my hands and kissed her lightly on the lips. I slowly sucked the tears rolling down her cheeks with my tongue, moving it slowly, lovingly. After tasting all the salty moisture, I was back on her lips. She kissed me back. The hug became tighter. Her tongue sought mine, and mine, hers.

A month later we got married. We have been married for twenty years now. "Just who do you think you are" continues to be a standing joke between us, a signal meant to indicate that the one saying it wants to be loved. Then and there.

What follows is the story of a good friend of mine. She did, in fact, marry her tiger.

Resume in hand, she marched through the front door, ready for a firing squad, ready to make that best first impression, ready for anything. Taking one last deep breath as the secretary said, "He will see you now," she strode confidently toward his office, unaware of the effect this meeting would have.

It only took one look and she faltered. His smile, deep and enticing, complemented by his smooth brown eyes, was the last thing she saw as her confidence evaporated into the mahogany of his desk. They shook hands, he asked a few questions and the job was hers. She floated out of his office in a school girl crush haze, a distant memory of the woman she was when she arrived.

In the weeks that followed, her affection grew from a morsel of infatuation into an undeniable attraction her heart and body could not hide for long. No one seemed to notice her longing blue eyes as he greeted her each morning, just as she failed to see his yearning in return. Gradually, lunch breaks would become their favorite time of the day, as they spent the whole hour talking about everything imaginable that was not related to work.

One afternoon, they learned two things about each other, that would change the situation forever. Work and play would never intertwine in his life and her career was the most important thing in hers. They both left the break room that day, a little disheartened.

Months turned into years, and the emotions never dulled. Secretly, each heart grew fuller and sadder with the love they had, but could never share. Then, the day she'd worked so hard for finally came. She was getting that big promotion. She felt so accomplished and proud, but something lingered inside that kept her from being truly happy. She knew what she had to do.

It was a Monday morning and he was the

by
Stephanie Rosseter

Belmar, New Jersey

One afternoon, they learned two things about each other, that would change the situation forever.

---

first to arrive. On his desk was a luxurious bouquet of flowers, filling and overflowing the intricate vase that held them. Bewildered, he searched for the card, certain that these flowers had found the wrong destination. Nestled deeply between the roses, he pulled the card from its stand. Written in a beautiful script were the words, "I quit."

She stepped across the threshold only moments later, smiling harder than she had in years, and said, "It has been a pleasure working for you, but I'd rather give playing a try."

His eyes lit up and he smiled, stretching out his hand to hers. As they stood in his office for the last time as coworkers, he sighed, "I've been waiting years to hear you say that."

81

by
Maggie Moran

Los Angeles, California

From the moment I locked eyes with his, I knew I had to have him. He didn't know me yet, but I had been staring at his picture for weeks. I was in charge of casting for a television series, and luckily for me, not only was my guy incredibly handsome, but also an amazing actor. I picked him for the initial casting session and the stars aligned when I learned my producers loved him, as well.

He lived four states away and we only had three days together during the shoot; I had to make the best impression I could during those short three days. I spent every possible moment I could with him, and neither one of us slept a wink. If we weren't working, we were deep in conversation. We sat up late into the night, sharing stories about family, friends, where we wanted to end up. We talked about anything and everything. I felt like I had known him in so many other lives before and that I had truly met my soul mate. I didn't think I would ever find anyone like him again in my life.

It was really hard to say good-bye, knowing I might not ever see him again. Having to go back to the guys I had been dating in the city made my stomach wretch. So we kept writing and calling. I'd call him from a bad date when the guy was in the bathroom, and he'd call me while he was out with his buddies.

One time we watched a movie together-over the phone, just to feel like we were on a date together. We talked every night from nine p.m. until three or four in the morning. We flew back and forth twice a month, for six months, before we couldn't stand the distance anymore.

Every time one of us left the other at the airport, our hearts broke a little more. The last time I had to leave him, I almost missed the flight because I couldn't pull myself away from his arms. I couldn't take the good-byes anymore, or the tears. I knew I had to do something to show him how serious I was about having him in my

> I couldn't take the good-byes anymore, or the tears. I knew I had to do something...

life forever. I thought, life is too short and we are young, with no strings attached. Why can't we be together? We both have jobs we don't care about right now. So I made up a story about a family emergency, took a week off from my job and put my plan into action.

I showed up on his doorstep for what he thought was a monthly visit and said, "You're coming with me!" I told him I had only bought a one-way ticket and he had better start packing up his car with his belongings. We spent the entire day packing his stuff in his car, and what we couldn't fit, we left behind with friends.

We drove all the way from Washington State to Southern California on what seemed like a Bonnie and Clyde mission. We slept under the stars, on the beach, in the redwoods and forgot about any other responsibilities. Of course, when we got to California we had some explaining to do! But we didn't care about the rest of the world. This was our time. We moved into an apartment together when we got into the city and this past February he proposed to me on the beach in Malibu.

Our wedding date is set and we couldn't be happier. He is my best friend, my most loyal companion and the greatest lover I have ever known. If I hadn't put aside my fears, doubts and second thoughts, I might still be counting the days until our next visit, instead of planning my life with the man of my dreams. I can't wait to be his wife and have children with this man. Some day we'll grow old together and look back at our adventure. We never let anyone stand in our way and we never let anyone tell us it wouldn't work, even though they all tried. I'll never look back with regret at the one who got away, because I didn't let him.

Go grab your tiger and take charge! If it's true love, he'll follow you to the ends of the earth. Or at least a few states away.

By the age of fifty-one, I'd read every book on men and relationships ever written. Finally convinced that I was the problem—not my live-in boyfriend of twelve years, Rick, I set on a path of rediscovery with the help of some therapy and plenty of yoga. I caught up with old friends, biked on weekends and learned to knit. Slowly, almost effortlessly, my self esteem started to build. I left Rick, and, after spending a few months alone doing things I enjoyed, I decided it was time to bring a man into my life—different from the selfish 'lookers' that had stolen my heart in the past. Crazy, I wasn't, however: He'd still have to get my engine going. But for the first time I planned to let my head, and not my hormones, lead me to him.

I thought about all the really nice men I'd turned away in my thirties and forties, as I waited for Rick to morph from bad boy to nice guy. Back then, I'd moan that good guys had no edge and I'd toss them aside like old newspapers. It seemed that men with the cunning ability to distract me with their glibness, while they dismantled my heart, were the men of my dreams.

But that was then. It was time to find a healthy relationship and I figured work might be a good place to start. My job, managing a large dental office, put me in front of hundreds of people each week: Unfortunately, few were in a good mood when they came in and even fewer were eligible, single men. I figured, all I needed was one, and decided Bob Nilson might just fill the bill. He'd been coming to our office for years, but it was like I was suddenly seeing him for the first time. At forty-eight years of age, Bob had a warm smile, reddish hair that was starting to recede, velvety blue eyes and loved spending time with his daughter. Plus, he was divorced. He was not the kind of guy I usually went for—he had that clean-cut, wholesome look—which is precisely why I decided to give him a try.

Over the next few months, I made a point of dressing well on the days he was coming in and chatted with him even more than usual when he came up to pay. I learned that he biked and

by
Elyssa Byers-Nilson

Minnesota

At 5'11", blonde and in her early forties, she was formidable competition— and she was my boss! It was time to make my move.

---

coached inner-city softball on weekends, was a die-hard Vikings fan, enjoyed good mystery novels and liked to go camping with his eleven year old. As we got friendlier, we'd discuss football, compare weekend activities and recommend books to each other—all through the open Plexiglas window. Talking to him was effortless and I found myself feeling sad when he would leave.

Chandra, one of the three dentists in our office, also had her eye on him. A fellow Swede, she insisted their families knew one another and I sensed she was trying to stake her claim. At 5'11", blonde and in her early forties, she was formidable competition—and she was my boss! It was time to make my move. So when he arrived for his next appointment, I lent him a book I thought he'd enjoy, based on our many chats. Into it, I'd tucked a note saying how hard it was to talk in the office and that I could use some advice on the kind of bike to get (which was absolutely true). I ended my note with "How 'bout joining me for a picnic at Lake Calhoun a week from this Saturday? I make a great fried chicken—and I might even share it with you!" I added a hand-drawn smiley face and my phone number to the bottom.

Two days passed; no call. To say I felt like a total jerk doesn't begin to describe it. Then, Thursday afternoon, I got back from lunch and Chandra handed me a bag; "Bob Nilson dropped this off for you Tuesday; it must have slipped my mind," she said, as she dropped the bag on my desk. Sure, right—that was two whole days ago. Inside the bag, was a velvet pouch; I opened the drawstrings and discovered a big, yellow smiley face pin. No note. Just a pin. I was puzzled.

Bob's next visit was the following Monday so, rather than call him, I decided to wait until then to ask why he'd left the button for me. He knocked on the plexiglass. "What happened?" he mouthed through the divider. I pulled it open, only to learn that he *had* included a note in the bag and it had apparently disappeared. He told me his note said that he would be in Chicago that weekend, visiting his daughter, but he'd love a raincheck on the picnic, and was I free for dinner that night?

Needless to say, I swiftly identified the culprit in this miscommunication, which I kept to myself, as I went on to enjoy a wonderful dinner with Bob that very evening. Exactly twenty bike- rides, dinners and picnics later, Bob proposed. Soon after we started dating, he confessed that he'd always wanted to ask me out, but Chandra told him I was in a serious relationship, so he never made a move. When he read my invitation for the picnic, he was overjoyed. To this day, I suspect my lovely office mate removed his note; but with all her manipulations, she couldn't eliminate me!

83

I used to choose men just like my brother and father—liars, con-men, not trustworthy, not reliable, cold, mean, selfish and heartless. I guess it's because that's what I was accustomed to and I didn't know any better. After years of heartache, I took a hard look at myself: Everything I was doing in my personal relationships was wrong and self-destructive.

I'd been used, abused, lied to, and worse, by my former boyfriends. I knew my only chance for happiness was to pick men who were different from the ones I had dated in the past. So I put an ad in a local newspaper and received a large number of responses. Having come from a dysfunctional background, my sole focus was to find a man with a completely opposite history. He would respect me and I would respect him. This was more important than height, weight, career and all the other nonsense I would be attracted to in the past. I stuck to my goal. And it worked!

I didn't meet Chuck until I was thirty-seven, and we married three years later. Beginning with placing the ad, it was I who pursued him. I also set some firm rules, telling him from day one I would not tolerate verbal or mental abuse or lies of any kind.

The last twelve years have absolutely flown by. Like all couples, we have fights, but we can resolve them by sitting down and talking like two adults. During this happy period in my life, I even found the renewed energy to complete a book I've been writing; it has been a rewarding time and well worth the struggle to get here. And at the risk of sounding boastful, I have myself to thank.

There was a time I thought I was doomed to be alone and miserable for the rest of my life. But I made a plan and I stuck to it. If I can do it, anyone can.

by
Gail Fonda

Beachwood, Ohio

> **Having come from a dysfunctional background, my sole focus was to find a man with a completely opposite history.**

Grab Your Tiger

84

by
Warren Bull

Kansas City, Missouri

Judy and I met twelve years ago on a blind date vacation. We didn't know it was a blind date. My sister, Peggy, Judy and Lisa used to work together in the Speech and Hearing Department at Kansas University Medical Center. When Lisa and Peggy started new jobs, the three of them made arrangements to get together for a week at Lisa's summer cabin in Bar Harbor, Maine. Lisa and Judy were single. Peggy was coming with her husband and three children. She asked if she could invite along her brother (that's me) who was sad because he was getting divorced.

I had no interest in getting into another relationship. Judy had been divorced for more than a decade. She had a successful life, an excellent job, an occasional boyfriend and she enjoyed being independent. If I had been looking, I would have been impressed that Judy was my sister's best friend and that my niece and nephews adored her. But I wasn't looking.

Once in Bar Harbor, we had to jam into one van to travel anywhere, and took turns doing everything. Judy was warm-hearted, smart, funny, cute and flexible. Not that it mattered to me. She was a good sport, doing things the children enjoyed, like miniature golf, which she would never have done on her own. Once, Judy and I volunteered to do laundry for the group. We ended up laughing the whole time, while Judy tried to teach me a card game she didn't remember the rules to. We got so distracted, that we forgot to wash one duffle bag full of dirty clothes.

When we dropped Judy off at a bus station at the end of the vacation, she gave me a hug that cut through my gloom. I thought she was someone I would have liked to get to know better if I met her at a different time in my life. She lived in Missouri and I lived in California, so why even think about it? She told me later that at that moment, she thought about canceling her ticket and getting back on the van. But she didn't.

I was surprised when, a week or so later,

At that moment, she thought about canceling her ticket and getting back on the van. But she didn't.

167

she sent me a book in the mail from, "The Library Lady." It was a used paperback book, *Tourist Season,* from one of her favorite authors, Carl Hiaasen, who we had talked about during the vacation. It was funny, ironic and surreal. Not everybody's cup of tea, but I loved it. Later she told me she thought that might either end any chance of a relationship or confirm that I was someone worth pursuing.

I wrote her a letter and sent her a used t-shirt with a picture of a sailboat on it, since she said she liked sailing but could not afford a yacht of her own. She responded positively. I thought it was a shame I met her at a time in my life when I did not want to get involved with anyone, and when we lived so far apart. With regrets, I was ready to write her off with an "If you ever get to my neck of the woods, look me up" statement.

Then she suggested that we meet in Seattle, where she was working on a research grant. She said she was from the area and offered to show me Washington, "through the eyes of a native." Still, with no expectations, and with the thought that this almost stranger might not even pick me up at the airport, I went to Seattle and the magic began. We've been together ever since.

We did a total of three dives that day and the Dive Masters came along on all of them. One Dive Master, in particular, caught my attention. He was kind, helpful, funny, and looked great in wetsuit, but there was one small detail: he had a kid along. A few weeks later, a friend of mine and I went on a road trip to buy a new diving suit and we casually invited my favorite Dive Master along to chauffeur and for his expert opinion.

Leaving the Capital, I asked about his daughter. When he asked: "What daughter?" I was no longer interested in diving; now I was going fishing. It ends up it was his God-daughter! He was, however, seeing someone. I couldn't help but find out. After all, she did call him every half hour to see what he was up to. As we continued on our way, I became more and more interested, and more and more interesting. I couldn't waste any time. I had to save him from continuing in a bad relationship with the neurotic, untrusting "girlfriend" before things got too serious.

When we were on our way back, I realized that time was running out, and I had to make my move quick. I tried witty conversation. I tried common interests. I tried it all. But he hadn't asked me out yet. Finally, I just broke down and told him that I thought he should ask me out. He was a little surprised, but invited me to go to the gym with him the next day. Since Murphy's Law rules, I had class at grad school, even though it was a Saturday. So, we left it at "call me."

I knew I couldn't let this one get away from me, but I didn't want to be overbearing, either. After class, I had to work on a project with a friend from school, and we decided to study at Subway at the mall. When we finished, he called his girlfriend to meet him. I decided to do the same. So, I called Dive Master and asked him out. To my surprise, he met us there and we had a blast. But the next day, he didn't call me.

On Monday, after class we all went to a clandestine bar across town, so I called and invited

85

by
Melissa S. Marchand

Canton, Ohio

I tried witty conversation. I tried common interests. I tried it all. But he hadn't asked me out yet.

him. I knew he had never been there and knew he wasn't the "bar" type, but it was worth a try. When I called his house, I was told he had gone to bed. I really wanted to see him, so I asked if they could please wake him up. I told him where I was, how to get there, and asked him to come join us. He said that he was really tired and probably wouldn't go. About an hour later, my phone rang and it was him. He was waiting outside. Once again, we had a blast and pretty much closed the place. The next day, I got the call. He invited me to the movies, and that night, he finally got hooked.

About six months into the relationship, a friend called me to go diving. On the early morning dive, he stayed behind because he wasn't feeling well. The three of us girls headed out, swam about 400 meters offshore and decided to meet at -42 meters. At -42, we started swimming back inshore and agreed to do a stop at the sunken Christ at -23 meters. When I got to the Christ, another diver grabbed my flipper. It was my boyfriend. Apparently, he was feeling better. He signaled his palm (which in diving means "how much air do you have?") and I signaled back that I was OK. He kept signaling his palm. When I got closer, I saw the words "Do you want to marry me?" written on his hand. I obviously signaled "yes" and he put a ring on my finger right there at -23 meters. We took off our regulators and sealed the engagement with a kiss, right there at the Christ. Not surprisingly, I ran out of air fast on that dive. A month later we were married, and the following year we moved to an island off the coast.

Speaking Up

I may be one the few women, if any, in the world who at one point actually dated a Tom (a few years my junior), a Dick (a few years my senior) and a Harry (about my age) during my early thirties.

One May Sunday in 1973, Tom had agreed to attend a Russian Art Exhibit with me in D.C., but arrived quite late, never calling to explain that he had broken a finger playing baseball. After waiting in line at the exhibit a boring three hours with him, I certainly didn't want to dine with him later, as well.

After he left, I did want to go out, though, so I called up Dick. We went out to dinner, but by the time we got back at nine, I still felt antsy. If I had then called Harry, my whole life would probably be different.

Instead I hopped in my car and drove to Georgetown to a singles dance I knew about. By the time I walked into the room and looked around, I realized there wasn't anyone of interest to me, so I just sat watching people.

About half an hour later, out of the corner of my left eye, I noticed a handsome black haired man walking the full length of the rectangular bar area. Then he continued going round and round and round. After I counted his tenth full circuit, I stopped him to ask, "Do you know you're walking in circles?"

Though I certainly didn't realize it then, that night was the beginning of a friendship which has lasted thirty years and counting. He's told me he intended to talk to me, but saw other guys talking to me, so he didn't.

If I hadn't gone out on that proverbial limb...

We had one movie date that month. Then over Memorial Day I attended a Folk Dancing Camp in West Virginia. Unfortunately, it rained most of the weekend. On Sunday I had a chance

86

by
Rose Gordy

Maryland

After I counted his tenth full circuit, I stopped him to ask, "Do you know you're walking in circles?"

---

to leave early if I could get a ride from Frederick back to my apartment an hour away. I racked my brain for someone to call who might pick me up and thought about Ed, the circles man I had recently met who had told me he always spent Sunday afternoons at his parents' house. Out of the blue I called him, and he agreed to drive two hours each way to pick me up! He soared in my estimation from that day on.

A few weeks later my sister in Baltimore set up a blind date for me for a certain Saturday night, but at the last minute the man backed out. I called my sister and asked, "Do you think it's too weird if I call up a guy I've recently met who asked me to go to a Ski Club picnic on the same day as that date that fell through and say my plans have changed so I can go now?" She quickly answered, "It's worth a try." So I did. He was still dateless. We went together. Our first really Big Date.

On the first day of Spring in 1975, we married and had our first son in October of 1976 and our twin sons an hour and two hours before my 39th birthday in mid-August of 1978. This past spring, we celebrated thirty years of walking in circles, together, on a four-island Hawaiian tour.

I was twenty-eight years old and back in my home town after a ten-year absence, along with my five-year-old son and my daughter, who was three. To make matters even more interesting for all the small town gossipers, I was recently divorced from a Navy sailor. As I situated my family into a new home and became complacent in a new job, I found myself longing for male companionship once again.

One summer evening, I was having dinner with my kids at McDonalds, which is next door to a martial arts studio. As I watched children enter the studio with parents, I also saw a few men enter, dressed in karate attire. It looked like time for classes to begin.

At that moment, my son, Chris, informed me that he wanted to learn karate. As we talked about the commitment it would take from him, a Harley Davidson motorcycle roared into the lot and a very tall, well-built guy with a dragon tattoo on his shoulder parked and entered the studio. He really caught my eye but I didn't get a good enough look at him.

So, after dinner, I decided that I needed to go check out karate lessons for my son and check out this guy a little bit more. The owner of the studio was there and so was the cute instructor with the Harley. We discussed the benefits of having a child take karate lessons, and, since I was a fairly fresh divorcee, another plus of the lessons was that my son would have a good male role model in his life. I listened carefully to the information passed on to me by the owner, but was really so intent on watching the instructor's movements that I probably seemed like a real idiot to the owner who was trying to complete the registration forms. He was so tall and graceful. He had a deep sexy voice that sent chills down my spine when he talked. He also did not pay a bit of attention to me the entire time I was in the studio.

There was a week in between my visit to

87

by
Loren Estes

Central Kentucky

**We finished
with the details
of our planned date...
I realized I knew
absolutely
nothing about
this guy
but his name and
where he lived!**

173

the studio and Chris' first lesson. A whole week to think about this guy. I was really obsessed with him. The bad boy look, his powerful movements, and some sort of vague familiarity, made me think about him all the time. Several times, I thought about calling the studio to talk to him, but I never got his name and didn't know who to ask for. All I could do is wait until Chris' first class to see him again.

On Tuesday evening, we arrived for class just a little early; my plan was to introduce myself to this mystery man, and to learn a little more about him while my son took his lesson. Well, my plan was foiled, as my hunk turned out to be my son's instructor and was tied up the entire class teaching twenty five-year-olds how to throw punches and kicks. I did manage to get a "Hello" out, which he responded to with a nod of his head.

I left that night with my karate kid, hungry to know more about this guy. I pumped my son for information but all I learned was that his name was Greg and he was very strong. Well, at least I had a name. Chris would not have another class until next Tuesday and I could not wait that long to meet Greg. It took me three days to do it, but I finally mustered the courage to call the studio to ask him out.

The conversation was awkward, "Hi Greg, you don't know me but my son takes lessons from you. I was wondering if you'd like to go out for dinner Friday evening?" I think I held my breath the entire time he was responding to my offer.

"Sure, if you don't mind driving; my car is in the shop and I only have my bike."

We finished with the details of our planned date, where and when to pick him up, and said our good-byes. I realized I knew absolutely nothing about this guy other than his name and where he lived! I was mortified for the next forty-eight hours, wondering how this date would go.

Well, the date went absolutely great, and the weirdest part of it all was that I went to high school with Greg and never recognized him until we actually had a chance to talk at dinner. My mystery man turned out to be an old friend from years ago.

Greg and I were married three years later. That was ten years ago. We both have children from previous marriages, and one of our own, and we are very happy together. I am still intrigued by him and still like to watch his tall, graceful movements as he practices at the studio.

The moral of the story? Never let an opportunity pass you by. You never know what wonderful person may walk into your life.

Field Of Horses

The year I turned thirty-nine, I divorced my husband of twenty years, bought a gas station and fell in love for the first time in my life.

Larry was my first customer the day I took over the small country store in a neighboring county. He is seventeen years my senior, but doesn't look a day over forty-five. There's not a trace of silver in his wavy, chestnut hair and the sun-kissed skin around his gorgeous eyes is smooth and wrinkle free. His six-foot physique is trim and athletic, with broad shoulders and bulging biceps.

I'll never forget the first time I saw him. He pulled up to the gas pumps in an old green pickup truck that looked ready for the junk yard. I stood by the cash register and watched him put twenty-dollars-worth of unleaded fuel into his gas tank. Very quickly, he walked inside towards the coolers and grabbed a can of Mountain Dew.

With one hand in the back pocket of his well-worn Wranglers, he looked up and all was lost. The air was knocked out of my lungs and forced into my throat. I was hot and cold at the same time and the friendly greeting I had planned was lost somewhere in his penetrating gaze.

I had always heard that love will find you when you are least looking for it, and I darn sure wasn't in the market for the complication of another relationship, after getting out of one so recently. But, something just clicked when my royal blues met his baby blues. I held my right hand towards him. "Hi, I'm Sandy Driver, the new owner."

He reached for my outstretched greeting and clasped my hand tightly in his. My small fingers were lost in his palm, and I felt calluses and hard living. He released me abruptly. "Larry Holsonback," he said in a soft voice, dropping a twenty dollar bill and a few coins into my open palm.

He came in every day for weeks, with al-

by
Sandy W. Driver

Crossville, Alabama

Before I could lose my nerve, I picked up the receiver and dialed. "Larry, this is Sandy from the store..."

175

most the same routine. Occasionally, he paused and made small talk with another customer, but he was usually in a hurry, and barely spoke to anyone.

Very casually, I began making inquiries about him to some of the regular patrons living in the small community. I learned his age and that he was single—divorced twice, the last time for almost fourteen years. He had served our country in the Vietnam War, flying overseas, while I was still in diapers. He owned a lot of land, over a hundred acres, and raised horses; he had around ninety of the large animals that had always intimidated me a little.

Each day when he came into the store, I tried steering him into conversation, and finally succeeded one rainy afternoon. He bought his customary Mountain Dew, and almost reluctantly nodded when I asked him if he could 'sit down and stay a spell.' We talked for over an hour. Once he got started, he seemed hesitant to stop and leave, even when the rain subsided. Lord, I was in love with this man, and felt like a school girl sitting across from him.

I signed onto the Internet that night and found his phone number. Before I could lose my nerve, I picked up the receiver and dialed. "Larry, this is Sandy from the store," I said in a rush when he answered on the other end. "I'm interested in buying a horse."

We talked for almost an hour, and our conversations at the store grew longer each time he stopped in after that. I finally got up the gumption to drive over to his farm one evening—just to look at the horses, of course. We walked awhile and talked a bit. Finally, he looked down at me, and said with a smile, "You don't really want to buy a horse, do you?"

I shook my head and leaned towards him. He pulled me into his strong embrace and I've been there for the past eight months. The house next door to his went on the market recently. After discussing it thoroughly with him, I packed up a lifetime of memories and belongings from the house I'd lived in forever and moved towards the future.

The love that Larry and I share grows stronger with each passing day, and the nights get sweeter and sweeter, while his field of horses walk softly all around us, reminding me of how I finally found, and grabbed onto, the man of my dreams.

I worked at my parent's TV repair shop my sophomore year in college. Exciting though it may sound to be surrounded by televisions all day, I quickly learned that a girl can only watch so much TV before her brain fries. To relieve the boredom, I took to watching people instead, a much more entertaining diversion. Being in the middle of a busy shopping center, the shop was perfect for this.

One day I saw a gorgeous man walking toward the shop. He was tall—at least a foot taller than I, with strong arms and eyes the color of dark chocolate. His hair was sprinkled with gray, making him appear older than he was. Having always had a thing for older men, I immediately knew he was perfect for me.

I stepped back, praying that his TV was broken (cruel, I know). To my disappointment, he went into the Radio Shack next door. I anxiously waited for him to come back out, but hours later, when closing time rolled around, I was still waiting.

I walked by, staring into the small electronics store, only to realize that my dream guy worked there. He was standing behind the register, talking to a customer, and he had a smile on his face that made me melt. It was a smile that was innately masculine and so truly beautiful that I decided it should not be wasted on customers, alone.

I needed to meet him, and over the next few days I contrived to do just that. I got up early so I could "accidentally" arrive at work at the same time as him, but, after camping out in my car for several early-morning hours, I realized he was definitely not a morning person; this was perfect, because, I found, neither was I.

Then I waited for him to leave work, thinking to meet him in the parking lot, but that plan was flawed from the beginning, as our shop closed a good four hours before his. It would have looked ridiculous for me to stay at work so long.

by
Brandi Silva

Salida, California

Feeling mischievous, I retrieved the ladder and set it against the wall. I climbed up, water gun in hand...

What I should have done, was walk in and introduce myself, or try to buy something, so he would know I was right next door. But at nineteen, I wasn't so sure of myself, and I knew nothing about electronics. I was afraid I would make a complete fool of myself. Somehow that was not the image I wished to leave him with.

It's been said that if you wait, the right opportunity will eventually come along, and it's true. One day, while at the shop alone, I noticed something on the counter. My brother had visited earlier to show my dad his new high-powered water gun, and, lucky me, there it still was. I remembered something my dad had told me when I started working there; the attics of the buildings were all connected. Although walls separated the individual businesses at the lower level, above the oh-so-movable ceiling tiles, there were no such partitions.

Feeling mischievous, I retrieved the ladder and set it against the wall. I climbed up, water gun in hand, and cautiously lifted the tile, peeking my head through to the dusty area above. Noiselessly, I lifted another tile, opening it to look down on the electronics store. A quick glance revealed that he was standing right below me, so, without giving myself time to back out, I shot a stream of water at his head. He turned quickly, but I was already replacing the tiles, scurrying down the ladder. I had just enough time to stash the gun before he came running in.

"Hey, did you hear someone on the roof?" he asked.

"No, why?" I replied.

"I'm Tony from next door," he explained. "Someone just shot me with a water gun or something, and I think it came from the roof, but my back door's broken. Can I use yours to go look?"

He flashed me that smile, and I knew that I had made the right move. I dutifully went out with him to scan the roof, trying hard not to laugh as we searched for the naughty culprit.

Years later, when I confessed, he didn't think that it was quite as funny. He does admit, though, that had I not acted, he might never have met the woman who would one day be his wife.

We arrived just in time as the orientation began for Cub Scouts at my son's elementary school. Standing in front of the group was the most boyishly-handsome man I had ever seen. I felt shaken, as his attention was drawn to our entrance and he smiled at us.

I realized that getting my son involved with this group would be beneficial to him. Aaron had seemed lost since my husband passed away two years earlier. He really needed a male role model, and as I listened to this dark haired, charismatic man, I thought that it would be a good idea for me, as well.

It had been a long time since I had felt any attraction to a man, and I wasn't going to let the opportunity pass me by; I had mourned long enough. That night as I signed my son up for the "Tiger Cubs" I found out that the speaker, Jim, was not going to be in our group of Tigers. His son was in the Bear's Den, so our only contact was going to be at the pack meetings once a month. That was not going to be enough for me. I wanted to pursue this man and I was determined to find a way to put myself in his path.

The last announcement that was made by the Scout Master was about a camp-out the next month. Jim spoke briefly about the activities available for the scouts to earn their merit badges and advised that we speak to a member of one of the more advanced dens for advice on what to bring, and what to expect. Aaron was so excited, I didn't have the heart to tell him 'No,' even though I had never been camping in my entire life. As Aaron went to play with a couple of the other boys, I took the opportunity to approach Jim.

Jim said that he'd be happy to help me in any way possible, since he would be one of the Camp Master's team. He gave me his cell number to call if I had any more questions on what I would need to purchase for the trip. I thanked him and thought, with a blush, just how he could help me.

90

by
Florence C. Smith

Plantation, Florida

It had been a long time since I felt any attraction to a man, and I wasn't going to let the opportunity pass me by.

The next day I called him and asked if he could meet me at the Army-Navy Store on Saturday to assist me in making purchases for the camp-out; he agreed and we set a time of 11:00 in the morning. When he arrived at the store alone, I asked him where his son was. He said that he was with his mother for his weekend. He quickly went on to explain that he was divorced, but on fairly good terms with his ex-wife. My relief must have been evident on my face, because he just smiled at me and turned a little red himself. I explained that my son was not with me either, because he was staying the night with a friend.

I must have blushed as the thought of a night alone with him crossed my mind, because as I looked up at his smiling face I realized that his thoughts were coinciding with mine.

After we went through the store, selecting items for the camping trip, we decided to go for a cup of coffee and discuss what I should expect during the camp-out. We stopped at a Starbucks, and as we were talking, we realized just how much we had in common, camping experience aside. Jim offered to watch over us during the camp-out, to make sure it was a pleasant experience for Aaron and myself, and if it went well, we could try it with just him and his son on another weekend.

I've never before been one to be overly bold with the opposite sex, so I hesitated before stammering out that maybe he might like to join me for dinner, since we were both on our own for the night. He said it was a wonderful idea, with a smile that went from ear to ear so his dimples showed. He made me blush with anticipation. Anticipation that I still enjoy, except now, it is on a daily basis, as I wait for him to come home each day.

A Chance Meeting

I was home on my summer break, after finishing my first year away at college, when my old friend called. He was getting ready to attend his public speaking class at the local community college. He was looking for moral support, and since I was bored out of my mind, I agreed to go with him. I wondered why I thought attending a class during my break from college was a good idea.

That's when he walked to the front of the room. I felt my face become warm, and I knew I had to meet him after class. He was everything I ever envisioned in a man. He was tall, handsome, articulate, and funny. When his presentation was over, my mind drifted to how I would approach him after class; what we would talk about; what we would do on our first date.

After the last speech, the class was split into groups to discuss the presentations. To my delight, mystery man was in my friend's group. I decided to not make my move just yet; I needed more information. I discovered that my fantasy man, whose name turned out to be Robert, was majoring in criminal justice. Criminal Justice happened to be what I was studying, as well; that was the connecting link I was waiting for.

All too soon, it was time to leave. I was now faced with fear over whether to make a move. I decided I had nothing to lose, since I would be going back to college in a few months, so as my friend and I walked to the car, I mustered up the courage to approach Robert. The only problem was he was nowhere to be found.

I panicked! I begged my friend to slow down so that Robert could catch up. He resisted, so I did the only thing I could do. I grabbed everything out of his hands and threw the whole pile on the ground. My delay tactic worked a little too well. As I helped my friend pick up his multitude of note cards, Robert had managed to walk right past us.

91

by
Krista Harvey

Charlottesville, Virginia

I thought about calling him, but what would I say? "Hey, it's that crazy girl from the community college who always seems to be waiting for you after class. Wanna go out?"

Again, I panicked. I couldn't bear the thought of him driving away. I took off running towards him with arms flailing. Once I had his attention, I said "Hey, didn't you say you were a criminal justice major?" As the words left my mouth, I knew this was the dumbest thing I could have possibly said. I felt like such a fool. I couldn't move.

To my surprise, Robert looked at me and said, "Why, yes I did." A huge wave of relief washed over me. I proceeded to tell him about classes I had taken, and in the course of our chat, I learned that he was intending to transfer to the same college I was already attending in August. In that instant I thought, 'I may actually have a chance with this guy.' We exchanged information, and I promised to give him a tour of the campus once classes started in the fall.

I decided that I just couldn't wait two months to see Robert again, so I invited myself to the community college for three more public speaking classes. After each class I managed to talk with him for a few minutes. When I arrived for the fourth class, I was approached by the professor; she told me that while an outside listener is good for her students to practice presenting to, I would need to pay tuition if I continued to attend her class.

A month went by and I was growing anxious. I needed to see him. I thought about calling him, but what would I say? "Hey, it's that crazy girl from the community college who always seems to be around waiting for you after class. Wanna go out?" I decided that wasn't such a good idea, so I waited it out.

Finally, the first day of class came at my university. I was giddy with anticipation. And then it happened. I saw him coming down the hall. As he passed me, I grabbed him by the arm and yelled "Hey! Remember me?" What an idiot I was! Lucky for me, Robert is a gentleman. We talked, and he asked me out. We've been going strong for eight years and counting. True love is out there. Sometimes you have to walk up and grab it.

I first met Dave one night at our mutual friends' fraternity house. After spending most of the warm August evening dancing about on the front porch, I was becoming more and more irritated with the drunken wrestling and sloppiness festering outside. I decided to get some fresh air indoors, where I was sure there would be fewer drunken fools. To my surprise, there was only one person there, and he was cute. The hottie was leaning against the pool table by himself, seemingly staring into space.

For some unknown reason, I got the confidence to go up to talk to him. Before I knew it, my hand was resting on his chest and we were giggling about Michael Jackson and the 1980's. The fun would end, though. My best friend, Kim, came in, and knowing Dave had a reputation for being a "playa," dragged me away, with promises of a good party. I reluctantly went along thinking that was the end of my brief affair with the hunk in the white button down shirt.

When we got outside, however, my friend stopped to talk with some people who were going with us to the party. Somehow, in the three minutes we were waiting for someone to get back from the bathroom, I transformed into some hidden inner vixen I had never known.

I turned to my friend and simply asked, "Would it be all right if I just went and kissed him?"

She looked at me with the protective concern of that motherly friend everyone always has.

"Please, I'll only be like two minutes."

She caved, and before I really had time to plan my move, I was standing in front of Dave, who had just walked outside. I blurted out the first thing that came to mind.

"Kim said I have two minutes to kiss you." I held my breath and braced myself for the response.

With a shrug of his shoulders he just said, "Okay," and poof! We were kissing in front of everyone.

92

by
Brittany Rostron

New York, New York

I turned to my friend and simply asked, "Would it be all right if I just went and kissed him?"

Before I knew it, my two minutes of bliss were up and Kim was dragging me away. She scolded me, saying that he had a reputation and I shouldn't get involved with someone like him. In a loud, obnoxious voice, completely uncharacteristic of me, I screamed (so I was sure he could hear), "So what? I just wanted to kiss him! It's not like I'm going to marry him!"

It'll be two years in August since that night, and we're engaged.

Grabbing The Tiger: The Best Time Of My Life

I have made bad choices in my life, and I had reached a point where I didn't trust my own judgment anymore. When I decided that I'd had enough and there would be no one in my life, I met my man.

There was a group of us that all got together on the weekends, cooked out, shot pool, threw darts, played dominoes, and relaxed from a hard week of work. This was a pretty fluid group, with people coming and going depending on what their schedules were and if they were trying to date someone seriously. My man was part of the peripheral group. I had seen him two or three times before we really talked to one another.

He was, and still is, gorgeous. He has truly amazing blue eyes, which light up, and glow when he smiles, especially when he has a mischievous grin. He is tall, and his face and body are amazingly handsome. This I knew before we really got to know one another. So, based only on physical matters, I was, as the gambling term goes "all in." But, physical appearance wasn't enough for me.

I found out that he is painfully shy. I asked one of our mutual friends about him, and she said that he was a super nice guy, but we'd have a hard time of it, because he is so shy, and I am not.

One night, we are all at my friend's house. I had hoped he would be there; in fact, I had dressed a little sexier than normal. He was there, sitting on the couch, alone, with his leg crossed so that his foot was resting on the opposite knee. When I sat down next to him, I shoved his foot down. He didn't know me well enough to really know what to think.

He said: "Are you crazy?" I took this opportunity—at least we were talking—to gamble on his sense of humor.

I replied, "Yeah, I am crazy; do we need to go outside to settle this?" Then I grinned, and

93

by
Melinda McGuire Burson

Hughes Springs, Texas

He didn't know me well enough to really know what to think. He said: "Are you crazy?"

---

thankfully, he grinned right back.

That was all I needed. I knew, really knew, that while this might be difficult, this was the man I was supposed to be with. This was the man everything in my life had led me to. And, I knew it, instantly. It scared me, and there were times, when he struggled with where he was in his life. It was a rough road, but he is such a great guy, that everything is worth it. Everything I went through in my life that led me to him, was worth it.

If I hadn't been brave enough to put myself where he was going to be, and initiate a conversation with him, I wouldn't be married to him now. Every day I thank God that he is my husband and that we were given the opportunity to be together. He's the most amazing person I've ever met. He's wonderful.

My Rock Star

by
Sherri Gagliardi

La Quinta, California

From across the street I spotted him. The first thing I saw was his white fringed leather jacket. That style was all the rage in the world of rock and roll in the 1980's. Long hair, tight jeans and leather jackets for the girls and the guys! My best friend, Jeni, and I had just parked the car and were walking across Sunset Boulevard toward "The Strip" as everyone called it. The Strip was a famous four block stretch on Sunset in Hollywood. On these four blocks alone, were three of the most famous nightclubs in the history of the Southern California rock scene; Gazzarri's, The Whiskey-a-Go-Go and the Roxy.

Jeni and I spent a lot of time at those clubs on the Sunset strip. We were fresh out of high school, we had our own apartment and we had big dreams. My biggest dream was to marry a 'rock star' someday, not necessarily a famous one, but definitely an extremely good looking one! I didn't intend on marrying just any cool, foxy, rock-'n-roller either! He'd also have to be kind, considerate, sweet, selfless and romantic! In my naiveté about the real world of men and relationships, I had no idea what a tall order I'd put in. Little did I know that my order was about to be filled!

Jeni had stopped to talk to a group of our friends that was standing around outside of Gazzarris. She kept a close eye on me, though, as I approached the guy who had captivated me from all the way across the street. He was about six-feet-tall, had dark hair that fell in waves past his shoulders, and a face that was hard to resist staring at.

Generally I am not an overly confident person, but on that spring night in 1987, something, from somewhere, was urging me on, bolstering my self-confidence and enabling me—empowering me—to pursue this guy. I was persistent and persuasive without being overtly pushy or needy. Without hesitation I looked directly into his eyes and coolly asked the gorgeous stranger if he would like to walk up to the liquor store on

> **Was he playing hard-to-get? He seemed distant and preoccupied. I had no idea he was really trying to show me that he wanted to be left alone.**

the corner with me to get a soda.

"Uh. No, thanks. I'm just going to hang out here for a while." He said, motioning toward the nightclub.

Hmm…I wondered, was he playing hard-to-get? I asked him his name.

"Michael." He answered quietly. He seemed distant and preoccupied. At the time I had no idea he was really trying to show me that he wanted to be left alone.

With some persuasion, I was able to convince him to walk with me up to the liquor store. We made light conversation as we strolled back to the club. He was still guarded, but loosened up a bit when he realized that I wasn't a vicious, sex-crazed groupie who only wanted one thing. He told me he was from Toronto, Canada. Just ten days earlier, with only his guitar, a duffel bag full of clothes, and a few bucks in his pocket, he had boarded a Greyhound bus bound for Los Angeles. He was there, in Hollywood, to pursue his rock-and-roll fantasy of 'making it' in the music world.

I informed him that I knew a lot of the local musicians and I might be able to get him a few good connections with some of the bands. I also offered him my couch if he needed a place to hang out for a few days till he figured out what he was going to do.

"No strings attached!" I assured him with a genuine smile. He was appreciative, but didn't accept the offer…right away.

I asked him if he would let me buy his ticket to the club so we could talk more and listen to the bands.

"Sure. Okay…Why not?" He said, still a little hesitant.

In the club, we sat downstairs at a small table. He told me that there are a lot of differences between Hollywood and Toronto. He said that the girls were definitely more outgoing in California. I smiled self-consciously.

"Meeting girls is not my reason for coming to Hollywood. My motivation in life is music." He was obviously passionate about his talent. I liked that.

I met up with Jeni in the bathroom a little while later. We were powdering our noses when she asked me "How is it going with that cute guy?"

"Jen, I think I met my future husband tonight." I knew it was true. I felt it in my soul.

(Michael did end up staying on my couch that night. We stayed up way past three in the morning just talking (really)! We were comfortable together, and he opened up to me and told me his life story; I reciprocated and told him mine. Our friendship seemed to come naturally, as did the romance later. We did not share a bed until weeks after we met. Michael and I were married exactly one year and five months after that fateful night in Hollywood when I spotted 'that gorgeous guy' from across the street.

Three years later, I gave birth to our first child, Dawn Michelle. Two years after that came our second child, Marina Nicole. Michael did end up forming his own band back in the 1980's and gained quite a following. Ironically the very first place the band played was Gazzarris on the Sunset Strip.

Michael and I are still married, and he's still my kind, considerate, sweet rockstar. Oh, and that white fringed leather jacket—it still hangs in my closet to this day.)

To say my normally reserved wife made the first move would be a gross understatement.

We met at the now defunct Elm-Tre Pool & Tennis Club in West Caldwell, NJ on Labor Day, 1988. My father was there and called me to come down and join him and my three brothers for some basketball, tennis, etc.

My father happened to be passing through the lobby as I walked in, so together we headed to the basketball court where my competitive brothers anxiously awaited. On our way through the tennis area, my father introduced me to an attractive girl sitting in a chair next to the soda machine. She was wearing a white tennis skirt and a red top and had a nice smile. My father said, "Dianne, this is my son, Kevin." I said "Hi" and she said, "Looks like you're playing everything," referring to the tennis rackets, basketball and football I was carrying. I laughed, said "Yeah," and then heeded my brothers' demands to join them.

My father, three brothers and I made five, leaving us one short of a 3-on-3. My father quickly filled the void by yelling to Dianne to be our sixth, much to my brothers' dismay. "She can play on my team," I innocently said, simply trying to quell the growing displeasure with my father's unexplained inclusion of a female in what was sure to be a typically fierce Cronin basketball game.

Though never leaving her feet, and despite clearly being the smallest player on the court, Dianne made every shot she took and we won the game. But, before I could even talk to her about her exploits, she was called away for a tennis match. My oldest brother and I went out and hit some balls on the court next to her, and she and I talked a little in between points, but that was the last I saw of her that day.

About a week or so later, I came home to find a note that simply said, "Kev, Dianne called." I didn't have her number or even know

95

by
Kevin Cronin

**Green Township,
New Jersey**

**As Dianne
approached,
I playfully asked,
"Did you beat her?"
to which she replied,
"When do I get
to play you?"**

what town she lived in and figured she'd call again. Call again she did, leaving a number this time. I called; it rang and rang; and I waited patiently for an answering machine that never came on. Another week or ten days passed, I hadn't heard from her and figured I'd never see her again.

Then one night in late September, I went to play tennis at Grover Cleveland Park in Caldwell with three of my friends. As we waited for a court, four ladies came off and I knew one of them. She introduced me to her friends and, after hearing my name, one of the other ladies said, "Oh you played tennis with my daughter." I responded by asking, "Are you Dianne's mother?" resisting the urge to tell her it was basketball and not tennis. She said, "Yes" and told me that Dianne said I was nice. They left and we smacked the ball around.

The following night, the same three friends and I returned for more tennis. As we walked onto the first court, I was stunned to see Dianne playing two courts down. She was playing with another girl I knew, Janice, and I said hello to both of them. Then I turned to the friend I was partnered with and told him that Dianne was the girl I had told him about.

Dianne and Janice wrapped up their match shortly after we started playing, and as I walked back to the fence to retrieve a ball, they began walking towards me on their way to the gate. As Dianne approached, I playfully said, "Did you beat her?" to which she replied, "When do I get to play you?" Taken aback by her unexpected answer, I blurted out, "Whenever you want," a bit surprised by my own response. Dianne quickly followed with, "How 'bout tomorrow night?" to which I said, "Okay," to which she said, "Call me after work." "Okay," I said again, clearly under this girl's spell as I watched her walk to her car and drive away.

We hit some balls the following night and then went to Friendly's for ice cream. Before parting ways, Dianne asked me if I wanted to do something over the upcoming weekend; I said I did, if I didn't go to Pennsylvania as planned. As it happened, I didn't end up going anywhere, and found myself sitting at home Saturday night watching the Olympics when the phone rang. It was Dianne.

We went to the movies that night and I still have the movie section from the newspaper and the Skittles wrapper from the theatre. Eighteen years and four kids later, I am glad my normally reserved wife made the first move—three times!

Hi Chris,

Hope you're having a good week. Serena won't be able to pick me up from the airport on Sunday. Can you pick me up? Just let me know. Thanks, Laurie

Now, maybe asking a man to pick me up from the airport, because my friend couldn't pick me up, doesn't seem like that big, or bold, of a move. But, let me put it in context.

I was living in Prague at the time. I was flying into Washington-Dulles International Airport to move back to the U.S. Yes. Move back to the U.S.—with all of my worldly possessions on my back. I was essentially asking this man to be my port of entry and welcome wagon. I had pretty much set myself up to be the mail order bride.

And the man who was to be my welcome wagon…well, we'd met on two occasions the previous August, when my friend Serena, the one who couldn't pick me up at the airport, had introduced us. And then again, a week later, when he was my escort so that she could swing a first date of her own, without leaving me on my own while I was visiting.

My friend Serena, among her many other varied talents, is a notorious matchmaker. I was visiting her in D.C. with a fresh set of divorce papers in hand, and the dual purpose of moving the things I had in storage out of my ex-mother-in-law's basement and blowing off some steam. Serena, on the other hand, had decided that it was her mission to get me a man and get me over my post-divorce blues.

She put her best foot forward in this effort, and one evening of a two-week whirlwind of activities included a night out with her guy friends. (Granted, she got kudos from her single guy pals for trotting out her "hot and exotic" gal pal who was "just in from Prague.") She told me that John wanted to meet me, but I would like Chris. I was determined not to like Chris. Did I mention that Serena, in my experience, is a

96

by
Laurie Blanton

Washington, D.C.

I was determined not to like Chris. Did I mention that Serena, in my experience, is a notoriously *bad* matchmaker?

---

notoriously *bad* matchmaker?

I was so determined to not like him, that I engaged him with bitchy zest in a fiercely eye-locked debate over anything and everything. If he liked it - I didn't. I only realized that my plan was backfiring, when John politely interrupted us with a, "Um, can we join the conversation?" I internally gasped with indignation at my lack of will power, but as the evening continued, the more I tried to not like Chris, the more I did, much to my chagrin.

Later that evening, when I returned from the bathroom to discover that all the guys had left, I just looked at Serena and said, "Where'd Chris go?" in a pathetically tiny voice that oozed "I've lost my puppy." She rolled her eyes at me, and asked, "Do you want me to call him?" I feigned shyness and said no, but she called anyway and arranged a double date with her and a guy she had a crush on to go to the B.B. King concert at Wolf Trap.

Though the date went well, it was awkward when Chris dropped me off. I felt a bit like a sailor, flying off to Prague the next morning, and Chris probably felt relieved, as this was one date where the girl wouldn't expect him to call the next day.

We didn't even exchange phone numbers, but unable to stop thinking about him, I eventually pried his e-mail address out of Serena. Once he got past my flamboyantly honest e-mail style, he, too, opened up, and we shared the highs and lows of love, work, and life. It was a fabulous friendship that developed via e-mail. We could tell each other anything and everything and that's what made me realize this could be so much more.

Sure, it was a bit crazy, having only gone on one date six months earlier, to ask him to pick me up from the airport. But, I just had this feeling, and when the gates opened up after passing through customs, he was standing there waiting, with a luggage cart and a nervous grin…I knew that feeling was right.

We've been together for over two years, and I can't imagine my life without him.

In The Name Of Love

He was attractively tall, broad-shouldered, had dark features and was distinctly handsome.. She was fair skinned and had flawless beauty, chocolate brown, bouncing curls and an anthropologic style. Years ago, he had played football at Penn., and she'd recently studied Communications at the University of Houston. He had a boistcrous contagious laugh, and a dashing smile. She had sparkling eyes and seemed reserved, with an inner goofy side she only shared with perfectly special people. He loved football season, Shiner Bock and Cabellas'. She loved the fall, Starbucks and old movies.

She admired him from afar at the office, and luckily sometimes, up close at group lunches. He noticed her, too, naturally. Not only was he not married, he had never been married and had begun to think he would never marry. He traveled frequently and his absence at work stung her and bred curiosity and lust. She would tactfully bundle his mail with brightly-colored, speckled paperclips and would attach personalized sticky notes, in an attempt at subtle flirtation. The lack of any movement towards the dating game drove her mad.

After repeatedly conversing with my sister about this man of her dreams, I encouraged her to just "shoot him an e-mail" and ask him if he'd like to have a drink. She did. Subject: "Cold Budweiser or warm glass of Cab?" A bold being by no means, she went out on a limb and risked embarrassment, rejection, mortification, shame and all else in the workplace. He accepted with excitement and shock, never imagining she'd find interest in him. Their first date at a piano bar was fabulously pleasant and nearly perfect. A first kiss and a definite, mutual eagerness to see each other again was expressed.

Today, the two of them live happily, married for almost three years, with still the newness that keeps a relationship fun and the coziness of a blanket and a good book on cool, November weekend morning.

97

by
Kelly Crabb

Houston, Texas

Not only was he not married, but had never been married, and had begun to think he would never marry.

193

They anxiously await the birth of their baby girl, Anna. This sweet child will be loved so sincerely by her devoted parents, Bill and Wendy, as they have loved each other in a way that is puzzling to express through prose. They have so much love to give.

He likes her relaxed, easygoing side, she, his understanding, fun side. He accepts her super-sensitivity, and the fact that she might tend to over-analyze situations, as women typically do. She forgives him when he contradicts her or hurts her feelings by being honest, or tunes her out during a good game, as men typically do. They forgive each other for their faults, as they both should do, because no one is perfect and "everybody's different," as my nephew once said. On the inside, they are truly two wonderful people. On the outside, they are quite fun to watch.

Sometimes you take chances, make sacrifices and do things you wouldn't ordinarily do in the name of love. Props to her for making the first move.

I wasn't particularly looking for romance, a boyfriend or even a fling. All I wanted to do was go out to eat for my birthday. A college friend was visiting me and my roommate one January. We were a few months into our graduate program and looking forward to a relaxing dinner. We were so ready, in fact, that we were literally waiting by the door, when Sara arrived.

Before she even uttered the word "Hello," Sara insisted that we help some poor neighbor push his car out of the snow. My words exactly were "screw him." He did look rather pathetic, and my friends headed that way, despite my resistance.

Ryan was quite embarrassed and barely spoke a word as we rocked his car back and forth in its tracks. It wouldn't budge, but soon one of his roommates arrived, and with his help, we rescued the car. The roommate and his girlfriend invited us to a party they were having that night; we decided later not to go.

Two months down the road, we were having a party of our own, and my younger sister decided there was too much estrogen there. I recalled that there were a couple guys living across the street and suggested we invite them. It seemed rather bold, and nobody was daring enough to do it. Eventually, after having a couple of beers to lower my inhibitions a little, I made my way to their door.

I issued an invitation and then scurried home—unsure if they would take it seriously. After all, we never attended their party.

In no time, three guys arrived. Within minutes, I noticed that my eyes kept locking with Ryan's. It didn't take long for me to corner him with conversation. I discovered that he was a union worker and figured he was a Democrat. I had a deep interest in politics and soon we were trading views on issues like health care, campaign finance and party politics.

At the end of the night we exchanged num-

98

by
Anonymous

Illinois

I couldn't stop thinking about Ryan, and I was crushed he hadn't called me.

bers. Since we clicked so well, I figured I would get a call very soon. A day went by and then two days and then three. I couldn't stop thinking about Ryan, and I was crushed he hadn't called me. I truly thought Ryan was someone special, even though I wanted more than anything to remain single. I even canceled a date that I had made prior to meeting Ryan.

Finally, on the fourth day, I couldn't stand it any longer. I called Ryan, and we talked for an hour—maybe longer. (I found out later he was intimidated by me because I was a 'college girl,' and he was just a blue collar guy.) It seemed rather ridiculous to talk on the phone, since he lived across the street, so he came over. Ryan was at my apartment the next three nights.

It wasn't long before we were inseparable—the kind of couple I had privately despised. I didn't care, however, because there was just something about him. He was unlike anyone I had met.

On that first night, he had shown me a photograph of his family that he carried with him. He was very proud of them, and noted that although his mother was over-weight, he didn't care because she had three kids and was a fantastic mother.

Not long after that, we were watching "America's Funniest Videos" together, and he busted up about a dad who scared his two sons by putting on a Halloween mask and sneaking up on them in their bedroom.

"I can't wait to have kids and do that," Ryan remarked.

Suddenly, I knew I wanted to spend my life with this man and have his kids. Children were never in my life plan before that moment, and that's when I realized it had to be true love.

We dated long distance for a little over a year, while I worked across the state at my first job after college. He proposed on his birthday, just about a year after we met.

This October will mark our seventh wedding anniversary. Our daughter will be four, and our son will be two. It's not even close to the life I had imagined for myself, and yet I couldn't be happier.

Sometimes, You Just Need Patience. . .

It had been ten or eleven years since I had seen Clark. Thirteen years, three kids, and one broken marriage between the day I first met him, when we were both sixteen.

I knew on sight that he was perfect for me. I don't know why. He was blond, and I usually go for dark hair. He was pale, and I like tanned skin. He was baby-faced, and I don't remember ever liking baby-faced. But he was also the funniest guy I'd met in my whole life. And we just ...clicked.

Instead of letting him know how I felt, I waited until he fell in love with my best friend and married her. I couldn't be around either of them, so I drifted away and watched carefully from a safe distance. Predatory? Perhaps. But I would have died before hurting either of them.

Now that marriage was over. Totally. She left him for a married couple. Talk about a blow to the ego! And now he'd had time to recover.

I cautiously planned my attack. We were both science fiction fans, and we both went to one particular convention. I knew he'd be close to the gaming room, so I dressed carefully and planted myself nearby. You never saw anyone hang around as casually as I did! He had to come out eventually. . .

And he did. I "bumped" into him. "Clark?"

He blinked. "Jamie?"

After the mandatory "How are you?"s, we sat down and talked for two solid hours—not about me, or him, but about all the things we'd always discussed as kids: Science, politics, history, and fun. Before letting him go, I had his phone number, knew where he lived and worked, and had a very good idea he was not seriously involved with anyone.

I planned to wait a week—but he called within a couple of days. He still didn't get that I was more than just an old friend. So I came out

by
Jamie K. Wilson

Louisville, Kentucky

> You never saw anyone hang around as casually as I did! He had to come out eventually...

and asked. "What do you think would have happened if you and I had gotten involved, instead of you and Barb?"

He was clearly caught off-guard. "I don't know. But I admit, I always kind of wondered." So I asked him out. And I kept asking him out, until he started asking me. It didn't take long at all.

Fast forward to now. Seven years later, we've been married almost two years; he's in the Navy, and we're insanely in love with one another. With his support and encouragement, I'm living my lifelong dreams – writing, travel, and true love. How can I not be madly in love with him?

"Love," Clark tells me, "is a form of insanity."

And he's right. But sometimes you can be crazy like a fox.

100

by

by
Celeste Heiter

Napa Valley, California

It was a warm Saturday afternoon in Napa Valley in the spring of 1995, and a tall, dark, handsome artist was working on a graphic arts project, when I walked into Kinko's to make copies of some of my figure drawings. I got a key counter for the copier, and at first, I put it in a machine by the window. But I couldn't take my eyes off that gorgeous guy and wanted to be near him, so I moved to another machine, one right next to where he was working, vowing to myself that I would not leave Kinko's without knowing who he was and how I might find him again.

I placed my drawings conspicuously on the counter, and being an artist, he took notice and commented on them. I was also having trouble getting them to reproduce clearly, so he offered some suggestions. Before long, we were chatting away and exchanging business cards. His name was René, and he later told me that after I left Kinko's, his client, who had witnessed our little flirtation, said to him, "That woman wants you." To which he replied, "Really?" He still claims, to this day, that he had been oblivious to my advances!

Nevertheless, René called a few days later, and when he asked if I wanted to meet for coffee or lunch, I suggested dinner the following Sunday evening. By the time the day of our first date arrived, it had been more than two weeks since we met, but when I opened the door and saw him standing there in a butter-yellow turtleneck and soft leather jacket, he was even more gorgeous than I'd remembered. We chose a nice little Italian restaurant nearby that stayed open late, and got to know each other over wine and candlelight.

Throughout the evening, René was utterly charming, a real old-fashioned gentleman. He opened the car door for me and escorted me safely away from the curb as we walked along the sidewalks. After dinner, when we meandered downtown to peek in the gallery windows, the

> **"That woman wants you."**
> **To which he replied, "Really?"**
> **He still claims, to this day, that he had been oblivious to my advances!**

night air was a little chilly, so he took off his jacket and draped it around my shoulders. I was already in love.

When he brought me home, he came upstairs for a few minutes, and although it was tempting, I did not invite him to stay the night. But after he left, I was delighted to discover that he'd left his glasses behind… what a perfect excuse to see him again. So when he called about them the next day, I invited him to lunch, and at lunch, I invited him for a home-cooked dinner on Saturday evening.

Over roast chicken and rice pilaf, I asked him, "What's a handsome, intelligent, talented guy like you doing free on a Saturday night?" To which he replied, "I'm so dedicated to my work that I haven't found anyone who can lure me away from it."

Oh how I love a challenge.

After dinner, talking turned to touching, and touching to kissing, yet I still didn't ask him to stay the night. But I was now sure that I wanted to consummate our relationship, and when the time came, it was I who did the asking.

The following afternoon, he had been hard at work on a mural at an elementary school up valley, and it was no coincidence that I'd been thinking about him when the phone rang. But, when he invited me to drive there to see his mural, I had something else in mind.

"I was hoping that we could pick up where we left off last night," I suggested.

He knew exactly what I meant, and with only the slightest hesitation, he answered, "I'll see you in a moment."

While waiting for him to arrive, I prepared a moveable feast of finger foods that could be shared in bed. And when he finally arrived, wearing his paint-dappled sweatshirt with the sleeves ripped off to reveal his biceps, I greeted him with a kiss: coy yet explicit in its intention. Standing very near, in an effort to be polite, I offered him my hospitality.

"Would you like something to drink?"

"No thank you. I'm not thirsty," he answered, coming a bit closer.

"Something to eat?"

"No thank you. I'm not hungry," he replied, grazing my lips lightly with another kiss.

"A shower, perhaps?"

"No thank you," he said, inching his way with me toward the bedroom. "I have everything I want right here."

I felt myself floating backwards in his arms, across the room, and when I opened my eyes, we were standing next to my bed with the afternoon sun streaming through the window, bathing us both in golden light. In that moment, the world became very still, and I knew that my life was about to change. And long after the golden sun had set and the silver moon had traversed the starry heavens, we settled into a soft embrace and slept in bliss. The next morning, we awoke, still wrapped in each other's arms, knowing that a magical spell had been cast upon us. And the rest…is history.

On a beautiful fall morning in Bloomington, Indiana, I waited in front of Woodburn Hall
amongst friends for my first class of the day to
begin. It was early in the term—only the second
or third week—and the crowd of students gathered on the building steps had not yet become
familiar to me, as they would as the semester
progressed.

It was the typical, motley crew of students,
all expressing their individuality through attire
affiliated with the various counter-cultural groups
of the time. Hippies, Goth kids, and preppies all
mingled into a colorful swirl of diversity.

One student stood out. He wore a full length
black wool cloak. His hair was dark and long.
Amid the students that surrounded him, cliché in
their mid 1990's garb, he looked like a medieval
hunter or soldier. Having many childhood memories of attending Renaissance Festivals with my
parents, I was quickly able to classify this misfit
as a "Renny." I may have robbed him of some of
his uniqueness by imposing this categorization,
but, nonetheless, I was completely fascinated by
him.

Never one to be held back by social clas-
sifications, I forged a plan to meet this unusual
young man. A trip to the fabric store provided
me with the materials and patterns to construct
my own period garb. Seven yards of brocade and
velvet later, I assembled and donned my armor.
Three weeks had passed, and on an equally brilliant though cooler morning, those of us attending 11:15 classes in Woodburn Hall reconvened
on the steps of that building. The previously unknown faces had become friendlier, more unique
and distinct than they appeared a few short weeks
before. His form, in particular, became familiar.

On that day he wore, not a cloak, but a
leather vest, laced in front, and the flowing, short
pants of an English peasant circa 1580. I said
nothing. I just walked by him, caught his gaze,

101

by
Megan A. Marquart

**West Chester,
Pennsylvania**

**I was completely
fascinated
by him.
I forged a plan
to meet this
unusual young man.**

---

and smiled while dipping a small curtsey, subtle under my large skirts.

When I left class that day he was waiting for me. In two weeks we will celebrate our first anniversary.

I met my husband while playing in a pool league which met once a week. There were six teams in the league. He was on one, I was on another. The surprise of it was that my teammate pointed him out and mentioned that she'd like to get to know him. I expressed my interest, too, and, being friends, we decided to find out his 'status'. We asked the league captain to talk to him to find out if he was married, involved or otherwise spoken for. No, no, and no were the answers.

I waited two weeks for my teammate to make her move, and when she didn't, I asked her if she was going to talk to him. She admitted she was a bit shy about approaching him. I told her I really wanted to meet him; would she mind terribly if I proceeded? (I probably would have tried to meet him even if she had said yes, but she was a gracious teammate and gave me her blessing.)

He looked like the sort of guy who attracted a lot of female attention, so I knew I needed to do something different—a unique approach, not too pushy but definitely *something,* to show him I was interested in him. I decided mystery was the best approach. I asked his waitress if she wouldn't mind delivering a message. She agreed, so I sent my business card over with a note on the back which read "Like your hat" and my home phone number. (He was wearing a ball cap so I didn't think I was being overly flirtatious. I also indicated that I had noticed him and found him attractive).

I gave the waitress explicit instructions not to point out who I was, if he asked her who sent the card. I watched surreptitiously as she passed it to him. He read the front, then the back and put it in his shirt. Well, I thought, so much for that. He didn't even ask the waitress who had sent it (not that she'd tell him) nor did he look around the room. I left that night shrugging him off and headed home.

102

by
Kathleen Mozingo

Fairfax, Virginia

I knew I needed to do something different— a unique approach, not too pushy, but definitely *something,* to show him I was interested in him.

The very next evening, he called, and we talked on the phone for two hours! It was the Thanksgiving holiday weekend, and I was going out of town, so we couldn't get together until the next pool league night. When I returned from my vacation, there was a message from him, and he called me every day after that until pool night. When we finally met face-to-face, he immediately smiled, said he'd never been approached that way, and was glad I took the initiative. We finished our pool games and went out somewhere to talk and get to know one another.

That was over eight years ago. We've been married for the past two years, are expecting our second child and the sparks are still flying!

My advice is "Nothing ventured, nothing gained." After all, why let the men always have the thrill of the hunt? A victory, by either sex, is just as sweet in the end.

103

I was never an aggressor. But that was before I met "the" man. His name was Trevor and he was dating one of my friends. Don't get the wrong impression of me. I am not a bad person. Let's start at the beginning.

Vicki is my friend. She is a smart, beautiful and outgoing person. In many ways we are opposites. I am not beautiful; I am average—maybe even pretty, when I try. I'm not outgoing. I am generally shy. But being opposites makes our friendship work.

Vicki and I had another real difference. I believed in fidelity. Vicki believed in having fun and what a current boyfriend didn't know, didn't worry her. This fact never completely bothered me; I figured the men who dated Vicki knew what they were doing. This changed the moment I met Trevor.

One day, Vicki begged me to go out with her and her current male friend. She didn't think I should be spending my nights home, alone. They were going to club to listen to music. It sounded like fun, so I said yes. Then she mentioned that her current male friend was one of three guys she was seeing. I just shook my head and shrugged.

That night I walked into the club, searching for Vicki and a man. It only took a moment for me to spot them. I casually walked over to their table. The man politely stood up and I just stared at him. I used to laugh at people who believed in love at first sight. But as I stared at Trevor, I wasn't laughing. I was too busy falling in love. I knew in my heart that this was the man God had made for me.

It was more than his looks, not that his looks were a hindrance. The man was magnificent-looking. He was tall and slender. His hair was jet black, cut short on top, falling in curls in the back to his shoulders. His eyes were a sparkling blue.

"This is Trevor," Vicki said, as he reached his hand out to me.

by
Linda M. McCloud

Chillicothe, Ohio

I knew this could be the end of my friendship with Vicki. But I couldn't allow our friendship to ruin what I felt toward Trevor.

"Hello," I replied, as I reached out to shake his hand. Our fingers touched and I felt an intense electric volt. I looked up at him and saw a questioning look in his eyes. That was when I realized that he had felt the electricity, too.

"There are some interesting people here tonight," Vicki casually said, oblivious to what was happening between Trevor and me.

That night was pure joy and pure torture for me. I kept glancing at Trevor, finding that he, too, was glancing at me. Vicki continued to chat the night, away as Trevor and I just played our parts. But before the night was over I knew I was going to do something. I had to have Trevor.

Vicki finally excused herself and went to the rest room. She asked me to tag along with her. I told her I would be there in a moment. She left the table and I smiled at Trevor.

"I like you," I bluntly said.

"What about Vicki?" he asked, not even pretending not to know what I meant.

"I will handle it," I promised. I had the answer I needed. Trevor wanted me, too.

I was nervous, as I hurried to the rest room. I knew this could be the end of my friendship with Vicki. But I couldn't allow our friendship to ruin what I felt toward Trevor.

"Vicki, are you seeing other guys?" I bluntly asked, after finding her at the mirror brushing her hair.

"Yeah, I told you that I was. Trevor is okay. But that is all he is."

"Vicki, I want Trevor," I said in an earnest voice.

"You what?" she asked in surprise.

Now you're probably thinking that this was the end of our friendship. You probably think Vicki is one of those women who only wants a man she can't have. If you thought either of these things, then you are wrong, wrong, wrong.

"Wow, you usually hate the men I date, but you want this one?" she asked, grinning. "Go get him, girl, but invite me to the wedding!"

And that is what I did.

Trevor and I started dating that night. Six months later, Vicki was my maid of honor.

And what about Vicki and her love life? She is still dating at least two men at the same time.

104

Early in 1983, I was promoted to Installation Manager for General Dynamics Communications. I was handed a small pile of documentation for upcoming installations and for those in progress. At the top of the pile was a letter from the Executive Assistant to the President of Hughes Offshore, taking us to task for not performing as promised. I told my manager I was impressed at how this woman had ripped us to shreds in a completely professional manner. He replied: I am glad you're impressed, because it is up to you to "take care of the b*****."

I called and introduced myself and scheduled a meeting for the following day to address her issues. We met several times over the next two weeks, and over that period, took care of all open items to her satisfaction. At the end of our second-to-last meeting, she asked me if I liked quiche, to which I responded I had never tried it.

She then suggested we have lunch sometime. Suddenly the light went on! I realized that several times, since our first meeting, she had been flirting with me, but I was too dense and too focused on successfully completing the task I had been given, that I had missed the signals. (I must also admit that I thought this beautiful, six-foot-tall woman was out of my league). I then suggested dinner, instead, and we made a date for that Friday. That was twenty-two years, three children and two grandchildren ago.

If she had not made the first move, I don't think we would be where we are today!

**by
Fred Palacios**

**Moreno Valley,
California**

**Suddenly
the light went on!
I realized that
several times
since our first
meeting
she had been
flirting with me
but I was too dense...
I had missed
the signals.**

105

"Hey, it's the FBI guy!" I shouted across the open-air bar. All eyes turned toward the object of my future affections. He looked like a startled deer in the headlights. It didn't have to come to this. If he'd been more forthcoming with personal information when I first started flirting, there wouldn't be thirty people staring right now. Unfortunately he didn't realize I was flirting and I was forced go into a full-scale stalk.

It was a balmy evening in St. Thomas when "He" walked in. I wasn't looking for a man. I'd picked a couple lemons in the Garden of Love; I was doing very well on my own, thank you very much. I had no interest in involvements, but there was something about this guy. He was tall, tan, with sun-bleached hair and a piercing gaze. I had to know him. The trouble was, it meant flirting, and I'm just no good at it.

"Accidentally" spilling my drink provided an opportunity to sidle up close at the crowded bar. Casually brushing against him, I smiled my most provocative smile, and leaned in closely. Alas, my feeble attempts to engage this mystery man with my sparkling wit and beauty fell flat. He wasn't rude, just uncommunicative. And he would not tell me his name. Disappointed, I took my glass and slunk back to my table. Shortly after my ill-fated attempt at seduction, Mystery Man turned and left the scene.

Next open mike night, I arrived with a girlfriend in tow for support and grabbed a table near the entrance. It was a shot in the dark whether he would show up, but my silent prayers were answered. He strolled in carrying a well-worn guitar case. The wine I'd been drinking, reduced my usual inhibitions. That's when I shouted, and joined him at the entrance before he could head for the hills.

"What did you say that for?" he asked in bewilderment. There was a frightened look in his deep brown eyes.

"You wouldn't tell me your name last week.

by
Joan C. Peterson

North Fort Myers, Florida

Alas, my feeble attempts to engage this mystery man with my sparkling wit and beauty fell flat.

209

Are you an undercover agent or something?" I replied laughing. "Come sit at our table, I promise I won't embarrass you again."

It worked! Self-preservation on his part, perhaps, but he came willingly and took a seat. Now that I had him, I didn't know what to do with him. Tongue-tied and suddenly shy, I fidgeted in my chair. Carole managed to get a conversation started and pried out his name (Howard), and the fact he'd recently moved from St. Croix. Meanwhile, sitting like a mute lump, I listened and tried to figure my next move. Before I could formulate a plan, Howard excused himself to join the musicians on stage.

Sitting like a lump and eavesdropping sometimes pays off. I overheard Howard planning to meet friends at another bar following his set. Bingo! Time to change venues. It was walking distance from my condo, so it wouldn't appear suspicious to be somewhere so close to home. A little stalking would provide another chance to insinuate myself into his life. Off I went, to be in place when my unsuspecting prey arrived.

Lying in wait was tedious. The minutes crept by. Tired, half-sloshed and getting hit on by every weirdo in the place, I pondered going home in defeat. Suddenly, the doors swung open and the man of my dreams walked in. Life was good again; I'm instantly vibrant, engaging and thoroughly charming. We teamed up for Foosball. I'd never played before, but I jumped at the suggestion as if it were my favorite sport. My inebriated enthusiasm didn't make up for my lack of skill, but we had loads of fun. Later, I melted in his arms as we danced to bad music by a tone-deaf band. Bliss.

Eventually, it was last call. People started leaving. I feigned surprise that Howard's boat was docked across from my condo. I'd picked up that little gem of information by eavesdropping earlier. I asked for an escort home. The gentleman could hardly refuse. The exit crawled with crack dealers trying to make some last minute money. Howard was new to the area and didn't know they left the locals pretty much alone. He stepped in gallantly to run the gauntlet of seedy, wild-eyed crack heads. A little local knowledge proved a valuable tool. I also made sure he knew where I lived.

Howard eventually figured out what I knew at first sight. It was kismet. We've been together since, and married three wonderful years.

Roman Reunion

by
Lucy Welsh

Lewisville, Texas

"I know I can't afford it but I'm going anyway!" were my daughter's bold remarks as she crammed her luggage full of trendy designer clothes and strappy party shoes. The fearless quality she possessed to 'fly by the seat of her pants' was one I envied, and to which I'd grown comfortably accustomed, but this time I was a bit concerned. Even though I had strived to teach her the importance of courage and independence, and love to credit my committed hard work for her autonomous nature, I must admit, I worry about her incessant fearlessness. Despite her lean wallet, she was determined to fly to Rome, to join her friends for a college reunion and, per usual, her determination prevailed over the tedium of common sense. She was off!

The e-mail I received from her the following day proved her free spirit auspicious. Without hesitation, Emily proclaimed to me that she had met the man she was going to marry. Why was I surprised? I had predicted her marriage to a man from foreign lands years before. Nevertheless, to have met him so quickly, and known him so briefly, made her declaration shocking, not to mention a bit disconcerting! Were a romance novelist attempt to tell her 'fairytale-come-true story,' readers would probably think it slightly exaggerated, but because I am her mother, and I now have a strikingly handsome English son-in-law, I can validate her one of a kind love story as completely factual.

Upon her arrival to the historic city of Rome, Emily met with her comrades in their favorite local bar. It was a memorable spot, where years earlier, they had gathered to linger and relax over local food and drink. After much hugging and kissing, her attention was immediately drawn to a young man, whose penetrating eyes beheld her forthcoming future. Although he was, to her, a perfect stranger, the irresistible desire to

Although he was, to her, a perfect stranger, the irresistible desire to meet him was intense.

211

meet him was intense. She listened to that inner voice which had never let her down, and casually suggested moving closer to his table; the idea met with no resistance from her friends. Soon, she and the handsome foreigner were casually conversing. Thus, began a new life for my daughter. An evening of dinner, red wine and enlightened discussion soon led to a stroll through the charming streets of Rome. Each began to savor mutual feelings of attraction, respect and love; both readily accepted their encounter as predestined. She told him about her life in Dallas, her family and her heart's desires; he spoke of his Mother who lived in a suburb of London, his Father, whose passing still caused pain and sorrow, and his childhood memories.

Within two weeks, we welcomed Antony to our home in Dallas and very quickly began to understand why Emily so loved this handsome stranger. "Two years," she told me. "If we still feel this way in two years, we shall marry!"

On August 7, 2005, Emily and Antony celebrated their first wedding anniversary. Their wedding was the most glorious celebration of love and admiration I have ever experienced. I am so proud of them both. They live in Houston, Texas now and travel as often as they are able, to visit friends and family in England. Being Emily's mother has been one of my greatest joys, and celebrating the addition of another son into our family, has been an incomparable pleasure.

Theirs will surely be one of our family's greatest love stories, for indeed, their fortuitous encounter was one about which most people only dream. Many have commented on my daughter's good fortune. My reply? It has nothing to do with luck, but everything to do with the outrageous abundance of Emily's never-ending self-confidence. I derive much of my newfound inspiration from her example. Thanks, Em!

The Incredible Smile

by
Judythe A. Guarnera

Grover Beach, California

As the person who lined up speakers for the divorce support group I belonged to, I often had little time at meetings to meet new participants in the group. After the meetings, most of us went to a local coffee shop for dessert and a chance to talk in a more relaxed setting.

Once there, I made my way down the table, stopping to visit. I noticed a friend sitting with someone I had never seen before. As I chatted with my friend, I realized I was wishing he had an "off" button, so I could concentrate on the man sitting next to him. This new man's smile, which showed in the blue-sky color of his eyes, had caught my attention. My insides felt like an ice cube melting in a drink on a hot summer day, all liquidy and warm.

I had just finished a book entitled, "Smart Women, Foolish Choices" and I decided that I was going to be open to the endless possibilities that new relationships could bring. This was pretty brave for a newly divorced woman, fresh out of an almost thirty-year marriage. The above-mentioned encounter was my first opportunity to try out this new philosophy. My reaction not only startled, but scared me as well. I was not looking for a new romantic relationship, but something told me that this could be the romance of a century.

> **This was pretty brave for a newly divorced woman, fresh out of an almost thirty-year marriage.**

Unfortunately, he and my friend left a few minutes after I had found a place at a nearby table. I felt like a candle whose flame had been snuffed out without warning. The rest of that evening was a blur.

After a few days, I convinced myself that I had overreacted to that chance encounter. That night, however, I received a phone call from my friend, begging me to join a support group that he was in. He explained that the therapist leading the group said she would not continue, unless he could come up with one or two more people who could be counted on to attend regularly.

I thanked him for thinking of me, but said that I was ready to move on to some non-divorce type activities. Suddenly, I had a visual image of the man with the incredible smile. Trying to sound unconcerned, I asked my friend who was going to be in the group. He named a few people I knew, Mary, Sarah and then...Steve.

As my heart did flip-flops, I cleared my throat and asked, in what I hoped was a disinterested sounding way, "Who's Steve?"

"Oh, he's the new guy who was sitting next to me at the coffee shop the other night."

We then chatted for a few more minutes, my friend convinced, I'm sure, that I was disinterested in joining the group. Before I hung up, as casually as I could, I told him I would give the group a try.

As I stepped across the threshold the first night, I felt a jolt of electricity when I saw the smiler sitting on the couch, so I surreptitiously chose a seat at the opposite end of it. I remember little of that evening, other than the sensation of an electric current flowing between him and me. (Fortunately, no one sat between us to get caught in the crossfire.)

I left that night, plotting how I could see more of this man. When I heard that a well-known politician would be speaking at the university, I called several friends from the support group, suggesting that we attend the speech. I boldly added that I would be willing to call Steve, as we could all go in his van. I then asked Steve to pick me up first, so I could direct him to the homes of the others. I made sure that I sat next to him at the event, then hustled to reclaim my seat on the way back, as well as the one next to him at the coffee shop afterward.

What I discovered later, was that my bold tactics fit right into my smiler's plans. I wasn't the only one who had experienced that electricity! After almost fifteen years of marriage, I still feel warmed by that loving smile that seems to come from his soul.

The Kiss I Least Expected

It seemed complicated. I knew I was hooked, but then so was every female between the ages of twenty and fifty in our Long Island Government Agency. We admired Terry's intelligence and courageous independence. Ruggedly handsome at forty-two, this single dad had placed himself beyond reach. He staunchly opposed dating coworkers, especially subordinates in his department.

A widow, eighteen months older than Terry, I had acquired a horrible reputation, that of a 'whistle-blower.' Six months earlier, when I'd turned down overtures from "Ray," a married executive, the rejected creep quickly retaliated. He ordered my exile to the "Purgatory" of the Agency. Tripling my commuting distance, this outlying branch office sat upstairs from the County morgue.

With neither witnesses nor evidence to back me, my complaints to the Union resulted in fierce denials on Ray's part. Plus, my action sparked emphatic warnings from Upper Management to all male bosses: "Avoid even the faintest appearance of sexual harassment. Above all, stay far away from blabbermouth, Flo."

Unaware of the directive, and with two strikes against me, I reported to my new department, which Terry supervised. The smell of formaldehyde permeated the building, and greeted my arrival. To my cordial, "Good morning, Mr. Blake," Terry replied, "Comb your hair. You look like something the cat dragged in."

When I'd ask work-related questions, he'd answer with the terse pun, "I'd love to help you out, Flo. Which way did you come in?"

One afternoon several months later, a firefighter approached my desk. "You have to get out immediately," he said. "This building's on fire." Upon reaching the crowded parking lot, I asked

by
F. Calderone Blake

White City, Oregon

One endearing trait I'd noticed about Terry was the gallant side he exhibited around clients... Maybe he needed to view me in my moment of distress.

---

some coworkers, "Did Terry Blake make it out okay?"

The guys laughed, then one replied, "The first thing Terry Blake asked when he got here was, 'Did Flo get out okay?'"

Hmmm. Five hundred other people worked there, yet this grouch who was polite to everybody else, thought of *me*?

By that summer, my reputation for refusing to join Ray's harem had intrigued my coworker Carl, who regarded it a challenge. Back then, since I outranked him, he wasn't concerned about being accused of sexual harassment. He'd press for dates; I'd decline. He'd back off for two weeks, then start the pressure again.

One endearing trait I'd noticed about Terry was the gallant side he exhibited around clients—he loved to rescue a person in distress. Maybe he needed to view me in my moment of distress. At the close of this particular workday, I confided to him my exasperation with Carl.

"There's a simple solution," Terry said. "Tell him you're dating someone else."

"But, I'm not, really, Terry, am I?"

He put his arm around my shoulder, and said, "Yes, you are, Flo." Then Terry admitted that even before we'd ever met, he'd received orders from our former Commissioner to avoid me. Terry's extreme disdain for lothario Ray had labeled me heroic in his eyes, for rejecting the egocentric bully.

In the almost deserted parking lot, Terry walked me to my car. "What would you do if I grabbed you right now?" he said.

"I'd kiss you back," I replied.

Wow! I don't recall ever being kissed in broad daylight before.

The next evening we had dinner together. By the following Friday when Carl phoned, Terry and my future young stepson were present for supper with me. I could truthfully dismiss Carl with, "I'm dating someone."

Eight weeks later, despite the "official order" placing me off-limits, Terry and I were married. Many younger, prettier, shapelier coworkers were stunned that he'd picked me, rather than one of them. "That marriage can't possibly last six months," they wagered.

But, were they wrong. So far, we've had twenty-five happy years, and counting. Maybe it seems complicated, but nothing's too complicated for the God that helps make our fondest dreams come true.

Flash

"No way," I said firmly, shaking my head before I took another sip of wine. Caitlin and I were sitting in our local haunt having our usual after-work drink. As it so often did, the conversation quickly turned from office politics, shoes, and the astronomical cost of living in Paris, to men, or the lack of them, as it were. How was it that in the City of Romance, the only place to meet men seemed to be at work or in bars? Then Caitlin suggested trying a new Internet dating site she'd heard about. "Out of the question," I added for emphasis, as the waiter set down a fresh bowl of peanuts on our table.

It was true that my dating record since I'd arrived in France was less than stellar. I'd done the bar scene, meeting men and finding them interesting right up until halfway through my second drink.

What was I expecting, coming to this city with its romantic cafes, shady parks and bridges over the Seine? Certainly not this. The rituals of dating turned out to be the same as they were in every other city I'd lived, be it Toronto, Seoul or New York. Big cities hold the potential for excitement, but that excitement is quickly crushed by the realities of long hours at work, disagreeable weather, and great old movies on cable. The fact that just about every other person is in the same boat, leaves very little opportunity for getting out there, making new acquaintances, and meeting someone really special. Bars remain the popular choice for both those of us attempting to find a mate for the night or a mate for life—the only place where people feel comfortable enough to actually approach a stranger and strike up a conversation.

I, however, had had enough of going through the motions. No more spending the evening in yet another dark, smoky place, positioning myself in just such a way so that I appeared

109

by
Lise Charlebois

Paris, France

I, however, had had enough of going through the motions. No more spending the evening in yet another dark, smoky place...

---

approachable, but not eager, making eye-contact with, but not staring at, my chosen objective, having the internal dialogue about whether or not to make the first move, play it bold and confident or cool and aloof. No more mind-numbing small talk about work/place of birth/cinema/tastes/pets. There may be something to be said for the thrill of the hunt, but this girl was hanging up her bow.

"Not so fast," Caitlin said after we ordered a second round. "This girl at work told me that her sister, or was it her aunt? Anyway, someone she knows met a really great guy on this site. There are apparently tons of people logged on. Why not?"

Still skeptical, I nonetheless finished my second glass and headed home to see what this was all about. Within minutes I had my profile, picture, and a short introductory message online. Within seconds I got my first 'flash'; someone had seen my profile and contacted me. I was hooked.

After a week, I'd received and responded to dozens of messages, had spoken on the phone with a few guys, and had gone out on two dates. This was certainly turning out to be the easiest way yet to meet men. I still hadn't found anyone I really wanted to see a second time, however. Then I got a flash from Steve.

"Nice smile," Caitlin said as she bent over my shoulder to look at the photo that had appeared on my computer screen. I thought so, too, and answered yes, when he asked if I'd like to check out some of the good places to hear music in my neighbourhood, which also happened to be his. We made arrangements to meet at one of them the following Friday night. A little unsure if I'd recognise him in a crowded music hall, I walked in and hoped that my eyes would adjust quickly to the dim light.

I needn't have worried. That sexy smile met me at the door. I smiled back and introduced myself. We spent the evening talking until the lights came on and the wait staff was sweeping around our feet. Steve walked me the short distance home and by the way he smiled when he looked at me, I knew I wasn't the only one completely charmed.

That was a year and a half ago. Steve and I have been married now for five months, and waking up to that smile every morning is worth every bad date, every dull conversation, every tiring night at crowded bars. Getting here was a tough trek, and one I almost completely gave up on, until I got a flash.

by
Colleen Katana

New York, New York

I shuddered in embarrassment. Why did I have to be such a flirt? Why? Why? Why?

Damn it. My arm shook my pen violently back and forth in an attempt to make the ink come out. It didn't work. This kind of crap always happens to me. I scanned the room to see who looked friendly enough to ask for another pen. Our first day of work had not yet started, so most of us were involved in nervous small talk. In a room full of thirty new interns, most everyone looked anxious. A skinny boy who looked like Peter Pan with reddish brown hair that curled around his ears hung back in a corner. His weight kept shifting from one foot to the other, and he jingled his keys in his pocket. I was a little afraid that if I went up to talk to him, he might vomit on me. So, I kept scanning.

On the other side of the room was a tall, beautiful girl, about my age. She had high cheek bones and long blonde hair that fell just below her collar bone. I smiled and began to get up and walk over to her. She acknowledged my presence with a roll of her eyes, took off her sweater, and revealed her cleavage: two gigantic breasts that were bound unnaturally in a Victoria's Secret push-up bra. If you listened closely, I swear you could have heard her boobs cry for help. Her look said, "C'mon and try to talk to me. I dare you." I took this as my one warning and diverted myself over to the coffee table to get another cup.

I strolled up, grabbed a mug, and let the steam and smell of the Columbian brew fill my nostrils. With a subtle glance, I noticed the man to my left, who must also have had an addiction to caffeine. He reached across me to grab a packet of sugar, and for a split second our eyes met. What great eyes he had—they always do. They were a very light shade of brown, honey even. He had strong features, manly features, an angular nose, a strong jaw line, and a dimple in his chin. In fact, he looked a bit like John Travolta in Saturday Night Fever, but in place of bellbottoms, he wore gray dress pants and a power tie.

"Good Morning." He had the whitest, straightest teeth I'd ever seen, like he'd come to this meeting straight from the orthodontist.

"Mornin'." I flashed a genuine smile. I have

never been a morning person, but I'm pretty good at pretending.

"I swear they must lace this coffee with crack," he said. It's my second cup, and we haven't even started yet." He threw his head back very slightly and laughed a little.

It wasn't all that funny, but it would have been rude for me not to acknowledge the joke. So I smiled in a humoring way. "Hey, do you have a pen I could borrow?"

He reached into his breast pocket and pulled out a cheap Bic pen, handed it to me with his right hand, and crossed his left hand over top to shake mine.

"I'm Michael, by the way."

I felt as though I were receiving my diploma, and shaking my school president's hand. "Caitlin." I gave him a shy smile and bit my bottom lip a little teasingly. The other guys in the room were decent looking, but there was something about Michael's confidence. I held up the pen, and shook it a little. "Thanks. I probably won't need it, but it looks good to have one, ya know? I can at least doodle now, and look like I'm paying attention. Anything not to fall asleep." I gave him a wink. He didn't say anything, and his expression grew unreadable. He was just nodding a little. Not smiling. Not frowning.

I have a terrible tendency to keep talking until somebody stops me. So, I swallowed, and continued. "I mean, these first meetings are always so boring. Just the same old, 'Let's go around the circle and introduce ourselves.'" I opened my eyes wide like a doll's and put on a plastic face, bobbing my head about. "I mean, come on, that's what I did in second grade. Can't anyone be a little more original?" I raised my eyebrows and forced a smile.

A grin cracked through his indifferent face. A small relief to me. He took a sip of his coffee as he nodded. "Yes, yes, I know what you mean. But what else is there to do at the first meeting?"

"I don't know. Anything we do is going to be considered 'lame' by everyone here. So we might as well 'Lame it up!' We could go around and say which fairy tale character we think we are the most like, or something like that."

He laughed, revealing his pearl teeth. I swear I could've made a necklace out of those things. "That's so much worse than going around the circle giving names!" I laughed too.

"But at least it's original!" I poked his arm flirtatiously. "We should hang out sometime, you and me. We're all new to the area, so it would be nice to have a friend, or something."

He nodded as if amused and opened his mouth to say something. As he did, our boss, Tara, clapped her hands together to get our attention.

"Everyone! Everyone please take your seats! We're going to get started!"

She had an extremely booming voice for such a small person. I shrugged at Michael, and pursed my lips together in a "no teeth" smile. He went and sat right next to where Tara's chair was. I went back to my seat somewhere in the middle of the circle. Watching him from across the room, Michael seemed to be giving one hundred percent of his attention to Tara's welcome speech. He was probably the only intern in the entire room that cared enough to pay attention. The crush I had for him deepened inside my chest, a tighter feeling than was there before.

I put the black Bic pen he gave me between my glossy lips and began to chew the end. I tried to focus hard on Tara, and what she was saying. "We have a very special treat today for everyone!" Her voice echoed throughout the room, bouncing off the large French windows and back again. "The President of Cougar Photo Imaging and Phototicket is here with us today!"

Great, there's some arrogant man here, older than Jesus himself, and we'll all have to wait in line after the work day to kiss his ring and his ass. Can't wait to meet him. I exhale and lean back in my chair as cynicism invades my mind. "So, let's give a nice welcome to Mr. Michael Cohen!"

I turned and looked at the door, half expecting to see a grand entrance with a red carpet roll out. No such thing happened. Creases formed on my brow line in confusion, as I turned back around in my seat and noticed that everyone else was looking to the center of the room. There he was, my Michael, the modern day John Travolta, staring back at me. I shuddered in embarrassment. Why did I have to be such a flirt? Why? Why? Why? I rolled my shoulders back, and cracked my neck to each side.

Confidently, I sat a little straighter up in my chair. This was fixable. I took the pen out of my mouth and wiped the glitter and sticky gloss off of the cap. No more being sexy around my boss. My hand slid across the notepad I held in my lap, and covered the doodles of barnyard animals I had been drawing. Then, I made eye contact with his honey brown eyes, and tilted my head slightly, raised my eyebrows and smiled professionally, as if saying, I knew all along.

His welcome speech was much longer than Tara's. He introduced himself, and went into his past with the company, how he moved up to his current position, etc, etc, etc. I was just beginning to think how this was no big deal, when he said, "I had the plan to go around the room and have everyone introduce themselves," he glanced at me, "but earlier I was informed this was 'lame.' So now, instead we're going to go around and say which fairy tale character we think we are most like, and why." Hearing my idea out loud, I realized just how stupid it actually was. The room filled with audible groans.

As we traveled around the circle, all the girls compared themselves to princesses, and all the boys compared themselves to heroes, except the nervous Peter Pan boy, who, ironically enough, compared himself to Peter Pan. Irony can be your friend if you let it, I suppose! Eventually the circle made itself around to me. Triumph was sparkling in Michael's gorgeous eyes. I cleared my throat, and returned his gaze. I looked directly at my new boss, as I spoke slowly. "Since I must compare myself to a fairy tale character, I would have to say I am most like…Dopey from Snow White."

To Our Readers,

Always keep a sense of humor. Life holds many surprises, as well as the occasional glitch but don't let that stop you. Resilience and winning spirit will never you down.
Congratulations to Colleen, and to all women who dare to try!

Editor

Grab Your Tiger

QUIZ
Are You Ready To Grab Your Tiger?

Or is your attitude keeping you from meeting the right guy?
Discover your real views about making the first move.

1) Smart women know men love the chase. It's the male's biological imperative to pursue the female. T__ F__

2) I can learn a lot about a guy by the way he approaches me. Plus, I hold the power because he's already shown his hand. T__F__

3) He'll think I'm looking for sex if I make the first move. T__ F__

4) If a guy can't figure out how come over to me, he's not worth my time. T__ F__

5) I have to do some serious flirting—touch his arm, laugh at his jokes, hint I'd like to see a new movie, for a guy to know I'm interested in going out with him. T__ F__

6) If he's not approaching me first, if he's not getting my number or calling me within two or three days of our date, it's because "he's just not that into me." T__ F__

7) Most men want pretty girls. If it's between me and a gorgeous gal, I don't stand a chance. T__ F__

8) There are actual signals a guy will make to encourage me to walk over to him. T__ F__

9) If I steer clear of the guys that are better looking than me, I'll have a good shot at this first move stuff.   T__   F__

10) If I make the first move, he's going to expect me to be in control all the time and that's not the kind of relationship I want. T__ F__

Turn the page to see how you scored.

1) FALSE. Both sexes have the innate capacity to do the hunting. And, it's a turn on to a secure man when you get the ball rolling, not to mention very flattering.

2) FALSE. Psychologists say you need to spend at least six months with him to really have a bead on him. As far as power goes, real power is going after the guy you want, not limiting yourself only to guys who want you.

3) FALSE. Regarding the expectation of sex: Men think about sex every seven seconds, i.e., most men hope to score, no matter who initiates the date.

4) FALSE. You'd be surprised at how many wonderful, accomplished men are shy around the opposite sex. Famous shy guys: Richard Gere, Jim Carrey, Johnny Carson, Brad Pitt. Would you miss out on a chance to meet *them*?

5) TRUE. But you're several gestures short if you want flirting, alone, to get your interest across. There are fifty-two flirting maneuvers in a female's arsenal and she must use approximately nine of them to ensure her target guy will get the message. Even then, there's no guarantee he'll walk over.

6) FALSE. Men have their own distractions. They get lazy about calling, bummed out from tensions at work—all the things you know to be true about them once you have them as a boyfriend. So assume nothing. Most of us are bright enough to intuit when a guy likes us. When he doesn't call, and it seems out of sync with the vibes we felt when we were with him, we need to 'go for it.'

7) FALSE. Social scientists have found that men are more receptive to high-flirtation women who are average or less than average-looking than they are to women who are more attractive but who emit fewer signals.

8) TRUE. Men subconsciously emit signals when they like you. Even if the rational part of their brains is telling them to stay away, because of nervousness or a recent breakup, they can't stop their bodies from talking!

9) TRUE. Scientists at the Social Issues Research Center have found that you increase your chances of a successful hook-up if you focus on men who are roughly on the same attractiveness level as you. However, since over 80% of women have a poor body image, try flirting with better looking men.

10) FALSE. After the first couple of dates, no one cares who made the first move, and the men in the stories in this book are living proof. They say they are grateful to the women because, but for their approach, they might not be together today.

How did you score on the Are Your Ready To Grab Your Tiger quiz?
8-10 correct: Keep it up. You'll find your special guy.
4-7 correct: You need practice; read the stories in this book for inspiration.
3 or fewer correct: Bulletin: The knight has dumped his armor, set his horse free and he'd like you to join him in the 21st century. He can be found at movies, sporting events, lectures, parties, work, parks, and he'd really love it if you came over and said "Hi."

For ideas on *where* to meet your tiger, visit us at www.grabyourtiger.com.

Index of Contributors

Grab Your Tiger